DATE DUE

UNDERSTANDING SCOTLAND

Scotland stands at the centre of sociological concerns in the late twentieth century. Rather than being an awkward and ill-fitting case, a nation without a state, it is at the centre of the discipline's post-modernist dilemma. Scotland has been part of the United Kingdom, a highly centralised and unitary state for nearly three hundred years, yet has survived the Union in 1707 as a distinctive civil society. Its sense of difference and identity has, indeed, grown rather than diminished. In many respects Scotland is a society with an unmade history, for its history seems incomplete and unpredictable. In a world where the nation-state is losing its *raison d'être*, Scotland provides an important test-case for the proposition that the quest for self-determination occurs in the context of major shifts in political and social arrangements at the global level.

David McCrone is Senior Lecturer in Sociology at the University of Edinburgh.

INTERNATIONAL LIBRARY OF SOCIOLOGY
Founded by Karl Mannheim

Editor: John Urry
University of Lancaster

UNDERSTANDING SCOTLAND

The sociology of a stateless nation

David McCrone

London and New York

First published in 1992
by Routledge
11 New Fetter Lane, London EC4P 4EE

Simultaneously published in the USA and Canada
by Routledge
a division of Routledge, Chapman and Hall Inc.
29 West 35th Street, New York, NY 10001

Phototypeset by Intype, London

Printed in Great Britain by
Mackays of Chatham PLC, Chatham, Kent

British Library Cataloguing in Publication Data
McCrone, David
Understanding Scotland: the sociology of a stateless nation. –
(The international library of sociology)
I. Title   II. Series
941.1

Library of Congress Cataloging in Publication Data
McCrone, David
Understanding Scotland: the sociology of a stateless nation/
David McCrone.
p.   cm. — (The International library of sociology)
Includes bibliographical references and index.
1. Scotland—Social conditions. 2. Nationalism—Scotland.
3. Regionalism—Great Britain. I. Title. II. Series.
HN398.S3M38 1992
306'.09411—dc20
91-34756
CIP

ISBN 0–415–06747–2
ISBN 0–415–06748–0 (pbk)

CONTENTS

v

TABLES AND FIGURES

TABLES

vii

FIGURES

ACKNOWLEDGEMENTS

This is my country, the land that begat me . . .

A number of people have shared, sometimes unwittingly, in the writing of this book. Since 1975, students taking the 'Scotland' course have taught me almost as much as I have taught them about our country. Their interest and enthusiasm in our shared commitment persuaded me that the book was necessary.

My colleagues, Frank Bechhofer and Steve Kendrick, shared the responsibility for carrying out sociological research on Scottish social structure which was funded by the Economic and Social Research Council, and by the Nuffield Foundation. I hope they will not dissent too much from the interpretation I have placed on our common work.

I have benefited more than they know from the perceptive and critical comments of Brian Elliott and Lindsay Paterson, who kindly read the draft manuscript when they had much better ways of passing their time.

Above all, my wife, Mary, has had this passion for Scotland inflicted on her for long enough, and managed to put up with it with patience and good humour.

I am grateful to the following copyright holders who have allowed me to make use of the following material. Chapter 3, 'Is Scotland different?', draws upon an earlier piece in H. Newby *et al.* (eds) *Restructuring Capital: Recession and Reorganisation in Industrial Society* (London: Macmillan, 1985); and Chapter 4, 'Getting on in Scotland' on D. Robbins (ed.) *Rethinking Social Inequality* (Farnborough: Gower, 1982). Chapter 6, 'Politics in a cold country', uses material first published in *Political Studies* 27, 1989; and my early thoughts on Scottish culture (Chapter 7) first appeared in D.

McCrone *et al.* (eds), *The Making of Scotland: Nation, Culture and Social Change* (Edinburgh: Edinburgh University Press, 1989). For Table 6.1, I am grateful to Richard Parry for permission to reproduce a table from his book *Scottish Political Facts* (Edinburgh: T. & T. Clark, 1988).

INTRODUCTION
The sociology of Scotland

Scotland stands at the forefront of sociological concerns in the late twentieth century. Rather than being an awkward, ill-fitting case, it is at the centre of the discipline's post-modern dilemma. The historic task of sociology has been to analyse 'society', to understand how social systems operate and lay down the rules for people within them. In this regard, 'society' can be treated at a high level of abstraction, as 'Society', as it were. The specificities of actual or 'real' societies can be ignored in favour of broad, common patterns. Hence, sociologists have talked about 'human society', or 'industrial society' or 'capitalist society'. In this perspective, the common features of societies are judged to have much more theoretical or predictive importance than their specific features.

The other, and probably most common, way of handling 'society' is simply to refer to nation-states. Hence, we have 'British society' or 'American society' and so on, meaningful abstractions which short-circuit the analytical problem of what, in sociological rather than political terms, a society actually is. As Norbert Elias put it,

> Many twentieth century sociologists when speaking of 'society' no longer have in mind, as did their predecessors, a 'bourgeois society' or a 'human society' beyond the state, but increasingly the somewhat diluted image of a nation-state.
>
> (1978: 241)

This common-sense approach, which has long had problems in handling internal variations within these states, is rapidly becoming problematic in a more fundamental way. The conventional nation-state, treated as a self-contained and bounded social system,

1

is rapidly losing its *raison d'être* in the modern world. In political terms, the nation-state is too small to solve some major problems, and too large to handle others. It is under pressure to cede decision-making power upwards to supra-national bodies (like the European Community or International Monetary Fund), and downwards to regional or national units seeking greater control over their own affairs. Clearly, these political pressures are connected with economic and cultural forces most commonly described as 'globalisation'. The assumption that politicians could manipulate the levers of economic power in the interests of the 'national economy' began to fail as trans-national corporations and supranational organisations asserted their considerable influence. In military terms, too, the capacity of the individual nation-state to control its own means of destruction and defence – its very *raison d'état* – is falling apart in a nuclear world. Similarly, the simple association of the nation-state with national culture – the essence of nationalism – loosened considerably under pressure from multicultural and multi-ethnic forces. In short, the useful assumption that nation-states, at least in the 'developed' world, had economic, political and cultural coherence – that they were self-contained 'societies' – has begun to seem less sure.

The assumption that the nation-state is equivalent to society no longer seems a valid one. This presents sociology with considerable difficulties. Of course, its practitioners can still continue to talk of 'society' in the abstract, as reflecting the broad, common patterns in all human societies (even conventions like 'capitalist society' become less meaningful with the collapse of the political-economic order in eastern Europe). On the other hand, the easy equivalence of state and society seems increasingly redundant. To some, of course, this redundancy is long overdue. As Michael Mann has pointed out in his critique which we review in the next chapter, 'societies are much messier than our theories of them' (1986: 4); he proposes that we jettison the notion of 'society' altogether.

Closer to the ground, as it were, the breaking up of the old assumptions as well as the real challenges to existing nation-states provides as many opportunities for the sociologist as it does problems. 'British society' has long occupied a central place in sociological discourse, but it contains a highly problematic assumption, that state, society and nation are coterminous. We are able to see with the hindsight of the late twentieth century that this is not so, that the British state formed in 1707 continued to harbour quite

2

distinct civil societies which kept alive institutional variations in the instruments of government, as well as providing the seed-beds for alternative national sentiments to survive and prosper. As writers such as Tom Nairn have pointed out, there has been something 'pre-modern' about the British state insofar as it did not bring state, civil society and nation into firm alignment. (One might even argue that this lack of articulation has a 'post-modern' feel to it, that Britain contains the loosely aligned structures which will be most appropriate in a post-modern world, assuming that it can manage the complex political changes necessary to adjust to this new world.)

It is indubitably clear that Scotland survived the Union of 1707 as a separate 'civil society' and as a nation, and that, if anything, its sense of difference and identity has grown rather than diminished. That this has happened may, on the face of it, seem strange because Scotland has been part of a highly centralised, unitary state for nearly three hundred years, governed from Westminster and submerged in a population which swamps it by nearly ten to one. Nevertheless, as we shall see in this book, Scotland has retained a remarkable degree of civil autonomy, and its relationship with the British state has allowed considerable control over its own affairs. The agenda, then, of this book is as follows: to construct a sociological account of a society and a nation which is struggling to assert its identity out of an older nation-state; to understand how it is that a distinct society and culture could survive and be periodically remade even within a highly centralised economy and polity; and to appreciate how and why it has diverged from certain English trajectories. Scotland seems poised to provide the specifically British example of those fissiparous tendencies which signal the radical remaking of political orders everywhere.

ANALYSING SCOTLAND

What tools of analysis, what perspectives, do we have to hand with which to understand Scotland? The two dominant modes have been the historical and the cultural, both focused upon Scotland as 'past'. This is not difficult to comprehend because 'Scotland' as an object of academic study seems to belong there. Much historical work has the rationale that because Scotland had its own political independence until 1707, and because many of its institutions, notably law, religion and education, survived that Union there was a self-defined field of study available. This study was, of course, institutionalised in the academic division of labour, although it was not without its contradictions as separate departments of 'Scottish history', 'economic and social history', and even 'history' make plain. Cultural studies of Scotland, its literature, language and folklore especially, formed the basis of another academic industry, one which extended beyond the academic world into that of the enthusiastic practitioner. One problem with this division of the intellectual map was that culture has seemed cut off from political, economic and social developments in contemporary Scotland. The task was too readily defined as one of conservation rather than development, of protecting the legacy rather than planning the future.

Sociology has both an old pedigree and a recent history in Scotland. On the one hand, there is a strong case for claiming that sociology was invented in Scotland, for the Scottish Enlightenment founded its knowledge upon 'sociological' assumptions about mankind (Brewer 1989). Enlightenment thinkers such as Adam Ferguson and Adam Smith wrote histories of 'civil society' based upon analyses of social structures and social institutions. People, said Ferguson, are in essence social creatures who derive happiness, ease and a sense of identity as well as security and sustenance from society. While this 'science of man' took in more than the social sciences currently defined, such a science was predicated on a sociological vision of human nature. Adam Ferguson, who was one of the earliest sociologists, anticipated the negative effects of the division of labour to be found in the writings of Karl Marx. Ferguson analysed different forms of society as they were affected by different social structural factors. Histories of sociology, however, seem to have written out his contribution in favour of the writer Auguste Comte, who is usually credited with founding the discipline, at least its name (in 1838). Ferguson's sociological ideas were themselves subsumed in the minds of later generations into the dominant, and more optimistic, school of classical economy associated with the Scottish Enlightenment, and social ideas were lost in the welter of a more individualistic and economistic theory of society. It was not until nearly two centuries later that sociology made its way into universities and colleges in its own right.

In its modern sense, sociology came late to Scotland. The

academic establishment of Scottish education, always wary of new-fangled ideas particularly if they emanated from south of the border or from across the Atlantic, resisted its inclusion in the school curriculum. There was no Higher in sociology like the A level, and it was not until the mid-1960s that the first Scottish university department was set up. There seemed to be little justification for claiming that sociology would add much to an understanding of Scotland that 'British sociology' would not. Once sociologists were established in Scottish universities and colleges, they set about applying the concepts and perspectives fashioned in 'Britain' and the USA. Infused as it was at the time with its Fabian legacy, British sociology simply accepted that 'society' was coterminous with the British state, unitary and highly centralised, driven by social change in the political and cultural heartland of southern Britain. If there was a particular sociology of the 'periphery' – in Wales, Ireland and Scotland – it had to do with analysing a 'traditional', pre-capitalist way of life. It was judged to be the task of the sociologist of these parts merely to chart its decline and ultimate incorporation into 'modern' society, or so it seemed.

For those working in Scotland, interested in the familiar social institutions and processes of the discipline – work, the family, deviance, the city, for instance – sociology was carried out *in* Scotland rather than *about* it. Sociology as a social science has traditionally operated by carving up these institutions and processes of the social world, and developing special literatures and expertise. Studying whole societies is much more uncommon and difficult, because it demands an understanding of how different sub-systems such as the economic, political, industrial, demographic and occupational interact with each other to produce a dense but comprehensive social reality. Much of the thrust of the social sciences in this post-war period was to pursue the universal rather than the particular, to identify what societies had in common rather than what made them differ from each other (Burns 1966). The assumption was that, apart from a little local colour, one society was much like any other. And if 'society' was defined as the British state, there seemed little point in focusing on its under-populated northern half.

On reflection, much of post-war sociology was ethnocentric, based on the imputed characteristics common to all 'developed' societies. What the United States did today, for example, the rest of the (developed) world would do tomorrow. Where the south of

England led, the rest of Britain would follow. This washing out of specificities, of what made societies different rather than similar, was not simply a reflection of post-war socio-political realities, but quite fundamental to the sociological project. As Poggi pointed out, 'The notion of society as normally used in sociological argument reflects historically distinctive circumstances associated with the advent of modernity' (1990: 182).

UNCOVERING MODERNITY

Modernism and modernisation have been quite fundamental to sociology. Its founding fathers, notably the sociological trinity of Marx, Weber and Durkheim, had set out to explain how societies became 'modern', whether in industrial, capitalist or bureaucratic form. In Kumar's words, 'all lived, wrote and theorised under the overwhelming impression that "a terrible beauty was born"' (1978: 54). In essence, sociology came into existence to make sense of the 'great transformation' to modern industrial society. Modernisation represented the process by which 'traditional' societies achieved modernity. Hence, in economic terms, improved technology, the growth of commerce and an increasing division of labour in industry were matched by urbanisation, the extension of literacy and the decline of traditional authority. In essence, industrialism and modernity seemed to be the same thing. 'To become modern was to go through the process of industrialisation, which is to say, to arrive at something like the state of society envisaged in the sociologist's image of industrialism' (Kumar 1978: 111).

These economic processes of modernisation were matched by political changes, notably the extension of the franchise and the binding of the population to the allegiance to the state. Processes of industrialisation and democratisation went together as part of a larger movement towards the 'nationalisation' of society. Virtually all individuals living within the borders of the state were identified with a national political order, usually via 'citizenship'. In its classical form, the nation-state claimed the notion of sovereignty, that it had supreme authority over the territory, which it did not share with another power. The population was bound to the nation-state by means of the ideology of nationalism through which people developed an emotive identity with this sovereign community. Classical sociology saw nationalism as the ideological cement which held complex industrial societies together, as the new secular religion of the modern state. In this scheme of things, then, 'modern society' was industrial, a vast productive enterprise, whose political expression was the nation-state which provided citizenship rights for the population and demanded its national allegiance in return. By the middle of the twentieth century, sociologists were struck by the sameness of the industrialisation process, by the similarities between those societies deemed to be industrial and modern. As Kumar pointed out,

> It appeared that the Western model of industrialism in its 20th century form was in the process of vanquishing all other competing models, and increasingly standing out as the common feature of the whole globe.
>
> (1978: 181)

In this model of things, Scotland seemed to have no special rationale for study, beyond it having been the second country (after England) to undergo the comprehensive process of industrialisation. Once it had crossed the great divide in the late eighteenth and early nineteenth centuries, there seemed little that sociology could say about Scotland which was of particular interest.

By the late 1960s, however, the general and the particular versions of the modernisation theories of social change were being challenged. The notions that all industrial societies were undergoing 'convergence', and particularly that differences between capitalist and socialist countries no longer mattered very much came under attack. Some writers had begun to argue that 'industrial' societies were being superseded by 'post-industrial' ones in which knowledge had become the new capital, post-scarcity had overcome want, service industry had replaced manufacturing. While critics argued that 'post-industrialism' was a very unspecified term, and seemed to involve simply adding another stage to the industrialising process, it was clear that old certainties were falling away, and that new questions were being asked. Post-industrial theorising was valuable 'more for re-opening certain questions to do with social change than for supplying much help in answering them' (Kumar 1978: 239).

From a more radical perspective, 'modernisation' too became a questionable concept. Nor only was it thoroughly ethnocentric, based on developments in the west, but empirically it was plain by the 1970s that it did not lead to automatic economic growth, particularly in Third World countries seeking to catch up with the developed west. Indeed, many radical critics of modernisation argued that low growth and social inequality resulted from precisely those processes of modernisation which were meant to be the harbingers of prosperity and plenty.

Although theories of modernity and modernisation seemed to have little to offer the student of Scotland, these critiques opened up new possibilities. By the 1970s a burgeoning sociology of development had lent a new perspective on Scotland. Abiding regional inequalities between Scotland and England might be explained, some argued, by the obstacles placed in the way of 'development' by economic and political structures, notably by the concentration of economic power in the south-east of England and the United States, and by the absence of political autonomy in Scotland itself. These new perspectives appeared to offer a way out of the traditional sociological blindness about Scotland, and to fuse new interests in the 'branch-plant' syndrome whereby much of Scottish industry was controlled beyond its boundaries, with the resurgence of political nationalism in the late 1960s and early 1970s.

By the 1980s much of the debate about the sociology of Scotland focused upon the extent of its similarities and differences with the rest of the UK. This was a debate not simply about how to interpret the welter of statistics on industrial, occupational and social change in general, but more fundamentally, about which sociological model fitted Scotland best. It was a debate which ran across the traditional boundaries between sociology and history in its search for appropriate data and models to fit them. Above all, it served to confront sociology with the 'problem' of Scotland. Much of the conventional wisdom had produced an 'us-too' sociology of Scotland, one which focused on its similarities with other countries, notably England. Instead, there was a new 'not-us' sociology, stressing the differences. Scotland was 'different', critics claimed, because it had followed a different trajectory of economic and social development; it had 'colonial' status *vis-à-vis* the metropolitan centres of power. Whatever the truth or otherwise of these claims, Scotland was appearing on the sociological map.

MODERNITY AND POST-MODERNITY

Since the 1980s the classical paradigms of sociology associated with modernity have continued to be questioned. The critique of 'post-industrialism' may have beaten off one assault, but the fundamental weakness of the structure remained, only to be attacked again under a new guise, labelled late- or post-modernity (Lash 1990). If the modernity thesis had stressed scientific rationality, post-modernity emphasised the erratic and unpredictable nature of much social behaviour. Modernity had associated itself with industrialism and organised capitalism; post-modernity focused on consumerism and 'disorganised' capitalism. Modernity had aligned the national economy, polity and culture in such a way that citizenship and an allegiance to the sovereign state provided a clear and unambiguous identity. Post-modernity, on the other hand, pointed to the limited nature of state sovereignty in an inter-dependent world, and highlighted the often contradictory and competing identities on offer. The plethora of new social movements with their limited and shifting aims contrasted with the predictability of class-based movements associated with 'modernity'. The debate about 'class de-alignment' and the broadening of politics beyond the narrowly material were but symptoms of major shifts in late-twentieth-century societies. These economic and social changes, it was argued, were leading to a radical redefinition of politics. Social movements, as Alberto Melucci (1989) described them, no longer operated as characters (as in the theatre), but as forms of symbolic challenge, with the consequence that traditional labels like Right and Left became increasingly vacuous in analytical terms.

Above all, and what is important for our purposes here, a new trans-societal order had emerged in which, argued Melucci, nation-states were extinguishing themselves:

> The decline of the nation-state is not due to socialism (the myth of the abolition of the state), but because nation-states are losing their authority: from above, a global, multinational political and economic interdependence moves the centre of decision-making elsewhere; from below, the multiplication of autonomous centres of decision-making gives 'civil societies' a power they never had during the development of modern states.
>
> (1989: 86–7)

The multiplication of contacts and the constant flow of messages was steadily destroying the homogeneity of individual cultures, and the media and mass tourism were eroding specific territorial cultural practices. On the other hand, ethnicity did not wither but revived as a source of identity to meet new emergent needs. It was well placed to do this because, according to Melucci, it had a vertical as well as a horizontal significance. Ethnic or national movements exposed problems relating to the structure of complex societies (the horizontal), while they were also rooted in history (the vertical):

> Unless we link their appearance with the transformations of complex societies, they become simple historical by-products of the process of nation-building or incidental events in the narrative of international relations. If on the other hand we ignore their origins in 'national questions' and in their conflict with the states, we risk reducing them to mere cultural appeals in the name of diversity.
>
> (1989: 91)

The resurgence of local or ethnic nationalisms came to be seen not as in direct contradiction to increasing globalisation of economic, political and cultural power, but as part of this process itself. While ethno-nationalisms are plainly rooted in the past, they also highlight continuing societal transformation and discontinuity. These are general processes at work in the contemporary world, but they forefront Scotland in a novel and interesting way. This book argues that the survival of Scotland as a nation and the assertion of nationalism more generally in the late twentieth century set it at the centre of current sociological concerns. The fact that it can claim to be a nation without a state in the conventional sense does not mean that it remains an anomaly in the modern world, as judged by the more traditional perspective of 'modernity'. Rather, Scotland becomes an example of those fissiparous tendencies threatening to remake the world political order, an order in which the correspondence between states, societies and nations is no longer clear-cut.

These, then, are the key themes which this book addresses. It will chart the ways in which Scotland emerged as the subject of sociological debate from the 1970s: first, in the context of whether or not it could be considered within the paradigm of Third World dependency and under-development; and second, as political and cultural changes highlighted the origins and nature of nationalism in Scotland. Its main task is to provide a sociological perspective – an understanding, as the title indicates, rather than a direct account of the social structure of modern Scotland, of its demography, occupational and class structure, its political and cultural formations. It would be foolhardy and arrogant to suppose that the sociology of Scotland can be encompassed within one text, and this book reflects the author's belief that setting out clearly the sociological perspective for 'understanding' is a prior and vital task. Nevertheless, we hope that much can be gleaned about the social structure of Scotland from the way the perspective is set out.

The first chapter will lay out some key ideas around the questions: What is Scotland? On what basis can we say that it is or is not a 'society'? Indeed, are we correct any more in referring to any territory as a society? What theoretical and analytical tools are available to us for handling Scotland? What do we mean, for example, when we describe Scotland as a 'nation'?

The second chapter focuses on the models of development which have been used to explain social and economic change in Scotland. Historians and sociologists, for example, have been involved in a lengthy debate about the role of Calvinism in Scotland, and whether or not the Scottish case confirms or negates Max Weber's thesis concerning the relationship between Calvinism and capitalism. Briefly put, Scotland seems to provide a test of the thesis that there is an intimate relationship between Protestantism and the rise of capitalism. The issue here is that while Scotland underwent a Calvinist revolution as early as the sixteenth century, it could not be described as a thoroughgoing capitalist society until at least the late eighteenth century, seeming thereby to break the link between capitalism and Calvinism. Scotland has also been a battleground for debates about the sociology of development, notably about whether at crucial stages in its development it was 'dependent', and if so, what the consequences were. This chapter will also assess the impact of capitalism on Scotland since its early point of take-off, and those accounts which try to interpret the form it took. The task here will be not to offer a history, but an assessment of the sociologically informed models of Scottish economic and social development.

The third chapter concentrates on attempts to treat Scotland as 'dependent' or as a 'colony', characterisations which framed much of the research agenda on Scotland in the 1970s. Specifically, we will ask whether Scotland has followed a distinctive path of industrial and occupational change. Nevertheless, while the broad

11

outlines of Scotland's class structure may be broadly similar to other advanced industrial or capitalist societies, how class is expressed in action, through politics and protest, is by no means comparable.

Systems of inequality and privilege are dynamic ones, and the fourth chapter discusses 'getting on' in Scotland, the systems of social mobility and the meanings which are attached to these. Beliefs about the relative openness of Scottish society have a long and deep historical pedigree, and these are not easily amenable to proof. So powerful are these 'myths' in sociological terms, that they seem to have infused the Scottish identity itself, set against what is judged to be a less mobile, status-conscious and more powerful society – England.

Scotland has often been described as an 'un-democracy', in which decisions are taken outwith its boundaries in both political and economic terms. The fifth chapter focuses on elites in Scotland, and the basic parameters of power. In economic terms, Scotland has moved from being a self-regulated 'economic' system at the beginning of this century when an indigenous and self-confident bourgeoisie held the reins of power, to an overtly 'political' system at the end of the twentieth century when the state has played a major part in economic decision-making, and in particular has encouraged a process of external ownership and control in the Scottish economy by multi-national corporations.

The sixth chapter examines the political sociology of Scotland in recent years. Over the last thirty years or so major divergences have occurred between Scotland and England with respect to electoral success for the main parties. While the Nationalist party has been a major distinguishing feature between the two political systems, it has been the rapid collapse of the Conservative vote which has been outstanding. Generally, it seems that the political agendas of both countries have moved in such a way as to weaken the social base of the Right, while not necessarily moving it to the Left. This chapter will assess the extent to which political divergence has been caused simply by socio-economic differences (for example, more manual workers and council tenants in Scotland), or by shifts in the character of the political agenda north of the border.

The last twenty years have seen a cultural renaissance in Scotland, in those aspects which confirm its separate identity. Yet the dominant analysis of Scottish culture remains a pessimistic and negative one, based on the thesis that Scotland's culture is 'deformed' and debased by sub-cultural formations such as tartanry and Kailyardism. The seventh chapter assesses the validity of this analysis, and argues that while media representations of Scotland are often simplistic and distorted, the search for a pure, national culture as an alternative is doomed to fail in a complex modern, multinational world.

The final chapter examines the future scenarios for Scotland in the late twentieth century. In many respects, Scotland is a society with an 'unmade' history insofar as its history seems incomplete and thereby unpredictable. Given that Scotland is dependent on external political and economic forces, its capacity to control its destiny and to become more of a self-governing society seems limited without major revisions of these constraints. Nevertheless, Scotland provides an important sociological test-case for the proposition that the quest for greater self-determination occurs in the context of the globalisation of economic and political power. In a world where the nation-state of the nineteenth century seems to be losing its *raison d'être*, Scotland's future seems bound up with major shifts in political and social arrangements at a global level.

A BIOGRAPHICAL NOTE

It is important for any author to give an account – an apologia – for any project in which he or she is engaged. While we tackle such with as much objectivity and clear-headedness as we can muster, most of us are drawn to subjects and topics for personal reasons, or through sheer serendipity.

My own interest in Scotland as the object of sociological study is a mixture of both. Born and brought up in Aberdeen, part of what Douglas Dunn has called 'the essential east', I stood outside that region of Scotland – the central belt – where most Scots lived, and shared the sense of separateness, even peripherality, of many folk in the north-east. My immediate family came from the north-east, and on my father's side, from the south-west, two regions of Scotland with their own pronounced senses of regional identity. My introduction to sociology was largely a matter of serendipity. Confronted in the mid-sixties with the bewildering choice of the Scottish university system, I opted to take sociology as a third or 'outside' subject, as part of a degree in Literature. Once hooked, there was no going back for me. It seemed to provide a way of linking personal biography and social account (C. Wright Mills was an early discovery). But there were puzzles. I learned a lot about gangs in the ghettoes of Chicago, and family life in Bethnal Green, but Scotland was not mentioned, except in the assumption that life was like that here too. It was 'us-too' sociology, in the main. Virtually everything I read assumed the homogeneity of British society (the phrase seemed natural), or that American society was the ideal-type against which to test theories and hypotheses. Society was society was society, and it was no different in Aberdeen either.

By the late 1960s and early 1970s, the old understandings began to unravel. Sociologists began to get interested in local communities, historians in people's history, and the old, easy assumptions made less sense. 'Bottom-up' rather than 'top-down' accounts reinforced the point that people's immediate surroundings were vitally important to them in making sense of even the most global of changes. Above all, political change began to happen in Scotland which the textbooks said was not meant to happen any more. British politics were, we were told, secular and homogeneous, then along came nationalism, which was supposed to belong to the dustbin of history. Many academics ignored it on the assumption that, rather than threaten cherished theories, it would soon go away. Some even predicted that, to their later confusion when nationalism returned. It presented problems for conventional theories because it undermined the supposed homogeneity of the United Kingdom; it made learning about life in Chicago and Bethnal Green seem less relevant and more distant.

To what extent did sociologists react to these changes within Scotland? Social scientists in Scotland were oriented towards wider academic networks at a British or an international level, and while many used Scottish material to flesh out their analysis, far fewer sociologists turned to analyse Scottish society itself. Of course, there are considerable difficulties in getting Scottish material published unless it is seen to have strong comparative links. It is deemed 'parochial' in a way English material is not, particularly because it has a smaller, limited market for publishers. There is considerable irony in that, because sociology in Scotland finds itself at the centre of immediate political concerns in a way in which Anglo-British sociology has ceased to be, after the fracturing of the welfare consensus. This consensus had been largely the outcome of political Fabianism, which in turn had underwritten both Labourism and British sociology. In Scotland, political issues and sociological debates could be more easily connected in a way they once were south of the border but are no more. Analyses of Scottish society by social scientists seemed to interact with political issues of identity and loyalty. As a consequence, academic definitions of Scottish reality – the terms of academic debate – appeared to find their way into political debate, and thereby were refracted back into the academic realm. This fusion of intellectual and political endeavours gives a charge to the sociological enterprise in Scotland, presenting both opportunities and problems for academic analysis. While there are obvious dangers of academic analysis getting swept up in the taken-for-granted assumptions of political debate, replete as these are with a plethora of myths, the momentum which this centrality gives for relevant research is obvious.

The lack of resources, however, for carrying out Scottish research is well known, as is the lack of career opportunities for young academics who have largely been responsible for developing these new ideas. Because the sociological study of Scotland does not mesh well with other specialisms of the discipline, it is difficult to provide a career structure in a country so dependent on external agencies for resources. Nevertheless, much valuable sociology has been carried out by historians, policy analysts, political scientists and others as a by-product of their own researches. It remains, though, a weak basis on which to fashion a proper sociological understanding of our country, particularly one in which sociology is largely invisible before university, for it is not a school subject.

If there is much to be done, there is much enthusiasm to do it. This book is a small effort at mapping out our knowledge of Scotland. Its deficiencies are clear; the rest lies in the future of both sociology and Scotland.

As Scots become more confident about their own culture and society, so there has been a revival of interest in language. Scots today see no need to apologise, like David Hume, for 'Scotticisms', and prefer to express themselves in the language they use. Non-Scots readers may encounter words like 'outwith', 'furth', 'thirled' and 'thrawn' whose meanings may seem at first unfamiliar, but which can be gauged from the text.

1

WHAT IS SCOTLAND?

What is Scotland? How are we to understand it sociologically? At first glance, this may seem like a non-problem, because at a common-sense level Scotland plainly exists. It is a territory, a place on a map with a long historical pedigree, even with a border which distinguishes it from its southern neighbour. To treat Scotland as in any way problematic might seem to many to be academic play-acting. And yet Scotland as a meaningful sociological category is highly problematic. If only nation-states are societies, and if sociology is the science of society, can we have a sociology of Scotland?

The challenge for the sociologist of analysing Scotland lies in assessing its claim to be a society in any meaningful sense. 'Scotland' exists at different levels of meaning, not all of them of central interest to the sociologist, but each with some sociological content. At the most basic, Scotland refers to a geographical place, a territory on a map, a collection of rocks, earth and water, defined by its topography, its climate and natural resources. Lest we dismiss this level as unimportant to a sociological account, we should remind ourselves of the powerful imagery of Scotland which draws on these resources. Scotland as land of mountain and flood is captured in literature and by the tourist industry in its representations of Scotland. It is, as it were, a landscape of the mind, which carries potent resonances for cultural and political action.

SCOTLAND AS COUNTRY

Deciding whether or not Scotland is a society is inextricably bound up with other notions of what Scotland is. For example, many who would hesitate to call it a society or even a nation are quite content to refer to it as a 'country'. While this seems to be a fairly neutral term drawing attention to territorial integrity, it resonates with other images. As Raymond Williams pointed out: ' "country" is both a nation and part of a "land"; "the country" can be the whole society or its rural area. In the long history of human settlements, this connection between the land from which directly or indirectly we all get our living and the achievements of human society has been deeply known' (1973: 1). 'Country' has come to stand for the essential values and images of place, hence the fusion of land and nation (1973: 296).

Central to identity is the sense of place: *where* is Scotland? Just as the idealised England is essentially a rural idyll, a place, where country and Country come together, so the 'real' Scotland (and Wales and Ireland) are essentially rural – 'Welsh Wales', the Gaeltachd in both Scotland and Ireland, the heartland of the culture. As far as Scotland is concerned, Scottish culture has adopted (or had thrust upon it) a 'Gaelic vision'. The anthropologist Malcolm Chapman (1978) showed how, as Scotland was becoming industrialised in the late eighteenth century, and its lowlands became much like other urbanised and industrialised regions, so the symbols, myths and tartans of the Highlands of Scotland were appropriated by lowland Scots in a bid to cling on to some distinct culture. The irony was that the part of Scotland which had been reviled as barbarian, backward and savage found itself extolled as the 'real' Scotland – land of tartan, kilts, heather.

Scotland as 'country' is, then, a landscape of the mind, a place of the imagination. As such, notions of the essential Scotland are what people want it to be. In this respect, many argue that Scotland is particularly prone to myths and legends about itself, because it lacks the formal political institutions of state autonomy. As we will see in Chapter 7, the image of Scotland as a divided, schizophrenic society is a very powerful one, corresponding in part to the separation of state (British) from society (Scottish). The analysis of Scottish culture is replete with the imagery and assumptions of division. There is a powerful sense of Scotland being 'over', as belonging to the past: the essential Scotland as consigned to history.

Accounts of Scottish history are disproportionately dominated by a highly romanticised and time-specific section of history. The late Marinell Ash, in her excellent and neglected *The Strange Death of Scottish History*, accused Scots of a 'historical failure of nerve':

The time that Scotland was ceasing to be distinctively and confidently herself was also the period when there grew an increasing emphasis on the emotional trappings of the Scottish past . . . its symbols are bonnie Scotland of the bens and glens and misty shieling, the Jacobites, Mary Queen of Scots, tartan mania and the raising of Scottish statuary.

(1980: 10)

As Scotland was losing its identity both politically, culturally and economically, so it appropriated that which had flourished in the currency of the Romantic movement – the Gaelic vision. And plainly, these images have been further appropriated and incorporated into the twentieth-century tourist vision of Scotland. In this respect, of course, Scotland is by no means unique in the modern world.

Certainly, historians have complained about the 'forged' character of Scotland. Following the English historian, Hugh Trevor-Roper (1984), we might be tempted to treat Scotland as a forgery, something got up by professional myth-makers and story-tellers. Many of the images of Scotland – kilts, tartan, heather, bagpipes – seem to have been purloined from the Highlands after 1745 to distinguish ourselves from our southern neighbour. Perhaps 'Scotland' is simply something invented by the heritage industry and the Scottish Tourist Board? Undoubtedly, 'Scotland' resonates with a powerful set of images, based on romance, sadness, defeat, hardship, conflict and struggle; there is certainly no shortage of raw materials.

Historians of Scotland have written at length about the distortions of reality which have passed for 'history' in Scotland. It seems to be an account which ignores recent events in favour of a highly romanticised version of the past. It is a history of personalities rather than people, of events rather than processes. In Marinell Ash's words,

Modern perceptions of Scotland's past are like a foggy landscape; small peaks and islands of memory rising out of an occluded background. The name of some of these peaks are Bruce, Wallace, Bannockburn, Mary Queen of Scots, Bonnie Prince Charlie and the Clearances.

(Ash n.d.: 1)

The result is that it is impossible for Scots to see or understand the connections between these isolated figures in the mist. Certainly, Scotland has what we might call a rich myth-history which is often at odds with 'history' proper. For example, historians have tried but largely failed to correct the popular notion that events such as the Jacobite rising of 1745 and the Highland Clearances were struggles between the Scots and the English. To take an example, Ash has pointed out the importance of the St Andrews legend in Scotland's myth-history as 'an understandable example of national hagiographical status seeking'. St Andrew, it seems, was pressed into service as Scotland's national patron about the thirteenth century. No self-respecting state could be without one, especially as it signified papal approval for the authority of the state itself. Such political opportunism on the part of the Scots had an internal as well as an external rationale. On the one hand, English territorial demands on Scotland required others to confer legitimacy and protection on the threatened state. Internally, adopting St Andrew, a foreigner, as the national saint avoided internal conflicts between regional pretenders among the indigenous saints, and had become 'a symbol that would unite two peoples separated by language and culture' (the Picts and the Scots in the eighth century). There was little objective evidence that St Andrew had much direct connection with Scotland (claims that the king of the Scots had received a heavenly visit from the saint on the eve of battle predicting victory were suspiciously similar to claims elsewhere, notably concerning the Emperor Constantine in AD 345). However, the key aim, it seems, was to prove that Scotland was an older Christian nation than England (which had a much more dubious patron in the Cappadocian dragon-slayer, St George, who suffered final demotion from the calendar of authentic saints by the Vatican in the 1970s).

Similarly, as Ash points out, the centrality of the 1320 Declaration of Arbroath, with its ringing sentiments about Scotland's freedom is of fairly recent pedigree. The declaration (which was unlikely to have been 'declared' anywhere, never mind at Arbroath) seems to have disappeared from Scottish historical consciousness for over three hundred years, only to be revived in the seventeenth century when Scotland's parliamentary union with England was on the political agenda. Anti-union forces found the statement and its rhetoric useful in rallying opposition to what they saw as the destruction of Scotland's identity.

The key point in these episodes is not that they represented a falsification of history, but that they provided historic legitimacy for claims that Scotland was indubitably a distinctive country. The pressing of history into the struggles of the present is a common phenomenon. As late as 1935 Lewis Grassic Gibbon was drawing on the difference in social origins between William Wallace and Robert Bruce to make the point that the struggle between the common man and the aristocrat had an older pedigree (Ash 1990).

We might be tempted to argue here that this falsification of history is a peculiarly Scottish trait, reflecting the fragility of Scotland's identity. But, as Neal Ascherson pointed out,

> We talk easily about the forging of a nation, but forgery has played a real part in the foundation and revival of many nations. In Scotland we should know that better than most. Ossian was a forgery, but the emotions about nations and history roused by James Macpherson's pastiche of genuine Gaelic myth cycles was real enough. Finland's national epic, the 'Kalevala' emerged rather later, but doesn't bear close inspection either.
>
> (1988a: 61)

The inventing of traditions is by no means confined to Scotland, for as Hobsbawm has put it, these operate to bridge the present with the past, to offer a legitimating continuity through suitable history. New nations from the nineteenth century onwards sought to invent or appropriate symbols and icons such as flags, songs and stories (Hobsbawm 1984).

The key point is a sociological rather than a historical one, that myth-history is a vital part of the story-telling of any country. Myths do not disappear when they are confronted with facts, because, as we shall see in this book, evidence does not drive out myths, for they operate on quite a different plane. In other words, myths validate experience and action independently of their truth-status. As Andrew McPherson has put it,

> Since Durkheim, sociologists have often wanted to reserve the term 'myth' not for beliefs that could simply be dismissed as false but for folk stories that had two simultaneous functions: to celebrate identity and values, and to describe and explain the world in which these are experienced or sought. Logically, myths may be expressive *and* true, or expressive *and* false; though the explanations that they offer and the

'facts' that may confirm or refute them are never closed to dispute.

(1983: 218)

The myths and legends which McPherson is addressing here are relatively modern ones, having to do with the supposed openness of Scottish society (relative to England), its egalitarian tendencies, its capacity to encourage mobility through education, crystallised around lads o' pairts in the nineteenth century and myths about the lack of racism in Scotland in the twentieth. Lest we try to sweep away much of this imagery as unhistorical and unscientific, we ought to ask why these images have such force, why they prove so resistant to debunking. One answer might be that in contrast to other countries Scotland does not demand the teaching of its own history in its education system; another, that because Scotland ceded political sovereignty to Westminster while retaining considerable civil autonomy, its identity is much more complex (even confused) than in those countries where state and society are one. Nevertheless, much remains of Scotland's political system.

SCOTLAND AS SOCIETY

Should we, then, describe Scotland as a society? As we saw in the introduction, this term increasingly carries problematic resonances of the political, social and cultural self-containedness of territories. Anthony Giddens, for example, defines society as 'a group of people who live in a particular territory, are subject to a common system of political authority, and are aware of having a distinct identity from other groups around them' (1989: 731).

On these geographical, political and ideological terms, Scotland is a society. However, it might be preferable to qualify the term somewhat by referring to 'civil society', a term usually used to distinguish the social realm from the political one. In other words, while Scotland surrendered its statehood in 1707, it retained much of the institutional apparatus of self-government. The Union of 1707 ensured that the 'holy trinity' of institutional autonomy, the law, the church and the education system, remained as key governing agencies. While these institutions have had their autonomy eroded as Scotland became a secular society, and as Westminster (and European) government imposed higher systems of governance on the country, other social institutions have grown in importance.

In many respects, the bargain struck in 1707 allowed Scotland to survive as a sufficiently different civil society within the confines of the unitary British state. In Lindsay Paterson's words,

> The Union had left intact all that really mattered to daily life in Scotland in the eighteenth century . . . the Union was, in Angus Calder's words, 'a rational solution to very dangerous economic and political problems', involving the abandonment of an already highly constrained foreign policy in the interests of maintaining independent control over domestic policy.
>
> (1991: 105)

In many respects Scotland remained self-governing in its civil institutions, and the British state did not overly interfere except when it perceived the military-political authority of the state to be under threat (as in the Jacobite rising of 1745–6), or at the behest of Scotland's ruling elites (as in the imposition of the laird's patronage over the appointment of Kirk ministers in 1712). Paterson argues that day-to-day life in Scotland and its governance remained in the hands of Scots, and were consolidated in the 1832 Scottish Reform Act and in the setting up of *ad hoc* governing boards to administer, among others, prisons, poor law, health, schools and the crofting counties. These boards were incorporated into the responsibilities of the Scottish Office in 1886, ironically raising the complaint that the last vestiges of Scottish nationhood were thus being eroded. In the last hundred years, increased agitation for reform in Scotland has resulted in increased responsibilities accruing to the Scottish Office to the extent that *de facto* Scottish self-government, or 'limited sovereignty' as Paterson calls it, has resulted. The demands for democratic accountability over this 'Scottish semi-state' in the late twentieth century represent recognition of the limits which bureaucratic devolution has reached.

The remarkable growth of separate political administration for Scotland since 1886 has undoubtedly helped to reinforce the sense of 'Scotland'. It is easier to visualise what a separate Scotland would look like precisely because by the 1980s the Scottish Office had become 'a Scottish semi-state with a powerful administrative apparatus' (Kerevan 1980: 24). The proponents of devolution in the 1979 referendum could set out their case for political autonomy in terms of the need to extend democratic accountability over this bureaucratic structure. Further, the emergence of a distinctively Scottish media agenda from the 1960s depended on the administrative apparatus governing Scotland.

At this level, Scotland undoubtedly exists as a political-administrative unit, as a governed system defined by the remit of the Scottish Office. In little over one hundred years of its existence, the Scottish Office has given a political meaning to Scotland. There is irony in this, because by treating Scotland as an object of administration, Westminster government has to live with its political consequences. If the Scottish Office had never been created, it would have been much more difficult to address Scotland as a meaningful political unit. The northern territory could have been handled as the 'North British regional province' of the central British state. The Scottish Office was itself the expression of a complex network of social organisations – a Scottish civil society – which have made political demands for democratic control of the bureaucratic machinery of Scottish government so much easier to make than in, say, the north of England which lacks this administrative framework. Scotland (like Wales) retains important historical and cultural residues of nationhood, but also sufficiently separate networks of interaction around which social and political consciousness can form.

Despite the overwhelming powers of the southern-dominated British state, the Scots have retained a sufficiently distinct civil society, articulated in assertions of national identity. Being 'Scottish' seemed to be more important than being 'British', particularly in the context of post-war decline in the British economy set against the discovery of North Sea oil in the late 1960s and early 1970s. The late John P. Mackintosh observed in 1974, at a new peak of Scottish nationalism, that Scots had to hand two identities:

> With dual nationality, there is a simple alternative if the pride in being British wanes; just be Scottish. It is an 'opt out' solution which allows each person to imagine the kind alternative to the disappointment of being British which he or she wants.
>
> (1974: 409)

Since Mackintosh wrote, this 'alternative pride' has, if anything, grown in salience. The continuing problems of the economy, the hopes and disappointments attached to North Sea oil discoveries, the destruction of much of Scottish manufacturing industry in the early 1980s, and, above all, the election of an ineluctably English prime minister in 1979, all helped to reinforce this alternative identity. In 1991, in an opinion poll carried out for the *Scotsman* newspaper, 40 per cent of Scots considered themselves to be Scottish not British, and a further 29 per cent more Scottish than British. Twenty-one per cent thought themselves equally Scottish and British. While such data tell us little about the depth of such feelings, or about their political implications, they do seem to confirm a powerful source of alternative aspirations. In the last decade or so Scottish politics appear to have become more 'Scottish' in their agenda. This change has been remarked upon by commentators such as Neal Ascherson, writing in the early months of 1989, some ten years after the ill-fated referendum on devolution. Scottish political theatre, he said, was no longer easily accessible to non-Scots:

> politics North of the Border operates inside a web of references – past and present manifestos, conference resolutions, factions and splits, psephological allusions in a country now used to a four party system, formal and informal institutions – which are simply not shared with the rest of the United Kingdom.
>
> (*The Observer* (Scotland), 12 March 1989)

One might, of course, argue that such a discourse simply reflects the curious world which is politics, but it seems more likely that this sea change reflects more fundamental social changes north of the border. It would be a curious politics which did not reflect these sociological shifts in the heart of Scottish society itself.

Having sought to establish our claim to talk of Scottish society in these terms, it is important to remind ourselves that the very word 'society' has grown increasingly problematic. In the early 1980s the French sociologist, Alain Touraine, expressed the conventional wisdom:

> The abstract idea of society cannot be separated from the concrete reality of a national society, since this idea is defined as a network of institutions, controls and education. This necessarily refers us back to a government, to a territory, to a political collectivity. The idea of society was and still is the ideology of nations in the making.
>
> (1981: 5, my translation)

24

Other sociologists have suggested that 'society' is far too problematic a term, and should be jettisoned. The account by Michael Mann is perhaps the most coherent and the most radical. He states, 'It may seem an odd position for a sociologist to adopt; but if I could, I would abolish the concept "society" altogether' (1986: 2). Using the term, he says, brings two problems. On the one hand, most accounts simply equate polities or states with 'societies'. Hence 'the enormous covert influence of the nation-state of the late nineteenth and early twentieth centuries on the human sciences means that a nation-state model dominates sociology and history alike' (1986: 2). On the other hand, the term ''society' implies a unitary social system, but, he says 'We can never find a single bounded society in geographical or social space' (1986: 1). Even nation-states are not 'bounded totalities'.

How, then, are we to understand 'society'? Mann argues that 'society' should be treated not so much as a unitary concept implying internal homogeneity, but a 'loose confederation', as 'overlapping networks of social interaction'. Hence a society is a unit with boundaries within which social interaction is relatively dense and stable, at least compared with interaction across its boundaries. The unitary conception of society, on the other hand, implies that because people are social animals, they are societal animals having a need to create a bounded and patterned social totality – a society in the strict sense of the term. Perhaps, then, we can have degrees of society.

Let us ask ourselves, says Mann, what society we live in. We may inhabit, at the highest level, 'western society', or 'capitalist society' and so on, and manifestly we live in 'British society' which implies that the national (*sic*) state forms a real interaction network. Of course, there are other 'socio-spatial networks of interaction' which we inhabit. Above all we participate in local 'societies', or communities which involve face-to-face interactions, as well as intermediate 'societies'. This 'mediating' world has been well described by the anthropologist, Anthony Cohen:

> A man's awareness of himself as a Scotsman may have little to do with the Jacobite wars, or with Burns, or with the poor state of the housing stock in Glasgow. It has to do with historical particular experience as a farmer in Aberdeenshire, as a member of a particular village or of a particular group

25

of kin within his village. Local experience mediates national identity.

(1982: 13)

We might invert the final sentence to say that national identity (in this case, being Scottish) also mediates local experiences insofar as these are made sense of in terms of the national level. The problems of living in an Aberdeenshire croft or in a Glasgow slum can be interpreted as the result of 'being Scottish', for example. Essential to this way of defining society as a series of partial, mediating networks of social interaction is the sense of belonging to them, and to what degree. In other words, these worlds are symbolically constructed; the sense of attachment (or detachment) is an important part of the definition.

If Scotland is a 'society' insofar as it provides a set of meaningful frameworks through which to judge social experiences, we need not deny that there are other levels of association – being a Gael, a Shetlander, a Glaswegian, for example. None of these necessarily negate, are at odds with, being 'Scottish'. This sense of national identity opens up the third level of understanding Scotland: its status as a nation.

SCOTLAND AS NATION

The concept of 'nation' belongs firmly to the ideological plane, and as such cannot be grasped directly. As Charles Tilly has put it, ' "Nation" remains one of the most puzzling and tendentious items in the political lexicon' (1975: 6). The final chapter in this book will address more fully the ways in which nationalism in its broadest senses helps to keep the idea of 'Scotland' alive, but it is important at this stage to set out the case for treating Scotland as a nation.

To say that 'nation' is ideological is not to imply that it is in some way false or inaccurate, contrary to material 'reality'. As Mann points out, we do not understand the world merely by direct sense perception, but by concepts and categories of meaning imposed upon what we perceive. In this respect, the ideological realm cannot simply be reduced to the material one, even although it may operate much of the time in close conjunction with these interests. 'Powerful ideologies are at least highly plausible in the

26

conditions of the time, and they are genuinely adhered to' (Mann 1986: 23).

Ideology is not 'false' even although, in Gramsci's words, 'the bad sense of the word has become widespread, with the effect that the theoretical analysis of the concept of ideology has been modified and denatured' (Gramsci 1988: 199). Ideology implies a source of power which is transcendent or immanent, deriving from a higher or 'sacred' form of authority set apart from secular structures. In this respect, it is vital that people share common beliefs in the legitimacy and potency of this higher order (religion is the obvious example), expressed through ritual and aesthetic forms. Mann quotes Bloch: 'You cannot argue with a song' (Mann 1986: 23).

The idea of the 'nation' has been in vogue since the Middle Ages and used to refer to a breed, stock or race, and only in the last few centuries implied a politically organised people. In the words of Raymond Williams,

> What has happened is that the real and powerful feelings of a native place and a native formation have been pressed and incorporated into an essentially political and administrative organisation which has grown from quite different roots.
>
> (1983: 181)

Its correlate 'nationalism' has been subject to shifting definitions and competing constructions, and has become, in Cohen's phrase, an ideological hatstand. Although today we associated 'nation' with the modern state, its usage is much older. Perhaps one of the most useful definitions is by Benedict Anderson, who outlines four characteristics. First, the nation is imagined insofar as it carries the image of communion, social interaction even with people one has never met. Second, nation is limited because it has finite, though elastic, boundaries. Third, it implies sovereignty in the sense that its members – the people – have the right to determine their future. This may or may not be in the form of a territorial state. Finally, nation implies community, a sense of deep, horizontal comradeship among people. Anderson talks of nations being 'imagined communities' because they require a sense of belonging which is both horizontal and vertical, in place and in time. The 'nation' not only implies an affinity with those currently living, but with dead generations. The idea of the nation is to be conceived of, says Anderson, 'as a solid community moving

27

steadily down (or up) history' (1983: 31). This idea of historical continuity is a vitally important part of the nation as imagined community. It implies links with long dead ancestors, and in Anthony Smith's words, 'the nation becomes the constant renewal and retelling of our tale by each generation of our descendants' (1986: 208).

There can be little doubt of the ideological power of 'Scotland' as a nation in these terms. It implies that Scotland is not simply a collection of rocks, earth and water, but a transcendent idea which runs through history, reinterpreting that history to fit the concerns of each present. In this respect, it is not unique. To say that Scotland (or Wales, Ireland or England for that matter) are 'figments of the imagination' is not to imply that they are 'false', but that they have to be interpreted as ideas, made and remade, rather than simply as actual places. Above all, they are places of the mind. In this regard, the term 'the Scottish people' implies a historical idea stretching back over centuries, implying that four-teenth century peasants and twentieth-century workers share some crucial identity. Nor is this unique to Scotland.

Consider the phrases 'the English people' or 'the German people'; these do not simply refer to those who inhabit the territory at one point in time, but to those who live elsewhere, and crucially those who once did (in history). Such phrases have been used to include as well as to exclude those who are deemed not to belong – those born elsewhere, those whose racial or ethnic characteristics are not accepted. Most obviously in the German case, the nation is not coterminous with the state, because until 1990 there were two states, to say nothing of those 'ethnic Germans' who live in other states and who claim some linguistic or cultural affinity.

'The Scottish people' presents problems of definition of those who would claim ancestry some generations ago, over against those living but not born in Scotland. The Welsh case shows nicely how conceptualising the nation can be time-bound and historically constructed. The late nineteenth century saw the remaking of 'Wales' as an ideological device for rousing 'the people' against the dominant foreigner – the English who were 'stealing the land' (Gwyn Williams 1980). In this context, language became a crucial 'cultural identifier' in Gellner's phrase, which included, and, of course, excluded. To borrow Anderson's comment, 'Seen as both a historical fatality and as a community imagined through

28

language, the nation presents itself as simultaneously open and closed' (1983: 133).

It is not necessary for nations to be linguistically distinct, but there are plenty of examples – not simply the Scottish one – of nations setting about constructing or, rather, reconstructing 'national languages' for political purposes: Hebrew, Norwegian, and even Irish, which was given a political significance out of all proportion to those who could actually speak it. The 'real' or authentic Ireland demanded that it should be politically asserted. Scotland's failure to mobilise an oppositional nationalism in the eighteenth century has been identified by Anderson as partly the result of the hegemony of 'English' in lowland Scotland, so eliminating 'any possibility of a European-style vernacular-specific nationalist movement' (1983: 86), although the distinctiveness of the Scots tongue might well have provided fertile political conditions for the re-assertion of nationalism (McClure 1988). Anderson's is an important point, but implies that other identifiers are less significant in generating nationalism. Language, however, carries disadvantages as well as advantages, because it erects a threshold, a tariff, which has to be met if one wishes to participate. Perhaps the strength of nationalism in Scotland *vis-à-vis* that of Wales reflects the fact that, despite (or because of) a lack of linguistic differentiation, nationalism can present itself as more than protecting a cultural past under threat.

The debate about the importance of language to nationalism masks a more fundamental point. There is a conventional wisdom that nationalism is simply the expression of fundamental, pre-ordained cultural and social differences. As Fredrik Barth puts it,

> We are led to imagine each group developing its cultural and social form in relative isolation, mainly in response to local ecologic factors, through a history of adaptation by invention and selective borrowing. This history has produced a world of separate peoples, each with their culture and each organised in a society which can legitimately be isolated for description as an island to itself.
>
> (1969: 11)

The point here is that nationalism is not the expression of objective differences, but the mobilisation of those which the actors believe to be salient. Barth is arguing that cultural differences should be seen, not as primary and definitional characteristics, but as the outcome or implication of social struggles. In this regard, 'the nation' is not a primordial form of social organisation, but an idea, an aspiration. It should be considered not simply as 'place' but as 'process'. We can, for example, ask meaningfully not simply 'Where is Scotland?', but also 'When was Scotland?'.

Nationalist movements usually have two answers to the question, one oriented to the past and one to the future; their task is to unite the two. In the case of the past image, the nation oftens exists in a Golden Age, as Raymond Williams points out, a romantic retrospect in which the nation and the society cohered. Sometimes this can be identified in history (before the loss of political independence, for example, when the country was 'whole') or more likely in the imagination. Secondly, it is necessary to project this image into the future, to imagine what the community will look like when it is whole and integrated again. Here the myths of history are a vital ingredient to the task. Traditions may be invented; symbols of national identity are manufactured. Perhaps there is a suggestion in the word 'invented' that myths and traditions are fabricated; what seems to happen is that the cultural raw materials are refashioned in a manner which gives coherence and meaning to action. The task is not to debunk these inventions, but to show how and why they are put to such telling use. Traditions and myths provide meaningful though partial interpretations of social reality and social change. They involve selective inclusion and exclusion, and thereby become a contemporary and active force providing a reservoir of legitimation for belief and action. Raymond Williams expresses it in this way:

> Tradition has been commonly understood as a relatively inert historicised segment of social structure; tradition as the surviving past. [However,] what we have to see is not just a 'tradition', but a selective tradition – an intentionally selective version of a shaping past and a pre-shaped present, which is then powerfully operative in the process of social and cultural definition and identification. It is a version of the past which is intended to connect with and ratify the present. What it offers in practice is a sense of predisposed continuity.

> (1977: 115)

Traditions, then, legitimise institutions, symbolise group cohesion, and socialise others into the appropriate beliefs and values. They

survive because they address present concerns. The growing literature on the 'heritage industry' (Wright 1985; Hewison 1987), for
example, shows how powerful the sense of a national past is in
the present. Above all, the past has an idealised air of a Golden
Age, and in mobilising this sense of the past, says Wright 'the
nation works to re-enchant a disenchanted everyday life' (1985:
24). What is on offer is 'ethno-history', a historicised, idealised
trajectory which provides a framework for social identity. In Scotland and Wales, different ethno-histories are on offer from the
dominant Anglo-British one, and these mobilise their own myths,
legends and traditions. In some instances, these ethno-histories
are built around powerful confessional identities which draw on
competing and oppositional political cultures. The two Irish identities typified by the Unionist 'No Surrender!' and the Nationalist
'Erin Go Brath!' are perhaps the best developed examples of these.

In examining Scotland as a nation, then, it is important to ask
what the mechanisms are which reproduce the necessary imagery.
We have to ask not only 'When was (or is) Scotland?', but 'Where
is Scotland?', and 'Whose Scotland?' There are, of course, competing versions of Scotland, using distinctions which have a mytho-
logical base: Scotland of the past and the present; Scotland of the
Highlands or the Lowlands; small-town east-coast Scotland versus
Scotland of the west-coast conurbation. At any point in history,
for example, some versions of Scotland may win out over others.
For example, the relegation of 'Catholic' history in eighteenth
and nineteenth-century Protestant Scotland (Ash 1980: 129); the
association of Scotland with Unionism in the nineteenth and early
twentieth century, and in the late twentieth their almost complete
dissociation.

Such images can, of course, be fought over and even 'captured'
by social interests who seek to turn them to material advantage,
but it would be a mistake to produce a simplistic association. One
of the most interesting developments of the last two decades, for
example, has been the way that the Scottish National Party has
turned a rich and diverse cultural meaning of Scotland into a
politically charged one, but one which frequently slips out of its
grasp. The party's problem for long enough was that it could find
no way of changing the idea of 'Scotland' into one of a politically
independent nation. 'Scotland' remained associated with the music
hall, tourism and cultural organisations. It was not until the discovery of North Sea oil that the SNP found the key to unlock

this rich source of political and cultural imagery. Similarly, the Conservatives in Scotland are genuinely perplexed that they have failed to mobilise what they see as 'Scottish' values of thrift, hard work and enterprise. The Thatcherite project was largely perceived north of the border as an alien, an English, political creed, despite its standard-bearer describing Adam Smith as 'a jolly good Scot'.

Other images of Scotland can be associated with material and political interests – the rural Scotland of the lairds, the industrial Scotland of the urbanised working class – all are images which compete against each other in the political realm, and all are constructed out of partial interpretations of Scotland. If Scotland is a nation, then we are entitled to ask, Whose nation? Whose image is being presented? And what are its political implications? 'Scotland' is above all a set of meanings, as is England, France, Germany and so on. Much depends on whose meaning wins out.

In many respects 'nation' is akin to 'community' insofar as the search for its 'real' parameters is less significant than the set of symbolic meanings which attach to it. In Anthony Cohen's phrase, community is essentially symbolically constructed; it does not reside in geographical or even social territory so much as in people's minds. 'People construct community symbolically, making it a resource and repository of meaning, and a referent of their identity' (1985: 118). The word 'nation' could just as easily be used instead of 'community' because the former is a version of the latter. Cohen again: 'People assert community, whether in the form of ethnicity or of locality when they recognise in it the most adequate medium for the expression of their whole selves' (1985: 107). Similarly, the notion of boundaries or frontiers takes on added significance, because these exist in the minds of the beholders as well as being material artefacts.

CONCLUSION

Nationalism is once more on the political agenda in Scotland and elsewhere, because rapid social and economic change has destabilised political conventions. The historic nation-state of the mid-nineteenth to mid-twentieth century is losing its *raison d'être*: in economic terms, there is a diminishing correspondence between political and economic systems. The nation-state appears to be losing its rationale in a world dominated by multinational corporations and trans-national organisations. Politically, the *raison d'état* of the nation-state, the control of violence and aggression, has been severely curtailed. In the field of culture, nations can no longer practise what Weber called *Kultur politische*, the political protection of cultural identity. Even in language, it has become very difficult for the modern state to continue to insist on mono-cultural language. Multi-culturalism becomes no longer desirable, but inevitable.

In this context, the claim to power of the nation-state is under pressure from two directions, from above from supra-national organisations (such as the European Community), and from below from national or regional autonomism. That such a phenomenon should happen within the United Kingdom simply reflects the special conditions which attach to British political and cultural life – its multinational legacy, the post-war paradigm of economic decline, the resurgence of English nationalism at the political centre, and Scottish and Welsh at the periphery. As Cohen puts it, the resurgence of ethnicity reflects 'the bankruptcy of the higher level entities as socio-psychological repositories of identity' (1985: 107).

The purpose of this chapter has been to examine the different levels of meaning which attach to Scotland – as country, as society and as nation. At each, Scotland has a distinct identity, and considerable cultural and political capital attaches to them. Because Scotland is a nation which is not a state, conventional sociological models – premised on the fusion of nation and state – are of limited utility. Nevertheless, as the nation-state loses its *raison d'être* in a world economy, polity and culture, so Scotland seems to provide a glimpse into the future rather than the past. Given that it is locked firmly into an ever-expanding world economy, the assertion of national identity and cultural distinctiveness comes at a most interesting time in its history. As such, Scotland stands at the centre of sociological concerns in this (post-) modern world.

2

UNDERSTANDING SCOTLAND'S DEVELOPMENT

Scotland presents problems as well as opportunities for sociologists and historians who would explain its 'development'. Even using this term seems to imply that certain assumptions are built into our explanation, concerning the trajectory of economic growth and social development. As this chapter and the following one show, the case of Scotland has attracted much interest from those who see it as an exemplar of certain general models of change, and as a result a number of key debates have been generated around the issue of development and social change in Scotland. Taken together, these two chapters provide a sociological account of Scotland's economic and industrial history, but their main purpose is to show how a particular conceptual and theoretical vocabulary has shaped the study of Scotland.

As we saw in the Introduction, the paradigm of 'modernisation' focuses on the nation-state and its internal workings. This 'internalist' perspective seeks to relate social and economic change to the workings of the political system in such a way as to show how that system both reflects and drives social change. In this context, Scotland has not figured except as part of the broader ('homogeneous') British state, and as such has been judged as having little separate rationale for sociological study.

In many respects conventional accounts of economic change are of limited applicability to Scotland. These are usually premised on the existence of a relatively self-contained nation-state, a 'social system' within which satisfactory causes can be located, on assumptions about the linear character of economic development, and on the supposition that nation-states are the 'natural' units which develop. Clearly, Scotland does not fit easily into this mould, not only because it lost its formal political autonomy in 1707, but

34

because even a superficial reading of its history reveals the extent to which its economic and social fortunes depended upon external factors.

In terms of its structural position in the historical development of the capitalist world economy Scotland is doubly unique. Britain as a whole was the first state to have a thoroughgoing capitalist revolution; second, Scotland's capitalist revolution occurred within a country lacking the political and institutional structures of statehood. Further, as Nairn has pointed out, such a transformation occurred before the ideological input of nationalism which was to inform the political and economic features of capitalist industrialisation in much of Europe (Nairn 1977). Scotland, he says, crossed 'the great divide' to become an industrialised society without the benefit or hindrance of nationalism, which usually acted as a political or ideological vehicle for much of the European bourgeoisie. Further, Scotland's economy was rarely if ever self-contained and independent. It was an open economy, reliant on external capital and technology, and subject to the vagaries of the broader economic and political environment, whether of Britain, or a wider European capitalist economy.

By the 1970s, Scotland became the explicit concern of sociology in two ways. First, the long-standing debate about the relationship between religion and the rise of capitalism made Scotland and what Allan MacLaren (1974) aptly called its 'Calvin factor', a natural subject for study. Second, the radical critique of modernisation theory, particularly by 'world-systems theory' opened up new models of development which seemed to fit non-states like Scotland much more appropriately. The lack of political statehood, the relative openness of its economy, and its reliance on external forces attracted a mode of theorising which has been termed 'externalist', and in this context versions of 'under-development' or 'dependency' theories have been applied to Scotland. Hence, in the 1970s, it became part of the analytical discourse when talking about Scotland to refer to it as a 'colony' (without being too precise as to which respects this was true), as part of the 'periphery' of the developed world. Borrowed as these terms were from accounts of Third World development (or, rather, under-development), such models had difficulty explaining why Scotland had been 'developed' or part of the 'core' in the first place. In strict terms, 'under-development' theory set out to show how much of the Third

World had been prevented from 'developing', rather than how it was that a 'developed' region could lose that status.

This chapter will focus on these debates and their relevance to Scotland. The next chapter will look in some detail at the most explicit version of these models, the thesis of 'internal colonialism', and ask whether Scotland actually took a different trajectory of economic development from the rest of Britain. This debate has proved to be crucial because the assumption that Scotland is a colony has largely rested on presumed differences with the rest of Britain, with the inference that Scotland was permitted simply to develop as a specialised region. The argument throughout these chapters is that while the new 'externalist' perspectives of world-systems theory and models of under-development have recognised the importance of a frame of reference wider than the nation-state, there is limited analytical value and not much empirical evidence for treating Scotland as a colony of England, the United States, or any other state for that matter. As such, these two chapters should be read together, although there is a rough chrono-logical division such that the following chapter focuses more on the 'modern' period, and this one sets out the debates in a more historical context. This chapter will review the major models which have been used to explain Scotland's development, and its purpose is to examine this in a sociological way rather than to give an economic history of Scotland, which others are better equipped to do. The key sociological question will be why it was that a poor, northern territory of north-west Europe – in the words of the economic historian, S. G. Lythe, 'la sterile Ecosse' (1960) – came to occupy a place in the forefront of economic development, and further, why it appears to have slid away from 'core' status in the twentieth century.

RELIGION AND THE RISE OF CAPITALISM

Religion has been one of the abiding cultural characteristics of Scotland which distinguish it from its southern neighbour. As the historian, Callum Brown, has put it,

> religion in Scotland has had an important bearing on national consciousness. For a people whose sense of nation-hood was removed early in the 18th century, religion

remained one of the few facets of Scottish civil life in which a collective identity could survive.

(1987: 6)

Furthermore, the role of Calvinism in Scotland has tended to be one of the main planks for those who would argue for the primacy of 'internal' factors in explaining Scotland's economic development, and in this respect it is difficult to make the connection between Calvinism and capitalism without mentioning Max Weber. As Gordon Marshall (1982) has shown, Weber only made passing mention of Scotland, but there seems little doubt that he saw Scotland as corroborating his thesis. Subsequently, his thesis has been subject to considerable criticism from historians as well as social scientists on the grounds that, if anything, Scotland disproves the link rather than confirms it. Two critical examples will, perhaps, suffice. In his authoritative *A History of Scotland*, J. D. Mackie states that 'Capitalism existed before Calvinism' (1978: 288–9), the implication being that the latter could not thereby cause the former. Similarly, Christopher Smout puts it this way:

> Max Weber's classic thesis suggests a close link between the rise of Calvinism and the rise of a capitalist economy in European societies. . . . Few countries were more completely Calvinist than Scotland, yet is hard to see how any support can be found for Weber's thesis from the situation in this country between 1560 and 1690.
>
> (1970: 95)

Such accounts, however, are careful to give credence in general terms to the link between capitalism and religion (or, specifically, Calvinism). Mackie again:

> What is true is that the regard for truth and honesty inculcated by the discipline of the Kirk was a good foundation for success in business, and that the Scottish people, trained to the 'economic' virtues in a long struggle against a hard environment, were quick to exploit the advantage offered by better conditions.
>
> (1978: 289)

Similarly, Smout agrees that 'if we take the long view of Scottish history it does become difficult not to believe that Calvinism contributed certain things which could hardly help but favour the expansion of economic activity and the enrichment of cultural life' (1970: 96).

Marshall provides an exhaustive and critical examination of the applicability of the 'Weber thesis' to Scotland in his book *Presbyteries and Profits* (1980). On the face of it, it might seem that the Scottish case does refute the thesis because, while no one can deny that Scotland was infused with Calvinism as early as the late sixteenth century, that it was a 'theocracy', it was not until at least a century or more later that it became in any meaningful sense a 'capitalist' country. There is considerable difference among commentators as to what Calvinism is meant to be explaining – the rise of an 'industrial', 'capitalist', or 'modern' society or whatever. While a number of historians line up against the Weber thesis (W. H. Marwick (1931); Hyma (1937); Fischoff (1944); Lythe (1960); Trevor-Roper (1963)), Marshall argues that they are 'collectively imprecise' about the consequences Weber reputedly attributes to the 'Protestant ethic'.

Weber, says Marshall, addressed two separate but related questions: that of determining the nature and origins of the 'spirit' of modern capitalism; and that of identifying the diverse origins of modern western capitalism itself. On the first issue, Weber argued that the origins of the modern capitalist mentality may well have been located in a neo-Calvinist ethos in the seventeenth century, while the 'spirit' of modern capitalism was only one of many factors which might explain material and economic changes. Hence, Marshall is able to show that

> Scots Calvinist-capitalists were amply imbued with an appropriate capitalist mentality (deriving, it seems, from their Protestantism), but their efforts had few discernible consequences for economic development because of the unfavourable circumstances in which they were made and which they proved unable to transcend.
>
> (1982: 138)

The nub of Marshall's argument is that Weber never claimed that ascetic Protestantism was a sufficient cause of economic transformation, which was dependent on a series of economic, social and political factors (what he called 'conditions for action'). Scotland, then, is not a 'refuting instance'. Marshall's purpose, however, is not simply to defend Weber in a negative way against his critics, but to show how, by the late seventeenth century, certain Scottish entrepreneurs (notably Sir John Clerk of Penicuik) not only adhered to the principles of capitalist business practice, but did so through the values and ideals of ascetic Calvinism. That Scotland did not 'take off' until the late eighteenth century and beyond reflected a series of adverse social, economic and political circumstances such as

> severely detrimental economic and political relationships between Scotland and certain neighbouring states, inadequate supplies of suitably skilled labour and of liquid capital for investment, and the inappropriate fiscal and industrial policies pursued by the state.
>
> (1982: 138)

It is perhaps difficult in late twentieth-century Scotland to grasp that Calvinism was not simply a religion in a narrow sense, but a social and political ethos rooted in distinct institutions. Calvinism was a highly flexible social ideology which could be used for diverse political purposes. The significance of 'Calvinism in one country', to use Harvie's apposite phrase, owed less to the all-persuasive appeal of such a religious belief than to its use by political and social factions as a means for grasping and legitimating power. By the second half of the eighteenth century, 'Calvinist' qualities of sobriety, frugality, industriousness and duty were stretched to some obvious material ends.

Allan MacLaren's study (1974) of the Disruption of the Kirk in Aberdeen after 1843 shows nicely how new social interests and an upwardly mobile elite took to the new evangelical Protestantism of the Free Church in part as a means to challenge the traditional merchants and the gentry. In many communities Calvinism became what sociologists today would recognise as a 'hegemonic ideology', reinforced by the social power of the Kirk to issue a 'character' – a reference – for access to jobs, housing, poor-relief, and even criminal justice. At its height, many Scots were indeed 'keppit by fear'.

Nevertheless, by the late eighteenth and early nineteenth centuries the power of the Kirk was in decline, while at the same time Scotland was becoming a thoroughly industrialised society. It is this disjuncture which leads Smout to conclude that 'Calvinism . . . seems to be released as a psychological force for secular change just at the moment when it [was] losing its power as a religion' (1970: 96). Such an apparent temporal disjuncture might seem to invalidate Weber's thesis, but as Marshall stresses, Weber was not pointing to a neat relationship between Protestantism and capitalism, but an 'elective affinity' between the ethic of Protestantism and the spirit of capitalism. It was not necessary for capitalists to be Calvinists. The social type, the *Berufmensch*, the man identified with his calling, belonged to an earlier age, but the secular legacy remained. In Weber's own words, 'The Puritan wanted to be a berufmensch. We have no choice but to be' (quoted in Poggi 1983: 87). As Poggi pointed out,

> A generation's moral project, embraced with a sense of its intrinsic validity (and perhaps of its religious significance) may become to later generations purely a set of tactical, expediential directives on how to adapt to objective constraints, followed purely because it would be impractical or foolish not to do so.
>
> (1983: 87)

The serendipity of social ideas allowed Calvinism, and not simply in Scotland, to become vital to the designs of key social groups. Wallerstein, who has found this country a particularly interesting test-case for his theories as we shall see below, argues that in certain societies in the sixteenth century on the fringes of Catholic civilisation,

> by a series of intellectually accidental historical developments, Protestantism became identified to a large extent in the period of the Reformation with the forces favouring the expansion of commercial capitalism.
>
> (1974: 153)

There does not seem much evidence, however, that the urban merchants were wearying of traditional methods and becoming thrusting capitalists, at least in the sixteenth century. The merchants and the burghs were conservative. As Lythe points out, 'By and large the townsman had his capital tied up in goods, houses and ships; his economic thinking was encased in tradition; neither mentally nor financially was he equipped for great adventures' (1960: 35–6).

The 'entrenched burghs' of Scotland were not the capitalist entrepôts of the sixteenth century, and the conservatism of the powerful Convention of Royal Burghs surfaced in opposition to the union of parliaments in 1707. Before the last decades of the eighteenth century there was little sign of indigenous capitalist enterprise within Scotland. After 1780 – a substantial time-lag from 1707 – new opportunities afforded by the Union were taken up by existing low cost, low overhead trades. The expansion of capitalism in Scotland seems to have owed more to external changes than to anything going on within its boundaries. From the late eighteenth century the influx of foreign capital and talent was stepped up. As Lythe comments, 'the inflow of foreign skill and of some foreign capital was, not surprisingly, a concomitant to each surge of domestic enterprise' (1960: 37).

Although by the 1620s Scotland was trying to align her mercantile practices to those of more powerful and sophisticated trading nations such as England, France and Holland, she was at a distinct disadvantage, and the 'notorious weakness' of Scottish government before the Union meant that no decisive and sustained commercial policy was followed. Even the nature of goods traded reflected the subordinate and semi-peripheral status of Scotland, especially the export of raw and semi-manufactured goods, and the import of finished and manufactured products. In the mid-sixteenth century, France was the major trading partner. Scottish merchants exported fish, raw wool, skins, some textiles and coal in exchange for quality textiles, provisions, and wines. By the early seventeenth century, the Low Countries formed the hub of trade, and in Lythe's words, 'to go to the Low Countries was to go to the emporium of Europe' (1960: 233). While the Scots exported essentially primary products to this core area of the world economy – skins, wool, fish, salt, lead and coal – imports consisted of crafted goods, manufactured products, and 'groceries'.

Important as trading links with Northern Europe were, they do not seem to have been the major factor in the penetration of capitalism into the Scottish economy. Scotland was a peripheral part of this central economy and probably would have remained so if new trading relationships had not been entered into with the burgeoning English economy. It became a truism that while the Union of 1707 was a military-political bargain for England, it was an economic one for Scotland. Trade with England in the early years of the Union continued to follow the traditional pattern, the exchange of Scottish raw materials for the more sophisticated products of England. The route to capitalism lay through fuller participation in the English core economy. The flow of ideas, of technology and of capital became the motor of Scottish capitalism.

41

The failure of the Darien Scheme in 1700 marked a significant turning point. Accordingly, the Union of 1707 took on an aura of inevitability despite the entrenched opposition of the merchants of the traditionalist royal burghs, who otherwise might have been expected to support it. Despite the fact that the burghs opposed the Union, the making of an indigenous class of capitalists began. In Smout's words, 'Both society and the economy would have been much more resistant to change in the 17th and 18th centuries if it had not been for the bourgeois leavening which such men provided' (1970: 172).

WHY SCOTLAND TOOK OFF

Inevitably, the makings of a capitalist economy was a fragmented affair. After the Union, for a considerable number of decades, the Scottish economy was relatively backward, and the promised prosperity failed to materialise. The penetration of anything resembling a modern form of capitalism was sketchy and regionally specific. Much of the thrust towards economic development came from the traditional social structure, and as Bruce Lenman points out, 'Successful growth was achieved by exploiting low overheads and existing trends' (1977: 87). Much depended on the inflow of skills, capital and technology, and on the post-Union opportunities of new markets.

Scotland's unusual dependence upon external factors for its development has attracted attention from Wallerstein and other theorists, who have applied the terms 'under-development' and 'dependency' to Scotland. In broad terms, a world-system level of analysis seems particularly appropriate to Scotland for three reasons. First, it is difficult to explain Scotland's economic trajectory in its own terms, given the importance of external forces; second, world-system theory claims to eschew analysis based on national states and national economies, arguing instead that, at least since the sixteenth century, a modern 'world-economy' has existed; and third, that such a theory, insofar as it was created in opposition to 'modernisation theory', has the potential to handle economic decline rather than simply growth. In this respect, it is possible for territories to move out of, and not simply into, the 'core' of the world economy.

Treating capitalism as a world-system rather than simply a characteristic of a national economy seemed, particularly in the

1970s, to provide a way of explaining Scotland's development. Some were not so sure. In 1980 a debate about the status of Scotland took place in the house-journal of world-system theory, *Review*, between Christopher Smout and Immanuel Wallerstein. Smout expressed scepticism about how useful it was to describe some territories as 'dependent', pointing out that there were excellent examples in history (Australia, New Zealand, Denmark) of territories which launched themselves by trading primary products to 'developed' countries, and which ultimately 'made it' into the core of the capitalist world-economy. In other words, 'dependency' was not necessarily a barrier to economic development (Smout 1980a).

In this context, Scotland seemed to provide an interesting test-bed. Smout applied to Scotland the four criteria of 'dependency' borrowed from the geographer, Alan Gilbert: namely, market dependency – a reliance on exporting a restricted range of goods to one richer area in return for the bulk of imports; technological dependency – a dependence on imported technology from richer areas; capital dependency – a reliance on injections of foreign capital; and cultural dependence – whereby the internal elite looked elsewhere for its cultural values.

On the face of it, eighteenth-century Scotland looked 'dependent'. It was significantly poorer than England, and if anything had grown more so since the sixteenth century. By the end of the eighteenth century, on a wide range of social and economic indicators Scotland lagged significantly behind England. Not only that, but on the four criteria it had grown more dependent since the sixteenth century. By the end of the eighteenth century, cattle and linen cloth made up the bulk of exports south of the border. The Union of the Crowns in 1603 still placed barriers on cross-border trade, but dependence had grown rather than diminished in the course of the seventeenth century. Similarly, virtually all new technologies came from the south, underlining Scotland's dependent position. Thirdly, while there was some primitive internal capital accumulation before 1700, the dramatic failures of overseas investments (Darien was by no means the only one) spelled out in stark terms the dearth of capital. Finally, 'foreign tastes' – in fashions, life-styles, and even education – preoccupied the social elite in the late seventeenth century.

All in all, Smout argues, by the eighteeenth century Scotland was indubitably 'dependent' on virtually any criteria. He comments,

> Early 18th century Scotland was, indeed, as much a dependent economy as any country could be in that age, tied specifically to England in commerce and decision-making, more generally to the core countries of England, the Netherlands and France in technology and culture, and tending to look to the same countries on the rare occasions when it needed exceptional capital inputs.
>
> (1980a: 612)

Nevertheless, Scotland, he claims, was not doomed to permanent 'under-development'. By the nineteenth century Scotland had embarked upon a programme of capital exports in per capita terms probably greater than England's, and its cultural dependency – particularly in education – had also been eroded. Smout concludes, 'The dependent status so obvious in 1700 indeed turned out to be a symptom of an early stage in development rather than an obstacle to growth' (1980a: 614).

He identifies six levers to economic growth. First of all, the cattle trade provided a limited opportunity for profits to be retained in Scotland, thereby helping to transform agriculture in Lothians and the border country in particular. Second, by means of the tobacco trade – a supremely 'colonial' activity – Glasgow was raised from the status of provincial centre to its later dominant position in the Scottish economy. Building on its native traditions, an indigenous bourgeoisie began to prosper in what was a considerably open system of social mobility. Third, the linen trade, was probably, in Smout's view, a more powerful boost to proto-industrialisation in Scotland. It was spread, north to south, over the expanse of lowland Scotland; its entrepreneurs were clearly Scottish; and it employed a large labour force – an embryonic proletariat. The fourth lever to economic growth north of the border, the cotton industry, was more recognisably a 'modern' industry, and while the English connection was important, Scots were able to win the initiative quickly. A similar situation occurred with regard to the mineral industry, the fifth lever. Finally, changes in lowland farming seemed to owe very little to English expertise and capital except in its early days. Scotland's exacting climate and topography allowed new indigenous developments to occur, with far-reaching consequences for the economic and social structures.

Smout concludes that 'dependency' *per se* did not block econ-omic development in Scotland, but rather was beneficial and benign: 'Dependency in Scotland's case was far from being a crippling handicap. Trade was not an engine of exploitation, but a cause of growth' (1980a: 628). Scotland, it seems, had been able to move (in Wallersteinian terms) from peripheral to semi-peripheral to core status because of its early 'dependency'. Five specific factors helped to bring this about:

- In the eighteeenth century, only small scale external capital requirements were needed (in contrast to under-developed countries today).
- The English were not interested in developing Scotland as a 'colony' (like Virginia or the West Indies) because Scotland had limited raw materials, and because the 1707 Union had served England's political-military purposes.
- Scotland's civil society had not been smashed by invasions and colonisations, unlike Ireland in the sixteenth and seventeenth centuries.
- Scotland's native culture remained strong, especially among its merchant class, the quintessential 'modernising' cadre.
- Scotland avoided over-rapid demographic growth (unlike Ireland and its own Highland periphery) by means of emigration and the discouraging of sub-tenancies on the land.

Scotland, claimed Smout, is a good exception to Wallerstein's rule that capitalism confines territories to peripheral status, and he points to other exceptions to the rule – New Zealand, Finland, Japan, Singapore.

In response, Wallerstein argues that Smout's own data can be used to prove his own point, namely that between 1600 and 1750 Scotland was undoubtedly peripheralised, but that in the century after, the process was arrested and reversed. His argument, in essence, is this:

> Scotland was a classic case – Lowland Scotland, that is – of 'development by invitation', the privilege (or the luck) of a very few, a case which offers few policy lessons for other states since it cannot be imitated at will.
>
> (1980: 633)

Of the factors which Smout identifies as important in accounting for Scottish development, Wallerstein argues that only two were significant. On the one hand, the fact that the native elite was not smashed, and on the other, that Scotland did not have resources worth having, both signify to Wallerstein that development by 'invitation' was operating. As to the six levers of economic growth, Wallerstein argues that while these may have been necessary, they were not sufficient. He insists that the choice to develop or not was not one made by the Scottish elite, but at the invitation of the English, and concludes,

> Scotland's secret was not structural; it was conjunctural. The Lowlands were in a position after 1745, in Hobsbawm's phrase 'to take advantage of the exceptionally favorable European and British conjuncture of the end of the eighteenth century'.
>
> (1980: 639)

It can be seen from this debate between Wallerstein and Smout just how difficult, even dangerous, it is to generalise to and from Scotland. While pinpointing lowland Scotland's 'development by invitation' as an important aspect of what happened it ignores the historical specificity of Scotland itself, and the double uniqueness of Scotland in its route to 'development'. Certainly, in its early stages, Scotland's conjunctural position seems to have been important; it found itself at a historic and geographical conjuncture which allowed it to pass, in Wallerstein's words, into the core and away from the periphery.

Using the words 'core' or 'centre' and 'periphery' carries ambiguity. Are these geographical, political, economic terms, or what? Do they imply an explanatory model, or are they merely metaphors? One commentator put the dilemma as follows:

> The opposition of the centre and the periphery seems to belong more to the category of expressive images than to that of coherent theories. Many spatial mechanisms of power show a tension between the margins and the heart of the system, but to lead everything back to that dialectic is unrealistic; it risks hiding the deeper causes of the lack of balance in the modern world.
>
> (Claval 1980: 70)

At a conceptual level, the imagery of core or centre and periphery is unsatisfactory because its vagueness allows the defining characteristics of these terms to be precisely those found in what is to be explained. The characteristics of the cause are bound up inextricably with those of its effect. At an empirical level, as we shall see in the next section, these terms have tended to overemphasise aspects of difference in economic and social development at the expense of those which are similar. Geographical imagery in itself does not provide an explanation. As Smout points out in a related article, also published in 1980,

> Neither the old slums nor the new got there because Scotland was a periphery; they were the consequence of the nature of Scottish Victorian capitalism and 20th century planning, just as the problems of Detroit or New York . . . are the products of the history of American capitalism and planning, not of any peripheral relationships within the USA.
>
> (Smout 1980b: 269–70)

The value of Wallerstein's world-system theory lies in its insistence – not always adhered to – that economic structure be viewed as a dynamic process of ebb and flow, in its startlingly simple but useful assumption that since the sixteenth century there has been but one capitalist world economy and a multiplicity of political and cultural systems, and in its characterisation of this economy as a single division of labour with core, semi-periphery and periphery, allowing surplus value to be extracted (sometimes literally) and retained by the core. World-systems theory is concerned with explaining broad changes at the level of the 'world-economy', and is less satisfactory when handling individual societies, which it tends to treat in a 'black box' manner, as if only external factors are important. As Roxborough points out,

> Most models of underdeveloped societies de-emphasise the extent to which the changing economic structure produces qualitative structural changes in the class structure and gives rise to changing patterns of class alliance which have repercussions at the level of politics and the state. The forms and histories of the class structures of underdeveloped societies vary greatly and form a central part of any explanation.
>
> (Roxborough 1979: x)

What, then, are we to make of the analytical value of the concepts 'dependency' and 'under-development'? In its strictest sense, 'under-development' is inappropriately applied to Scotland because it implies – in its Third World sense – that some territories

47

have been blocked or prevented from making the transition from feudalism to capitalism. Insofar as Scotland shared in the core status of England at the origin of the Industrial Revolution, that it unambiguously occupied 'core' status in the mid- to late nineteenth century, then 'under-development' strictly speaking is inappropriate. Nevertheless, the world-system perspective is attractive because it tries to get away from nation-states as the central actors (a guideline not always successfully adhered to), and because of the weight it places upon 'external' factors such as changes in exchange or market relations. In this respect, world-system theory belongs to a revisionist or neo-Marxian outlook, emphasising capitalism as a world-system rather than defining it as a mode of production. This perspective reflects its origins in the work of Gunder Frank who sought to show that plantations or latifundia in Latin America were 'capitalist' because they produced for a world market even although they used slave or unfree labour (A. G. Frank 1969).

World-system theory belongs firmly to neo-Marxian formulations rather than more orthodox or classical ones. Thus it emphasises exchange or market relations over production relations; relations of external dependence over traditional internal class relations; territorial or national formations over social formations of production; the (frequently geographical) transfer of surplus value over exploitation within the labour process.

Wallerstein's model in particular has come in for criticism on a number of counts, firstly, for being over-economistic, and ignoring the internal system of class relations which derives from the dominant mode of production (Brenner 1977). Secondly, in spite of his desire to jettison national states as key actors in the world system, his model seems to demand that they are just that. As Theda Skocpol observes,

> Wallerstein hoped to overcome the worst faults of modernisation theories by breaking with their over-emphasis on national states and their tendency towards ahistorical model building. Ironically though, he himself ends up reproducing the old difficulties in new ways. Thus strong states and international political domination assume crucial roles in his theory.
>
> (1977: 1080)

Even if we accept the theoretical validity of Wallerstein's theory, does Scotland fit? Or does Scotland, as Smout argues, actually undermine the theory by being the exception which does not prove the rule? And if Wallerstein has to modify his theory to include 'development by invitation', that conjunctural rather than structural factors explain Scotland's development, is there not a suspicion that the model lacks an empirical cutting edge? There is also a methodological problem of circularity in the argument insofar as 'dependency' tends to become a pseudo-concept which explains everything in general and nothing in particular. To caricature, as O'Brien does, 'Dependent countries are those which lack the capacity for autonomous growth, and they lack this because their structures are dependent ones' (Roxborough 1979: 44).

It was undoubtedly the case, however, that in the late 1960s and early 1970s, the intellectual climate in Scotland was receptive to such a theory, which implied that the country was externally controlled, was even perhaps a colony. The colonial metaphor seemed especially relevant at a time when the SNP was making headway with the electorate, and when concern about Scotland having a 'branch-plant' economy was beginning to surface. The words 'dependency', 'under-development' and 'colonialism' seemed to have a ring to them. They chimed with the prevailing mood of the times. An early example of applying a loose Frankian framework to Scotland (and Wales) came from Buchanan (1968) who assumed that these countries were simply 'dependent', a state of affairs ultimately measured by differences in the level of a series of socio-economic indicators. Similarly, a contribution by Bryden in the 1970s in a publication called, evocatively, *Underdeveloped Europe* used a range of indicators as both cause and effect of the state of 'under-development'. Perhaps the most sophisticated account was by Michael Hechter in his book with the resonant title *Internal Colonialism* (1975), a concept he borrowed from the Third World to study the 'Celtic fringe' of Britain. Because he treats Scotland, Wales and Ireland as 'ethno-nations', as surrogate classes as it were, discussion of his work will be held over until Chapter 4.

THE HIGHLANDS AS PERIPHERY

If treating Scotland as a whole as 'peripheral' and 'underdeveloped' is somewhat problematic, it is the Highlands of Scotland which have attracted the description most often. There is the added irony that the Highlands provide many of the images and meanings for Scotland as a whole in the late twentieth century. Perhaps more has been written by historians and social scientists on the Gaelic-speaking Highlands than the rest of Scotland put together. In cultural terms, its imagery dominates. As the anthropologist Malcolm Chapman says,

> We are faced with the problem that a language not understood by 98% of the Scottish people, with a modern literary tradition that only begins to assume importance in the late 18th century and is still very small ... and spoken by a people who have been regarded for centuries by their southern neighbours as barbarians should now be regarded as the quintessence of Scottish culture.
>
> (1978: 12)

Interpreting Highland history has become something of a cottage industry, with, broadly speaking, two opposing views: the orthodox one that Highland history since 1745, and particularly the Clearances of people from the land in the eighteenth century was economically necessary if somewhat socially unfortunate, and the radical stance that what happened in the last two hundred years was tantamount to class warfare in which people lost their birthright. So powerful has the imagery of the Clearances remained in Scotland that their resonances have been pressed into the service of modern political and industrial issues from factory closures to late twentieth-century emigration. It is not the purpose of this chapter (or indeed this book) to 'solve' the controversy concerning the original Clearances, but to examine the interpretations put on Highland history from the perspective of 'underdevelopment'.

In 1974, Ian Carter, then a sociologist at Aberdeen University, described the Highlands as an 'underdeveloped region'. His paper built on an earlier analysis in *Scottish Studies* in 1971 of economic models which had been applied to the Highlands. Carter used the concept of 'underdevelopment' that he had taken from the work of André Gunder Frank in Latin America. He argued that the conventional way of seeing the Highlands was as an archaic, pre-capitalist, even feudal region whose future lay in opening up its traditional way of life to the market forces of the modern economy. He then said that such a model was fundamentally flawed, because it was premised on a very narrow conception as to what 'development' was. Such an account, he argued, betrayed the assumptions of a 'dual sector' model, which set out two dichotomous economic sectors, the traditional and the modern. Such a dichotomy lay at the heart of modernisation theory which had dominated development economics for so long, but which by the 1960s was being challenged by radical perspectives linked, sometimes loosely, to 'underdevelopment' or 'dependency' theory.

The classical economic stance implied in the dual economy model saw the Highlands as unequivocally 'backward'. Here, for instance, is the explanation by A. J. Youngson in his book *After The Forty-Five* (1973) as to why the Highlands 'failed' in the nineteenth century:

> They (the peasants) clung to the land because it seemed their only guarantee of subsistence and of the continuity of life. These people were the remnants of a feudal system which had ebbed away, leaving them stranded in remote glens and straths.
>
> (1973: 179)

Committed, as he saw them, to traditional ways of life, they would find the answer to their plight in embracing modern practices. He goes on, 'The Clearances to which so much attention has been paid in Highland history were important; but they were no more than the visible, breaking crest of a long-travelling, irresistible wave' (1973: 185), or, if one can change the metaphor, the impact of the hidden hand of the marketplace. 'Progress' requires the setting aside of 'status' and 'tradition' (1973: 201).

Radical revisionists such as Ian Carter and James Hunter took issue with this characterisation. Hunter replied that 'the crofter has never been immune from the pressures generated by capitalist civilisation. Indeed, he has suffered from them more than most' (1976: 2). Carter applied a more sociological understanding by arguing that much of what was considered 'traditional' in the Highlands was nothing of the sort. Hunter and Carter both argued that 'crofting' was by no means a 'traditional' means of livelihood, but the rational response of a people moved off the more fertile land in the glens to the marginal lands of the coast. Farming with a little fishing (or vice versa) became a sensible adaptation to circumstances over which the crofter had little control.

Carter's analysis (1974) of the black cattle and kelp (seaweed) industries was undertaken to show that both of these were market-oriented, organised on capitalistic lines. The cattle trade was essentially a commercial operation with Lowland or even English markets. The kelp industry – which involved obtaining alkaline for the making of glass, fertiliser and soap – came into its own during the Napoleonic wars when the traditional sources in Spain were cut off. The escalation in price allowed Highland landlords to organise their people in what was a labour-intensive industry, largely because they held monopolistic control over their tenants' output. The driving force for the kelp industry was the desire of the landlord to maximise profit. Kelp, said Carter, was a paradigm case of what Barrington Moore Jr. called 'conservative modernisation'. In Moore's words, 'the landed upper class will use a variety of political and social levers to hold down a labour force on the land and make its transition to commercial farming in this fashion' (Carter 1974: 301).

Carter directly employed concepts borrowed from underdevelopment theory, referring to a similar controversy over 'modernisation' in Latin America. Gunder Frank had taken issue with modernisation theorists who treated latifundia (the fundamental institutions of Iberian colonialism) as archaic and pre-capitalist. Frank pointed out that there was no analytical difference between latifundia and plantations because both existed to maximise profit for the owner, while in the case of the latifundio, this purpose was concealed by seemingly non-commercial relationships between owner and peasants. Regions became locked into systematic under-development by means of the contradiction of metropolis-satellite polarisation:

> The metropolis expropriates economic surplus from its satellites and appropriates it for its own economic development. The satellites remain underdeveloped for lack of access to their own surplus and as a consequence of the same polarisation and exploitative contradictions which the metropolis introduces and maintains in the satellite's economic structure.
>
> (Frank 1969: 33)

Frank described this process of systematic exploitation as 'underdevelopment', pointing out that while developed regions may at some point in their history have been undeveloped they were not systematically prevented from developing, that is, they were not underdeveloped.

Applying these ideas to the Highlands, Carter concluded that characterising them as backward is historically inaccurate and sociologically limiting. His debt to Frank's analysis was acknowledged:

> A number of consequences follow from this on Frank's assumptions. Any attempt to strengthen the links between the Highlands and the 'modern' economy through a large-scale exploitation of indigenous Highland raw materials . . . will increase the underdevelopment of the area by reinforcing the satellization of the Highlands.
>
> (1974: 302)

Crucially, whether or not a region is defined as 'backward' is, he said, a matter of definition. The Highlands had embraced economic change with new trades (cattle, kelp, crofting), and had long since left traditional runrig joint farm systems behind. Nevertheless, because they had not produced a polarised social structure of capitalist farmers and landless wage labourers, such change could not count, in official circles, as 'improvement'. All in all, said Carter, 'it all depends what you mean by development' (1974: 303).

What is sociologically interesting about Carter's analysis is that it explicitly attempted to import Frankian, even Wallersteinian, modes of analysis. It is clear, for example, that he preferred to define capitalism as a system of exchange, as a market system rather than as a mode of production. Latifundia in Latin America and cattle rearing in the Scottish Highlands were therefore defined as forms of capitalistic activity in this way rather than because these systems employed free, waged labour. Interestingly, in his later work, Carter used a more 'orthodox' definition of capitalism in analysing 'the articulation of capitalist and pre-capitalist modes of production in the countryside' (1981a: 87). A peasant population existed in the late nineteenth-century north-east because capitalist or 'muckle' farmers needed essential supplies of hired labour power, and because peasant farmers supplied quality lean cattle for fattening. Their demise by 1914 resulted from the removal of these two necessary conditions for generating profit.

Carter's work represented an important attempt to apply a new revisionist Marxism to Scotland, or rather, to the Highlands of Scotland. His work shares much with the historical account of crofting published by James Hunter in 1976. Carter was careful not to imply that what is true for that region of Scotland is true for the country as a whole. In an interesting aside, written as footnote to his article on the Highlands as an underdeveloped region, he criticised Buchanan's analysis, described above, for treating the Highlands and Scotland as co-extensive: 'His [Buchanan's] argument depends on the Lowlands standing in the same satellized situation to the English metropolis that I am here arguing for the Highlands; and the argument will not hold' (1974: 306).

Somewhat surprisingly, he went on to produce an alternative form of the same argument:

> Lowland industrialisation was the result of the English allowing a place in the metropolitan sun for certain specialised heavy industries, provided that they were *complementary* with the English economy and *not competitive*, and Scottish capital was invested abroad – three-quarters of the foreign investment in ranching in the United States in the 1870s and 1880s was Scottish.
>
> (1974: 306, my emphasis)

We have here a distinct echo of 'development by invitation' as described by Wallerstein in his debate with Smout. The view that Scotland's economic trajectory was shaped explicitly by its relationship with England has proved to be a powerful if somewhat flawed analysis. It has implied that certain forms of economic activity were forbidden to the Scots, that Scotland's economy developed in a highly specialised form, and that its class structure was somehow deformed by an essentially 'colonial' relationship. The notion that capitalism in Scotland took a 'complementary' rather than a 'competitive' form took root in academic writing in the 1970s. We shall argue in the next chapter that this was an attractively powerful but highly contentious account of Scotland's development.

3

IS SCOTLAND DIFFERENT?

In the theoretical vocabulary of the late sixties and early seventies, Scotland was indubitably 'dependent'. In this chapter, we shall see that this view, implicit or explicit, guided many of the research agendas and commentaries on Scotland. The notion of Scotland as a colony echoed many of the political concerns of the day. The rise of political nationalism, the extension of foreign ownership into Scottish business, the coming of the multinationals – all seemed to fit the idea that Scotland was dependent. Such a perspective did not emerge from a careful assessment of Scotland's structural position in the world economy, but rather grew out of sense of a country which had lost control of its own economic, political, even cultural, affairs. To the question, 'What is wrong with Scotland?' came the chorus, 'Scotland is dependent'.

In this context, a world-system perspective provided many of the theoretical answers to the 'problem' of Scotland. Scotland was invisible because it was no longer a nation-state, and the conventional paradigms passed it by. It had become a region of a homogeneous state of Great Britain. The notion of a 'world-system' – a unit with a single division of labour and mutiple cultural systems, in Wallerstein's phrase, seemed to liberate Scotland from this analytical vacuum. National states, which had been conventionally treated as the organising categories of analysis, were relegated to bit-players in this system, because, according to Wallerstein, they were not 'societies that [had] separate, parallel histories, but were parts of a whole reflecting that whole' (1979: 53). Contrary to the prevailing wisdom of the time, all states were not in a position to 'develop' simultaneously, because the system functioned by having core and peripheral regions.

The notion of a nation-state becomes problematic, because the idea of a nation is essentially a political claim that the boundaries of a state should coincide with those of a given ethnic group. Hence, it is not very useful, according to world-systems theorists, to distinguish nations from other kinds of ethnic groups. Further, says Wallerstein and his colleagues, 'if we are to use a strict definition of the concept "nation", we would be hard pressed to find even one "nation-state" in the entire world-system' (Arrighi et al. 1983: 302).

If social classes are the key social actors, as in conventional Marxist thinking, deriving their position from the dominant system of production, then this revisionist neo-Marxian analysis elevates nations or rather 'ethno-nations' to a position of coequal strategic importance in social struggle. Indeed, said Wallerstein, 'both classes and ethnic groups, or status groups or ethno-nations are phenomena of world-economies' (1979: 24). Here Wallerstein was not implying that ethno-national groupings were the same as Weberian status groups, despite using the same term. While for Weber status groups, like social classes and political organisations or parties, were, theoretically, agents of social change and conflict, Wallerstein's view was different:

> I believe 'class' and what I prefer to call 'ethno-nation' are two sets of clothing for the same basic reality. However, it is important to realise that there are in fact two sets of clothing, so that we may appreciate how, when and why one set is worn rather than the other. Ethno-nations, just like social classes, are formed, consolidate themselves, disintegrate or disaggregate, and are constantly re-formed.
>
> (1979: 224–5)

Wallerstein distanced himself from Weber because he saw both class and ethnicity as manifestations of the workings of the capitalist world-economy, not as theoretical alternatives based on quite different stratification systems. Nevertheless, while 'class' refers to this worldwide economy, this global economic system, 'class consciousness' is essentially a political – a national – phenomenon, and takes different forms including both overt class consciousness and 'ethno-national' consciousness. Wallerstein pointed out that virtually all the social revolutions – in Russia, China, Vietnam, Cuba – have been both 'social' and 'national'. Again,

It is similarly not at all accidental that oppressed lower strata in core capitalist countries (Blacks in the United States, Quebecois in Canada, Occitans in France, etc.) have come to express their class consciousness in ethno-national terms.

(1979: 230)

Class action and ethno-national protest are, then, different expressions of the same underlying struggle, they are 'kaleidoscopic reflections of a fundamental reality' (1979: 230).

While classes 'in themselves' develop in the context of a capitalist world-economy, classes 'for themselves' make conscious claims to a place in a particular political, that is, national, order. Hence, said Wallerstein, E. P. Thompson writes about the making of the 'English working class' because he is interested in how a proletariat forms itself within the conditions set by a political structure. Irish workers (and, presumably, Scottish) were defined as a different group, because 'the construction of a "class" was *ipso facto* part of the construction of at least two "nationalities", the English and the Irish' (Arrighi *et al.* 1983: 301).

There have been similar attempts by others to incorporate ethnic or national groups into a class analysis. From a more orthodox Marxian perspective, John Foster sought to rehabilitate national or ethnic struggles by adapting the concept of 'ethnic social carrier' which is 'the specific historical carrier of the ethnic at a particular moment' (1989: 40). Foster was trying to counter the view of Tom Nairn and others that the theory of nationalism is Marxism's greatest historical failure (Nairn 1977: 1). Within both a neo-Marxian and orthodox Marxian perspective, then, attempts were made to rehabilitate national struggles as class struggles. Said Wallerstein,

One can see the recrudescence of ethno-nationalisms in industrialised states as an expression of class consciousness of lower caste groups in societies where the class terminology has been preempted by nation-wide middle strata organised around the dominant ethnic group.

(1979: 61)

SCOTLAND AND INTERNAL COLONIALISM

Perhaps the most explicit (and contentious) attempt to employ the language of colonialism and dependency to 'ethno-nations' in Britain was that of the American sociologist, Michael Hechter.

Published in 1975 and entitled *Internal Colonialism: the Celtic Fringe in British National Development, 1536–1966,* Hechter's book was an ambitious attempt – in both conceptual and methodological terms – to apply an explicit Wallersteinian framework to Britain: 'It would not even have been attempted without his example', he acknowledged (1975: xvii). Hechter argued that orthodox 'diffusionist' models of development imply that strong core regions, through powerful central governments, are able to establish one national culture. To the contrary, an 'internal colony' model argues that a spatially uneven wave of modernisation creates relatively advanced and less advanced social groups and territories. The stratification system which emerges generates a 'cultural division of labour':

> To the extent that social stratification in the periphery is based on observable cultural differences, there exists the probability that the disadvantaged group will, in time, reactively assert its own culture as equal or superior to that of the relatively advantaged core. This may help it conceive of itself as a separate 'nation' and seek independence.
>
> (1975: 10)

Hechter acknowledged the origins of the notion of 'internal colonialism' in the Third World – specifically Latin America – and refined it through its application to US race relations, before exporting it across the Atlantic to the 'Celtic fringe'. Like other versions of underdevelopment, internal colonialism implies that, in contradiction to a diffusion model, the 'backwardness' of the periphery can only be aggravated by systematic transactions with the core, not aided by them. Hechter borrowed from the anthropologist Fredrik Barth the notion of a 'cultural division of labour' whereby social roles are allocated differentially to different ethnic groups. From Ernest Gellner he adopted the idea of ethnic nationalism being generated by the uneven spread of industrialisation through territorial space so that cleavages of interest form around ethnic differences. Said Hechter,

> The superordinate group, now ensconced as the core, seeks to stabilise and monopolise its advantages through policies aiming at the institutionalisation and perpetuation of the existing stratification system. Ultimately, it seeks to regulate the allocation of social roles such that those roles commonly

defined as having high status are generally reserved for its members. Conversely, individuals from the less advanced group tend to be denied access to these roles. Let this stratification system be termed the cultural division of labour: it assigns individuals to specific roles in the social structure on the basis of objective cultural distinctions.

(1975: 39)

This lengthy quotation gives the essence of Hechter's argument, and points out some of the problems in applying it to 'British national development'. Despite some considerable statistical sophistication applied to handling a range of social and economic indicators at the level of counties, his thesis seems methodologically forced into its theoretical frame. He adopted broad ethnic definitions of 'Anglo-Saxons' and 'the so-called Celts of Wales, Ireland and parts of Scotland' (1975: 47). This division corresponds to a 'radical split' down the middle of Britain between highland and lowland zones, divisions not simply geographical but reflecting 'types of social organisation' (1975: 58).

Celtic nationalism is the political response to the persistence of regional inequality, and in particular to the process of anglicisation, especially in language and religion. Industrialisation alone does not effect the national integration of Britain, as predicted by the 'diffusion model', but performs a mediating role for the persistence of regional identities on the Celtic fringe. While diffusion models predict the demise of peripheral ethnicity, the internal colonial model is justified insofar as ethnicity has persisted and grown. Industrialisation did allow a degree of integration, but its later effects were limited:

Though the partial industrialisation of Wales and Scotland did permit the structural integration of these regions into the national society [sic], principally through the establishment of national trade unions and the Labour Party, persisting economic stagnation in the periphery has shaken much confidence in the class-based political organisation.

(1975: 265)

Hechter's analysis generated considerable interest and controversy, not simply on the 'periphery'. Critics pointed out, moreover, that Scotland was a poor fit for his theory. While at times careful to refer only to the Gaeltachd of Scotland, at other times Hechter slid into a more general equation. Scotland was described as 'the sole Celtic land to have been politically united' (1975: 71). More generally, Hechter was careful to distinguish between the Highlands, indubitably Celtic, and the Lowlands which were 'culturally anglicised' (in language and religion, most evidently). Because of this, Scotland, he admitted, provides a 'more complex' case than Wales and Ireland. His solution was to say,

> Because the rulers of the Scottish state were themselves culturally anglicised, their English counterparts felt it unnecessary to insist upon total control over Scottish cultural institutions, as they had done in Wales and Ireland.
>
> (1975: 342–3)

This is a revealing statement, not simply because it implies, dubiously perhaps, that the version of 'English' spoken by Scots before 1707 was the same as that in the south, but because it employs much the same kind of explanation as Wallerstein has in his encounter with Smout – development by invitation. In other words, because Lowland Scots adopted English manners and practices, they were 'allowed' to participate in British economic development. As such, while they were subordinate to wider British interests, they were dominant in their own territory, a point echoing Gunder Frank's analysis of Latin American 'underdevelopment' in which a chain of metropolitan or satellite relations operate. This point of 'dependent development' is explicitly reinforced by Hechter a few pages later:

> Industrialisation did not diffuse into the peripheral areas in the same form as it had developed in the core. When industrialisation did penetrate the periphery, it was in a *dependent* mode, consequently production was highly specialised and geared for export.
>
> (1975: 345, my emphasis)

We will return to this assumption of 'dependency' and 'regional specialisation' later, because it has become one of the key assumptions built into analysis of Scotland and other 'peripheral' regions of the UK. At the end of his book, Hechter has few doubts about the validity of his analysis. 'The Celts', he claimed, 'are an internal colony within the very core of this world system' (1975: 348). He was careful not to allocate them to the periphery, but to a special place in the cultural division of labour at the core. At this stage,

Hechter proclaimed the homogeneity of 'the Celts' and the supremacy of 'the world-system'.

INTERNAL COLONIALISM REVISITED

Some ten years later, Hechter had begun to modify his account of the Celtic fringe in the light of the criticism, especially from historians. His basic theme survived, namely, that nationalism was ultimately derived from the existence of a cultural division of labour, 'a stratification system giving cultural distinctions political salience by systematically linking them to individual life chances' (1982: 9). Southern Ireland remained, he thought, 'a stunningly clear example of internal colonial development' (ibid.), while Scotland – at least its Lowlands – had been more of an 'overdeveloped' peripheral region than an 'underdeveloped' one. The second, and more fundamental criticism, he admitted no answer to – that he could provide no direct evidence that a cultural division of labour existed.

Delving into US ethnic history, Hechter found a parallel to the Scots in the Jews (*vis-à-vis* the blacks, for example) who had become 'very highly occupationally specialised' (1982: 10). This led him to modify his theory, to say that the cultural division of labour has two dimensions: a hierarchical one in which groups are vertically distributed in the occupational structure, and a segmental dimension in which groups become occupationally specialised at different (theoretically, any) levels of the structure. In this way, ethnic groups may manage to retain a degree of occupational autonomy, even, as in the case of the Scots, of institutional autonomy, which generates what Hechter called a 'segmental cultural division of labour'. Similarly, he had to revise his theory of social action, of nationalism, by making it less dependent on common material interests which are a necessary but not sufficient cause of action. Instead, support for nationalist movements varies according to the degree to which actors face limited sources of benefit.

Despite these revisions, or indeed because he has to make them, Hechter's account remains flawed. There is more than a suspicion that his sophisticated statistical gymnastics are insufficient to validate his theory because, ultimately, his data are not actually about the cultural division of labour on which his thesis rests. His revisionist interpretation of Scotland as an 'overdeveloped peripheral region' as is Catalonia, has a touch of desperation about it. Describing Scotland as 'overdeveloped' as an explanation for neo-nationalism when 'underdevelopment' does not do the job does not ring true.

Tom Nairn (1977) has also used, albeit in a more sophisticated way, the distinction between Scotland as 'underdeveloped' and as 'overdeveloped' (North Sea oil provided at least the possibility) because his theory of nationalism is also classically 'externalist'. Nationalism is to be explained by the uneven development of capitalism at a world level. Nevertheless, Nairn does avoid the excesses of 'analytical Third Worldism' when it comes to Scotland. If 'underdevelopment' refers to a systematic blockage in development of the 'periphery' then Scotland does not fit, because, as Nairn points out, Scotland along with the rest of Britain made the great transition to industrial capitalism before it happened anywhere else in the world. To describe Scotland as 'underdeveloped' because it has been prevented from crossing, in Polanyi's phrase, the Great Divide, makes neither analytical nor empirical sense. What cannot be denied, however, is the powerful imagery which 'dependency' and 'colonialism' brought to academic study as well as to political practice. Its power is that of the metaphor rather than explanatory concept, and it is these concepts that have shaped academic work on Scotland, by both historians and sociologists alike.

Much of the debate on Scotland's status *vis-à-vis* the British state has hinged upon the degree of divergence in economic development since the Union of 1707. Specifically, did Scotland simply become a specialised economic region of Britain, or did it develop as a diversified industrial system, albeit with internal regional specialisation? What can we read into patterns of industrial and occupational change about Scotland's political and economic relations with the rest of Britain?

INDUSTRIAL AND OCCUPATIONAL CHANGE IN SCOTLAND

Between 1750 and 1850 Scotland became not simply an industrial society, but one of the world's foremost examples. In particular, as Christopher Smout points out,

> the central belt of Scotland became ... one of the most

intensively industrialised regions on the face of the earth. By 1913, Glasgow, claiming for herself the title of 'Second City of the Empire', made, with her satellite towns immediately to the east and west, one-fifth of the steel, one-third of shipping tonnage, one-half of the marine-engine horsepower, one-third of the railway locomotives and rolling stock, and most of the sewing machines in the United Kingdom.

(1987: 85)

Other cities in Scotland had also captured markets, the most notable being Dundee, which processed virtually all the jute that came to Britain. Dundee became known as a 'women's town', not simply because there were three women to every two men between the ages of 20 and 45 in 1900, but because a very large proportion of women worked (in 1921, 24 per cent of married women worked in Dundee compared with only 6 per cent in Glasgow and 5.6 per cent in Edinburgh) (Smout 1987:88). On the other hand, Glasgow had produced a male-centred working class culture in which it became a mark of skilled status that wives did not work.

Given that prosperity (for a few) rested upon a small number of industries, it is tempting to conclude that Scotland's development depended on its becoming regionally specialised. The dominant image of Scotland's industrial structure was, in the words of the historian Bruce Lenman, that 'by the 19th century, Scotland had developed a very specialised regional branch of the British economy, heavily oriented towards the manufacture and export of capital goods and coarse textiles' (1977: 204).

We find this assumption of regional specialisation in Marxist and non-Marxist accounts alike. For example, one of the most influential and comprehensive histories of capitalism in Scotland, *Scottish Capitalism*, underlines 'the commitment of Scottish industry to the production of a relatively narrow range of specialisms, like ships and other heavy engineering equipment, which were so essential to the growth of world trade' (Dickson 1980: 194). The authors of this book explain this specialisation in terms of the way capitalism developed in Scotland:

In relation to Britain as a whole, what were to emerge in Scotland were *complementary* rather than *competitive* forms of capitalism, their interdependence being regularised under the political domination of Westminster. Such were the roots of the dependent or *client* status of the Scottish bourgeoisie.

(Dickson 1980: 90)

This distinction between 'complementary' and 'competitive' forms of capitalism echoes exactly that made by Carter in his analysis of the Highlands of Scotland. In each book, the supposition is made that Scottish capitalists were allowed only to develop those forms of economic activity that did not conflict with those of their more powerful counterparts in the south. But this distinction seems somewhat superfluous, even misleading, as an account of the development of capitalism in Scotland (or even in England, for that matter). In what was perhaps the quintessential free market economy, there is little need to import the notion that economic activity was managed by the state (or 'Westminster', in the words of the previous quotation). Insofar as capital would flow into those sectors where profits were to be made, and capitalists would invest in areas on strictly economic terms, the notion of 'complementarity' (with its implication of explicit intervention in the workings of the market) does not ring true. Such a perspective seems unduly influenced, albeit implicitly, by Wallerstein's notion of 'development by invitation': that Scottish capitalists were permitted to take on certain forms of economic activity which would not 'compete' with those of English capitalists. It is difficult to see what the mechanism would be for permitting or forbidding such activity.

While it is true that simply comparing the industrial structures of Scotland with those of the rest of Britain will not itself tell us whether or not Scottish capitalism was 'complementary' or 'dependent', such an exercise does give a much more accurate guide to industrial development in Scotland *vis-à-vis* England and Wales. Using the reclassified data in the work of the economic historian C. H. Lee (1979), it is possible to estimate more precisely than hitherto the differences in the industrial structures of Scotland and Britain. To do so is not to betray a sense of insecurity that Scottish economic development cannot stand on its own, but to set this development in the firm context of British patterns. Given that much of the interpretation about Scotland has depended upon such comparisons (implicit or explicit), the task is an informative and a necessary one.

Lee reclassified the industrial and occupational data in the censuses from 1841 to 1971 according to the 1968 Standard Industrial Classification (SIC). There are, of course, methodological difficulties in handling changing categories and classifications across such a span of time, particularly when industries themselves have undergone such massive change. The textile industry of 1841, for example, was not that of 1971. Nevertheless, Lee's data are incomparably better than anything else we have, and do allow a degree of comparison between regions which casts light on whether Scotland was 'different' from other 'Standard Regions' in the UK. Certainly, treating Scotland, Wales and other standard economic units in this way seems methodologically preferable to dealing with such imprecisions as 'the Celtic fringe'.

1851–1911

Table 3.1 gives the structure of industrial employment (the sixteen manufacturing orders plus mining and quarrying) for Britain as a whole and for Scotland and Wales individually in 1851 and 1911.

Table 3.1 Industrial orders as percentage of total industrial employment in Britain, Scotland and Wales, 1851 and 1911

Industrial order	Britain		Scotland		Wales	
	1851	*1911*	*1851*	*1911*	*1851*	*1911*
2. Mining and quarrying	9.5	14.8	9.3	16.6	36.9	51.9
3. Food, drink and tobacco	10.0	13.6	9.0	13.2	8.1	10.2
5. Chemicals	1.2	2.1	0.9	1.9	0.6	1.1
6. Metal manufacture	7.2	7.1	6.3	9.3	17.3	11.9
7. Mechanical engineering	1.9	6.2	1.7	7.8	0.9	3.0
8. Instrument engineering	0.6	0.5	0.3	0.3	0.3	0.2
9. Electrical engineering	–	1.4	–	0.8	–	0.7
10. Ships and marine engineering	0.8	1.9	0.8	5.1	0.9	1.1
11. Vehicles	1.2	2.3	0.6	1.1	0.9	1.1
12. Other metal goods	2.4	3.9	1.0	1.9	1.0	1.5
13. Textiles	32.2	18.1	44.4	19.3	7.1	2.9
14. Leather, etc.	1.5	1.5	0.9	0.8	1.2	0.4
15. Clothing and footwear	22.3	15.0	18.3	11.0	20.3	9.7
16. Bricks, pottery, glass	2.4	2.2	1.0	1.3	0.8	1.1
17. Timber and furniture	4.7	3.8	3.5	3.8	3.1	1.6
18. Paper, printing, publishing	1.8	4.8	1.9	4.9	0.7	1.4
19. Other manufacturing	0.5	1.1	0.2	1.1	0.1	0.2
	100.0	100.0	100.0	100.0	100.0	100.0
	N = 4,022,135		578,974		181,993	
	8,350,684		1,008,550		498,484	

It is clear that while there are differences between Scotland and

Britain, they are nowhere as great as those between Wales and Britain. The simplest way of comparing industrial employment structures is the positive percentage difference, or the index of dissimilarity. To calculate this index for Britain and Scotland in 1851, one simply adds together the differences between the British and Scottish percentages for those industries for which the British figure is higher. If the structures were identical, the index would be zero. If they were completely different, the value would be 100. In 1851, the index of dissimilarity between Britain and Scotland was 12.3, and in 1911, 10.2. The comparable index for Britain and Wales, on the other hand, was 37.6 in 1851, and 41.9 in 1911.

It should be remembered, of course, that the positive percentage difference (ppd) has to be interpreted with care, because its size is determined by the number of categories, not just by the degree of dissimilarity. Nevertheless, because we are making comparisons based on a fixed number of categories, it is an appropriate measure to use in these circumstances. Similarly, while we can make comparisons between Scotland (and Wales) and Britain, it makes little sense to compare England and Britain because, given its relative size, it would be bound to show very low positive percentage differences. Nevertheless, the ppd does provide an intuitively straightforward measure for our purposes here. Hence, if one calculates the indices of dissimilarity between the industrial structures of the ten Standard Regions of Great Britain, Scotland in both 1851 and 1911 appears as the closest to the overall British structure. In 1851 the mean value of the index between the regional structures and that of Britain as a whole was 25.4 compared with the figure for Scotland of 12.3, and in 1911 the mean was 25.7 compared with 10.2 for Scotland.

A representation of Scotland's pattern of industrial specialisation and industrial change relative to that of the other nine Standard Regions is achieved by muti-dimensional scaling (Coxon 1982). The data upon which the scaling is based are the industrial employment distributions of the ten regions at four time points: 1851, 1871, 1891, 1911. Positive percentage differences were calculated between all pairs of the forty industrial employment distributions. The multi-dimensional scaling programme tries to reproduce the rank ordering of the dissimilarites between the industrial structures in terms of distances between the corresponding data points in the plotted space. The result is that similar industrial structures will tend to be closer together in the solution

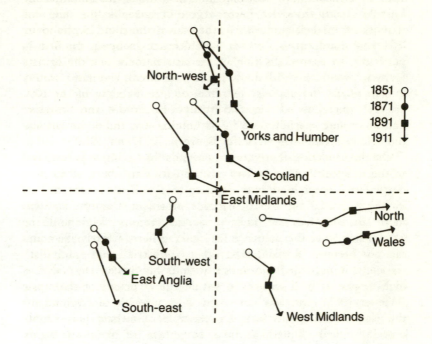

Figure 3.1 Two-dimensional MINISSA scaling of positive percentage differences between industrial employment structures (Industrial orders 2–19) of ten British regions

space. Thus a spatial assessment can be made of the relative magnitude of shifts across time as compared with differences between regions at one point in time. Since the positive percentage differences on which the solution is based are generated by the distributions of the seventeen industrial orders which make up the industrial sector, different areas of the multi-dimensional scaling solution space will tend to correspond to specialisation in particular industries or groups of industries with similar regional and temporal distributions. The two-dimensional solution for the British regions at the four dates are given in Figure 3.1.

The four data points (1851, 1871, 1891 and 1911) for each region have been joined up to facilitate the tracking of the region's trajectory through 'industrial space'. The group of regions at the top of the plot consists of those whose industrial workforces in 1851 were most heavily concentrated in textiles. Scotland and the East Midlands showed a lower degree of specialisation, and this is reflected in their positions further down the plot. In the lower left-hand quadrant is another well-defined grouping marked in particular by a specialisation in the manufacture of clothing and footwear, combined with a low proportion of employment in heavy industries. At the opposite extreme, on the far right of the plot, are the two regions – Wales and North of England – whose massive and increasing specialisation in coalmining was the dominant feature of their employment shifts between 1851 and 1911.

On this evidence, there are no grounds for saying that Scotland in the nineteenth century had an industrial structure which was particularly specialised with respect to the British economy. If anything, Scotland mirrored Britain's industrial structure, and was more 'British' than the other economic 'regions'. We should be careful in noting the point we are making here. Clearly, Scotland did not become 'British', but rather 'industrial' and 'capitalist'. As such, it remained a country within the British state with a high degree of civil autonomy within the structure of that state (Wiener 1981), and was not reduced to a region of England (as the North of England was, for example). Scotland was simply especially well-adapted to take advantage of Britain's highly advantageous structural position within a world economy itself shaped around Britain's interests. As Kirby put it,

> The distinctive nature of Britain's industrial structure was in fact one of the most outstanding features of the pre-1914 economy. In 1907 the old-established staple trades of textiles, coalmining, iron and steel, and general engineering accounted for approximately 50% of net industrial output and employed 25% of the working population. Most were heavily dependent upon an increasingly narrow range of export markets located mainly within the British Empire, South America and Asia, and coalmining, textiles and iron and steel alone contributed over 70% of the country's export earnings.
>
> (1981: 3)

Insofar as Scotland was so well adapted to imperial opportunities in the nineteenth century, the collapse of the post-World-War-One economy was more catastrophic for Scotland. The roots of

68

Scotland's decline are to be found in a 'surfeit of imperialism' rather than, as is more commonly supposed, in a position of clientage or dependence. When the international order collapsed, Scotland – locked firmly into it – suffered in the way experienced by Britain as a whole.

The extreme localisation of the effects of this collapse within Scotland in the 1920s and 1930s stemmed from the degree of regional specialisation which had occurred within Scotland prior to the war. Significant specialisation had taken place within Scotland in the nineteenth century. From a generally shared specialisation in textiles in 1851, industrial specialisation rapidly took place along two main axes, as shown in Figure 3.2.

The first shift, focused in particular on Renfrewshire and Dumbartonshire (more correctly, on Clydeside) was into engineering and shipbuilding, represented by a move down towards the bottom of the plot. The second was into coal and steel, represented by those areas moving towards the top right-hand side of the plot. By 1911 there was thus roughly a tripartite pattern of regional industrial development formed by shifts along these two axes and the relatively unchanged position of those regions which had maintained their specialisation in textiles, primarily around Paisley, Dundee and the Borders.

(Again, we should draw the reader's attention to the categories being used here. The towns and counties of Scotland are, to a high degree, units of comparison which are administratively derived, and contain internal differentiation which their simple categorisation ignores. Nevertheless, they do provide useful comparative units as long as we recognise that they are administrative rather than sociological constructs.)

The Inter-War Period

Largely because of the switch in 1921 from an occupationally based to an industrially based classification in the population census, it is much more difficult to trace industrial employment changes from 1911 to 1931. Campbell's work on the Censuses of Production of 1907 and 1924 conveys a picture of stability, in which the industrial structures of Scotland and the UK changed rather little, and remained on the whole alike (Campbell 1980). However, such differences as did exist in this period were to prove highly significant in the future. In 1907, 27 per cent of Scotland's industrial

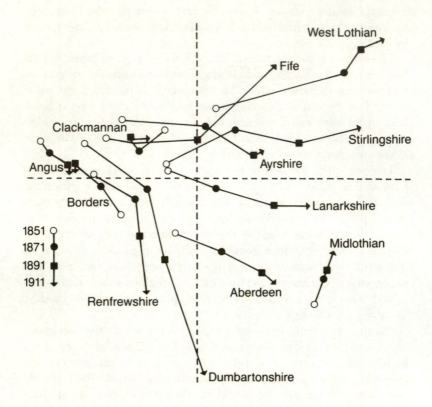

Figure 3.2 Two-dimensional MINISSA scaling of positive percentage differences between industrial employment structures (Industrial orders 2–19) of twelve Scottish industrial areas

workforce was employed in 'iron and steel, engineering and ship-building' compared with 22 per cent for the UK as a whole.

1931–1971

In these four decades in the middle of this century, the industrial structure of Scotland appears to have been marginally more differentiated from that of Britain as a whole than was the case in the nineteenth century. The indices of dissimilarity between Scottish

Table 3.2 Industrial orders as percentage of total industrial employment in Britain and Scotland, 1931, 1951, 1961, 1971

Industrial order	Britain				Scotland			
	1931	1951	1961	1971	1931	1951	1961	1971
2. Mining and quarrying	14.9	9.5	7.9	4.6	16.4	11.4	10.8	5.0
3. Food, drink and tobacco	9.1	8.4	7.7	8.7	11.6	11.1	10.4	13.7
4. Coal and petroleum products	0.4	0.5	0.6	0.7	0.6	0.5	0.5	0.4
5. Chemicals	2.8	4.5	4.8	5.4	2.1	3.9	3.9	4.2
6. Metal manufacture	5.2	6.4	6.9	6.5	7.2	7.2	7.9	6.8
7. Mechanical engineering	6.4	10.5	12.4	13.2	8.0	12.2	14.6	14.0
8. Instrument engineering	0.7	1.3	1.6	1.7	0.5	1.0	1.4	2.5
9. Electrical engineering	3.5	6.3	8.3	9.9	1.2	2.1	4.0	7.2
10. Ships and marine engineering	2.2	3.1	2.6	2.1	4.9	8.8	7.9	5.6
11. Vehicles	5.8	8.3	9.2	9.3	3.3	4.2	4.0	5.1
12. Other metal goods	4.6	5.7	5.8	6.9	2.2	3.4	2.8	4.1
13. Textiles	15.5	11.1	8.7	6.9	17.8	13.5	12.3	10.4
14. Leather, etc.	1.1	0.9	0.7	0.6	0.7	0.7	0.5	0.5
15. Clothing and footwear	11.8	7.6	6.0	5.5	6.3	4.6	3.5	4.5
16. Bricks, pottery, glass	3.4	3.5	3.5	3.6	2.0	2.5	2.6	3.0
17. Timber and furniture	3.9	3.7	3.3	3.5	5.5	4.5	3.5	3.8
18. Paper, printing, publishing	6.2	5.8	6.7	7.2	6.8	6.0	7.1	7.3
19. Other manufacturing	2.5	3.0	3.2	3.8	2.7	2.4	2.4	2.2
	100.0	100.0	100.0	100.0	100.0	100.0	100.0	100.0

and British industrial employment structures were as follows: 1931, 15.4; 1951, 16.1; 1961, 18.2; 1971, 14.6. Table 3.2 gives the pattern of industrial employment for Britain and Scotland from 1931 to 1971.

The indices of specialisation, shown in Table 3.3, reveal that there was a convergence at a regional level in Britain in general. The first index is the mean index of dissimilarity between all pairs of regions; the second is the mean index of dissimilarity between the ten regions and the British structure.

Table 3.3 Indices of British regional specialisation

1931	29.1	30.2
1951	24.5	26.0
1961	24.1	24.9
1971	21.1	20.0

In 1931 and 1951 Scotland remained the region with the industrial structure closest to the British mean, and in 1961 and 1971, only north-west England was closer. Generally, the other British regions were converging with Scotland. A three-dimensional scaling plot, Figure 3.3, shows this tendency clearly.

The rate of industrial change in Scotland seems to have accelerated in the 1960s (the percentage points difference is 12.0 compared with 6.6 for Britain as a whole), reflecting the fact that Scotland caught up to some extent in the electrical engineering category. By 1971, 9.7 per cent of Scotland's industrial employment was in these two orders compared with 11.6 per cent of British.

Nevertheless, the general process of convergence in the industrial regions of Britain in the twentieth century is not mirrored (up to 1971) within Scotland. In many respects, as Figure 3.4 shows, the traditional specialisations of the nineteenth century remained in the regions of Scotland well into this century.

The temporal trajectories suggest that the regions retained in the twentieth century the relative positions bequeathed to them by the nineteenth. In most respects, industrial differentiation within Scotland has been of a higher order of magnitude than the industrial differentiation of Scotland from the rest of Britain. Perhaps the tendency to write the economic history of Scotland from the

72

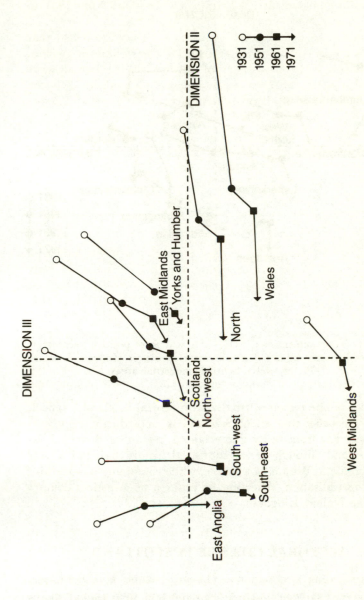

Figure 3.3 Three-dimensional MINISSA scaling of positive percentage differences between industrial employment structures (Industrial orders 2–19) of ten British regions

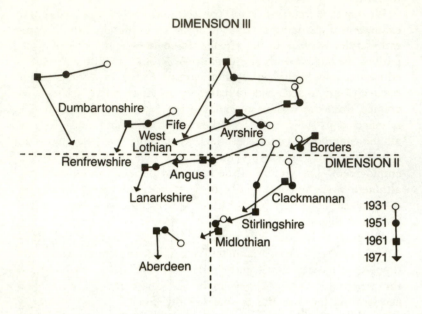

Figure 3.4 Three-dimensional MINISSA scaling of positive percentage differences between industrial employment structures (Industrial orders 2–19) of twelve Scottish industrial areas

standpoint of one region – usually west central Scotland – reflects itself in the belief that all of Scotland is, accordingly, regionally specialised. Far from being a specialised 'region' of Britain, however, Scotland throughout its industrial history has had a very similar profile to Britain as a whole, while containing considerable internal specialisation, reflecting its position as a distinct country within the United Kingdom.

SECTORAL CHANGE IN SCOTLAND

In understanding occupational change, change at the broader sectoral level has been much more important than change in the industrial structure. Table 3.4 shows the long-term trends in sectoral employment structure for Britain and Scotland from 1851 to 1981.

We have to remember, of course, that the service sector for example is a changing category, consisting predominantly of domestic-service workers in the nineteenth century, and today of occupations associated with the expansion of state functions, notably education and health. A further caveat is that in 1911 a major recategorisation occurred (a category of distributive trades was created from the various manufacturing orders), and this change is reflected in the table. Nevertheless, in both 1851 and 1911, of all the Standard Regions, Scotland's structure was the closest to the British one, once more mirroring the patterns for industrial employment. The picture of the inter-war period is more complex, although a slight convergence of sectoral employment structures takes place, both between Scotland and Britain, and between the Standard Regions in general.

Although it is from 1951 onwards that the 'occupational transition' – the shift from manufacturing to service employment – is thought to have occurred in advanced industrial societies, only in the 1970s does this happen in a fairly unequivocal way. The accelerating increase in the share of the service sector – from 24 per cent in 1951, to 26 per cent in 1961, to 33 per cent in 1971, and finally to 43 per cent in 1981 – is undoubtedly the greatest single shift in sectoral employment which Scotland has experienced in modern times. The growth of the service sector has been by far the greatest single identifiable motor of social change in Scotland since 1945. The changes in occupational structure, patterns of female employment and social mobility right through to household structure, demographic behaviour and political orientations can be traced back to this single transformation.

OCCUPATIONAL CHANGE IN SCOTLAND, 1921 TO 1971

Paralleling the belief that Scotland's industrial structure has been characterised by 'regional specialisation' (reflecting its 'dependency') is the view that its occupational structure has also been shaped by external relationships with England. Specifically, we encounter in the literature the view that Scotland has undergone a process of 'de-skilling' or 'proletarianisation' *vis-à-vis* its southern neighbour. This is often linked to the increasing dominance of

Table 3.4 Sectors as percentage of total employment in Scotland (top line) and Britain (second line offset), 1851–1981

| | Sector | | | | | | |
	Agriculture, Forestry and Fishing	Mining and Quarrying	Manufacturing	Construction	Intermediate	Service	Index of dissimilarity
1851	26.0	4.4	43.2	5.5	5.0	15.9	5.2
	23.2	4.3	40.9	5.7	5.8	20.1	
1871	23.6	5.6	40.9	6.6	6.5	16.8	8.0
	16.7	5.1	40.3	6.8	7.0	24.2	
1891	15.3	6.3	43.2	6.4	9.3	19.6	6.5
	11.7	5.8	40.8	6.8	10.1	24.8	
1911a	11.4	8.7	43.9	6.0	10.3	19.8	6.8
	8.4	7.2	41.6	6.8	10.5	25.5	
1911b	11.8	8.0	36.5	5.9	18.5	19.3	7.5
	8.7	6.6	33.5	6.6	19.6	25.0	
1931	10.1	6.0	30.3	4.2	25.4	24.0	5.5
	6.4	5.6	32.1	5.0	24.0	26.8	
1951	7.4	4.5	35.1	6.9	21.9	24.1	4.3
	5.1	3.8	36.3	6.3	21.4	27.2	
1961	5.8	3.9	32.5	7.9	23.7	26.2	5.0
	3.7	3.1	36.1	6.9	22.6	27.7	
1971a	4.1	1.7	32.2	8.2	21.0	32.8	2.5
	2.7	1.7	34.6	7.1	21.0	33.0	
1971b	2.7	1.9	33.4	7.9	20.6	33.4	3.2
	1.9	1.8	36.4	5.6	20.6	33.5	
1981	2.3	1.9	25.4	7.5	19.8	43.1	4.3
	1.7	1.6	28.6	5.3	20.9	41.9	

Scottish manufacturing industry by foreign multinational companies in the post-war period. These elements are appropriately fused in the following:

> in importing production line branch plants requiring, in the main, semi-skilled workers and a disproportionately low number of technical and skilled workers as against indigenous employers, US firms reinforced the de-skilling processes already at work in the economy. This de-skilling led one writer to conclude that by the mid 1970s, Scotland was 'more working class, and its population . . . less skilled, *vis-à-vis* England, than at any time since the First World War'.
>
> (Dickson 1980: 246)

This quotation is drawing on the evidence of the Scottish Mobility Study at Aberdeen University in the 1970s. Geoff Payne's analysis of trends in the occupational structure is a classic instance of the influence of internal colonialism models. He wrote,

> Hechter's ideas of internal colonialism, or the models of dependency and exploitation of the periphery seem better suited to the explanation of the impoverishment of Scotland's manpower than the grand but unworkable theories of convergence and technological determinism.
>
> (Payne 1977: 35)

Payne's claim that Scotland was being de-skilled compared with England was taken up by other writers as the most significant characterisation of the Scottish occupational structure (Watson 1980: 154; and Watt 1982: 222). We will see later, however, that Payne's conclusion has been taken out of context and given a new interpretation by later writers.

The problems of constructing a long-term series showing changes in the occupational structure are even more daunting than in creating an industrial series because the bases of occupational categorisation have been much revised. Nevertheless, we have two fairly reliable series with which to chart occupational change in Scotland. First of all, the Scottish Mobility Study reclassified the occupational distributions for 1921, 1931 and 1951, according to the socio-economic classifications used in the 1961 and 1971 censuses. Naturally, caveats must remain. A system of categories constructed on the basis of one set of criteria – the 1921 census, for example, cannot be translated simply into a similar system for socio-economic categories in 1971. Secondly, if we are to make such comparisons, we are forced to accept the assumption that terms like 'skilled' in 1921 meant the same in 1971. Clearly, the nature of work has changed to such an extent that we cannot be sure that such meanings stand the passage of time.

Bearing these problems in mind, these data do give us certain pointers. For instance, there has been a continous decline in skilled manual workers as a proportion of the non-farm workforce – from 35.3 per cent in 1921 to 24.3 per cent in 1971. Second, there has been a continuous rise in the number of non-manual employees.

The general impression given in Table 3.5 is once more of parallel development between the socio-economic structures of Scotland, and England and Wales. The percentage points differ-ences (ppd) shows no systematic divergence over time. Scotland does have a larger proportion of unskilled manual workers. Trevor Jones (1977), in his debate with Payne over interpreting these data, performed calculations on the 1971 industry by socio-econ-omic group matrices to show that this was not the result of a peculiar industrial structure, but reflected a higher proportion of unskilled workers within industries. The same was true of Scot-land's preponderance of skilled manual workers.

What light do these data shed on the assumptions about Scot-land becoming 'de-skilled' and proletarianised? It has to be said that there is some analytical confusion involved. The comment made by Dickson and his colleagues earlier is presumed to refer to de-skilling *within* the manual labour force, principally in the form of a swing away from skilled manual to semi-skilled manual work. What Payne, on the other hand, meant by Scotland being less skilled than England and Wales was a change in the relative balance between non-manual ('more skilled') and manual (less skilled, but, crucially, including *skilled manual* workers). In other words, Dickson *et al.* see a relative diminution of skilled manual workers as a proportion of the *manual* workforce as evidence of de-skilling. Payne actually refers to the fact that Scotland has rela-tively more skilled and unskilled manual workers as a proportion of the *total* workforce.

The fact that Scotland's industrial structure is close to the Brit-ish mean suggests that its occupational structure would be also, and so the data show. Only that of the north-west of England is closer to the British mean. Scotland's proportion in most

Table 3.5 Socio-economic groups 1 to 12 (non-farm, non-armed forces), each shown as a percentage of total, in Scotland, England and Wales, 1921–71

Socio-economic group		1921	1931	1951	1961	1971
1 and 2 Employers and managers	Scot.	6.1	5.6	6.2	6.8	8.0
	E + W	7.2	6.3	7.3	8.2	9.7
3 Professional self-employed	Scot.	0.6	0.4	0.4	0.7	0.7
	E + W	0.5	0.6	0.4	0.6	0.6
4 Professional employees	Scot.	1.3	1.1	1.6	1.8	2.8
	E + W	1.0	0.8	1.6	2.4	3.2
5 Intermediate non-manual	Scot.	3.1	3.1	4.4	6.1	8.2
	E + W	3.2	2.9	4.0	6.2	8.1
6 Junior non-manual	Scot.	14.7	15.9	19.5	21.9	21.6
	E + W	12.9	15.3	19.6	21.8	22.6
7 Personal service	Scot.	7.7	8.9	5.7	4.7	5.7
	E + W	8.8	9.7	5.8	5.0	5.5
8 Foremen and supervisors	Scot.	1.4	1.5	1.9	2.5	2.6
	E + W	1.4	1.3	1.8	2.5	2.6
9 Skilled manual	Scot.	35.3	31.3	29.0	28.2	24.3
	E + W	33.6	30.1	28.3	25.5	22.4
10 Semi-skilled manual	Scot.	15.4	14.1	14.9	15.8	13.9
	E + W	16.7	14.4	14.8	16.1	13.5
11 Unskilled manual	Scot.	10.3	13.9	13.8	9.6	10.3
	E + W	9.1	13.2	12.1	8.4	7.8
12 Own account workers	Scot.	3.9	4.2	2.5	1.9	2.0
	E + W	5.6	5.4	4.4	3.4	3.9
ppd between structures		5.1	3.2	3.0	4.1	5.2

Source: Payne 1977

Table 3.6 British regions: socio-economic groups as percentage of all economically active men, 1971

Socio-economic group	Great Britain	England and Wales	Scotland	South-east	East Anglia	South-west	West Midlands	East Midlands	North-west	Yorkshire and Humberside	North	Wales
1	3.8	3.9	3.6	4.5	3.1	3.3	4.0	3.5	3.7	3.5	3.3	2.7
2	7.9	8.1	6.2	10.0	7.7	8.4	6.7	6.7	7.4	6.8	5.6	6.6
3	0.9	0.9	0.9	1.1	0.9	1.0	0.7	0.7	0.8	0.7	0.7	0.9
4	4.2	4.3	3.7	5.6	3.5	3.8	3.8	3.6	3.8	3.0	3.2	3.1
5	5.7	5.8	5.0	6.9	5.0	5.8	4.9	5.0	5.3	4.6	5.0	5.2
6	12.2	12.3	11.1	14.9	10.1	11.5	10.2	10.6	11.9	10.5	10.5	9.6
7	1.0	1.0	1.1	1.4	1.0	1.1	0.6	0.6	0.9	0.8	0.8	0.8
8	3.6	3.6	3.5	3.2	2.9	3.0	4.0	4.1	3.9	4.3	4.1	4.1
9	30.6	30.3	33.1	25.4	27.1	26.7	35.4	36.4	31.7	35.1	36.1	32.5
10	13.0	13.0	13.1	11.4	11.7	11.8	15.6	13.1	14.8	14.3	13.1	14.2
11	7.8	7.6	10.2	6.4	6.8	6.6	7.1	6.7	9.6	8.7	10.1	9.8
12	4.6	4.8	2.5	5.6	5.3	6.1	3.8	4.1	4.5	4.0	2.6	4.4
13	0.8	0.8	1.1	0.4	2.1	1.8	0.7	0.9	0.4	0.7	1.0	1.1
14	0.8	0.8	1.0	0.3	1.7	2.1	0.8	0.9	0.5	0.7	1.2	2.8
15	1.6	1.4	2.7	1.0	6.3	2.7	1.2	1.9	0.5	1.4	1.6	1.4
16	1.5	1.6	1.3	1.9	5.0	4.1	0.7	1.2	0.3	1.0	1.2	1.0
ppd from Great Britain			6.6	10.2	11.1	8.3	7.9	6.9	5.1	7.3	9.0	8.3

Source: 1971 Census, Great Britain, regional economic activity, pt IV, table 31

socio-economic groups occupies a fairly median position with respect to the other Standard Regions.

Scotland does have the highest proportion of unskilled workers as well as the lowest proportion of *petit bourgeois* groups: SEG 2, employers and managers in small establishments, and group 12, own account workers. In terms of white-collar employment, however, the divide is not between Scotland and the rest, but between the south-east of England and the rest. In Scotland, as in other Standard Regions of Britain, the expansion of white-collar employment has been by far the most important transformation since the Second World War.

OCCUPATIONAL CHANGE IN SCOTLAND, 1961 TO 1981

The considerable revisions of the occupational classifications that took place for the 1981 census make simple comparison of this year's data with previous ones difficult and dangerous. It has been possible to apply an adjustment factor to the published figures to compensate for the effects of the changed classification. This involved adapting cross-classifications of the old 1970s socio-economic groups against the new ones for 1980 codes which had been produced for England and Wales and applying these to Scotland (for a fuller account, see Kendrick 1986: 267, note 3). The socio-economic group is the basic unit of classification in the censuses, and is based on a combination of occupation and employment status. The comparable changes over time are reproduced in Table 3.7.

The expansion in non-manual employment was occurring before 1961, but has continued subsequently, notably for professional employees, intermediate non-manual workers (such as teachers, nurses, and 'non-managerial' non-manual workers). Manual work has continued to decline, especially the skilled manual group, from 27.6 per cent in 1961 down to 19.8 per cent in 1981. However, Scotland is by no means extreme in this regard, lying in a middle band along with Wales and the north-west of England. It is, once again, difficult to escape the conclusion that Scotland's occupational structure largely mirrors that of Britain as a whole. In his review of occupational change in Scotland, Kendrick concluded:

81

Table 3.7 Socio-economic groups as percentage of total employment in Scotland, 1961, 1971, 1981

		1961	1971	1981 adjusted	1981 published
1.2, 2.1	Employers	2.6	2.2	2.3	2.2
1.2, 2.2	Managers and administrators	3.9	5.6	7.0	7.4
3	Self-employed professionals	0.7	0.7	0.8	0.6
4	Professional employees	1.7	2.7	3.8	3.2
5	Intermediate non-manual	5.8	8.1	10.8	11.3
6	Junior non-manual	20.8	21.1	21.9	20.9
7	Personal service	4.4	5.5	6.4	6.4
8	Foremen and supervisors (manual)	2.4	2.5	2.7	2.7
9	Skilled manual	27.6	22.8	19.8	19.2
10	Semi-skilled manual	13.4	12.9	10.8	12.1
11	Unskilled manual	8.3	8.9	7.0	7.0
12	Own account workers	1.7	2.0	2.4	2.4
13	Farmers, employers and managers	1.4	0.8	0.7	0.7
14	Farmers, own account	0.8	0.8	0.7	0.7
15	Agricultural workers	3.0	2.0	1.2	1.4
16	Armed forces	1.0	1.0	1.0	1.0
17	Inadequately described, not stated	0.4	0.5	0.7	0.7
Total (thousands)		2,216	2,164	2,104	2,104

• that while Scotland has a higher proportion of manual workers, its diminishing share reflects the general trend for the rest of Britain;
• that the shortfall of non-manual workers in Scotland consists in the main of a relative shortage of managers, especially in the private sector;
• that Scotland has a much lower level of non-agricultural own-account working (2.4 per cent compared with 4.3 per cent in England and Wales).

He pointed out,

It could be said that in addition to the obviously politically relevant manual/non-manual divergence, Scotland's occupational structure has what could be called a collectivist bias relative to England and Wales – away from own account

82

working and management in the private sector, and towards employment in a state sector widely defined to include central government, local government and nationalised industries.

(Kendrick 1986: 259)

The low proportion of private sector managers also seems to reflect the weakness of Scottish owned companies since the war. Given the concentration of headquarters in London, and the significance of overseas companies in manufacturing in Scotland, it is unsurprising that Scotland is well down the scale of Standard Regions, significantly perhaps along with Wales and the north of England.

WOMEN AND EMPLOYMENT IN POST-WAR SCOTLAND

In 1951, 34 per cent of women above school-leaving age in Scotland were economically active. By 1981, this had risen to 47 per cent. The increase was even greater if we take a narrower definition of 'working age' – 20 to 59 – from 35.2 per cent to 61.6 per cent in 1981. The number of economically active women in Scotland has risen by 38 per cent between 1951 to 1981 (from 688,000 to 950,000), while the number of men in the labour force has fallen by about 9 per cent (from 1,585,000 to 1,439,000).

Since 1945, the single most important shift has been the entry of married women into paid employment. The expansion of employment in the service sector coupled with the declining number of single women in the population at large (more women marry, and at a younger age), has brought more married women into the labour market. This phenomenon is common elsewhere but has been particularly striking in Scotland because historically single women were a higher proportion of the population in Scotland. Until well after 1945, the economic activity rate for married women in Scotland was only two-thirds that of the rest of Britain. It was not until the 1970s that the Scottish participation rate caught up. By 1981, 57 per cent of married women in Scotland under 60 were 'economically active', and certain low paid occupations were overwhelmingly female. The expansion of new occupations for women runs alongside the 'feminisation' of certain occupations. For example, clerical work has seen a major shift in only 20 years so that the percentage of women rose from just over half to three-quarters, as set out in the figures for 1961, 1971 and 1981.

	1961	1971	1981
males	87,000	69,000	60,000
females	121,000	148,000	181,000
% females	58	68	75

Why did Scotland have a lower rate of economic activity for married women? The main reason seems to be the historic 'surplus' of single women north of the border. Until recently, a lower proportion of Scottish women were married than in England and Wales (in 1861, for example, 44.3 per cent of Scottish women over 15 never married compared with 36.9 per cent in England and Wales), and this higher percentage of single women seems to have kept married women out of the labour market. By 1981 any differential was largely confined to older age groups.

Scotland has gradually swung into line with the rest of Britain because its proportion of single women has decreased; the shift from manufacturing to service employment was, if anything, faster in Scotland in the last two decades than elsewhere; and because the shift in the age structure of married women in Scotland was increasingly favourable to married women becoming economically active. By 1981, the profiles of female employment north and south of the border did not look all that different.

These data show that while the percentage points difference for males in Scotland and England and Wales stood at 7.4, that for women was 4.9. The thesis that Scotland has become increasingly de-skilled in comparison to England and Wales is difficult to sustain. Not only are the similarities north and south of the border much greater than the differences, but the patterns of women's employment mirror those of England and Wales more than those of men. If women are quintessentially 'unskilled' workers, whether in manual or non-manual categories, then it is even more difficult to make a case that Scotland has become unduly proletarianised.

Table 3.8 Socio-economic groups as percentage of total employment in England and Wales, and Scotland, 1981

	Males		Females		Total	
	E & W	Scot.	E & W	Scot.	E & W	Scot.
1.1, 2.1 Employers	2.7	3.0	1.4	1.2	2.2	2.2
1.2, 2.2 Managers and administrators	13.0	9.6	5.4	4.2	10.0	7.4
3 Self-employed professionals	1.0	1.0	0.1	0.1	0.7	0.6
4 Professional employees	5.0	4.8	0.9	1.0	3.4	3.2
5 Intermediate non-manual	8.0	7.7	15.0	16.4	10.8	11.3
6 Junior non-manual	10.2	9.4	38.8	37.4	21.6	20.9
7 Personal service	1.1	1.3	12.4	13.9	5.6	6.4
8 Foremen and supervisors (manual)	3.8	4.2	0.7	0.7	2.5	2.7
9 Skilled manual	26.1	29.7	3.9	4.1	17.3	19.2
10 Semi-skilled manual	13.3	13.9	10.3	9.6	12.1	12.1
11 Unskilled manual	4.9	6.0	6.9	8.5	5.7	7.0
12 Own account workers	5.8	3.3	2.0	1.1	4.3	2.4
13 Farmers, employers and managers	0.7	1.1	0.1	0.1	0.5	0.7
14 Farmers, own account	0.7	1.0	0.1	0.1	0.5	0.6
15 Agricultural workers	1.2	2.1	0.5	0.4	0.9	1.4
16 Armed forces	1.7	1.6	0.2	0.1	1.1	1.0
17 Inadequately described, not stated	0.8	0.7	1.1	0.8	0.9	0.7

Source: 1981 Census, Scotland and Great Britain, Economic activity (10% sample), table 18b

CONCLUSION

Much of the discussion about Scotland over the past decade or so has focused on the relationship between Scotland and England (and the rest of Britain), and, more specifically, on the extent of divergence, parallelism or convergence between the two countries. The debate over the similarities and differences between Scotland and England with regard to patterns of social change is in many ways a proxy for a deeper debate about whether or not Scotland exists, and its status as an object of study. Crudely put, there is a suspicion that if Scotland is 'different', then it exists; if it is similar to the rest of Britain in certain crucial respects, then it does not. The argument here, however, is that it is not necessary for Scotland to be 'different' in terms of its social structures to be a proper object of sociological study. We do not negate its existence by pointing out that it has far more similarities with other advanced industrial countries (including England) than differences. As such a society, it will share mechanisms of social change, while its particular structural position within the international division of labour will be distinctive. Above all, how these changes are interpreted, what they tell Scotland's inhabitants about themselves and their country will depend much more on cultural and ideological systems of understanding.

The argument here is that it is quite possible to produce an explanation of electoral divergence which is rooted in changing material conditions without having to postulate any significant differences in social development between Scotland and England. It is important to remind ourselves of the point made in the Introduction that material change in itself does not generate automatically social or political change. Much depends on how these changes are interpreted, and whence they come. As we shall argue in Chapter 6, the political agenda in Scotland has diverged significantly over the past thirty years from its southern counterpart. In Scotland, for example, social changes have released new social forces (such as a loosening of class identities) which are associated with political change (such as voting SNP). Material change, then, does not have automatic effects on political or social perceptions, but is embedded in broader interpretations of social processes.

In the following chapter, we will see just how important interpretations of social change are. While Scotland shares patterns of social class and social mobility with other advanced industrial countries, how these are embedded and interpreted in social consciousness is quite distinctive. Investigating social structures is only one part of the sociological enterprise; how these impact on people's understandings, how they fit their interpretations of social reality is a crucial task for the sociologist. In the next chapter, we will focus on patterns of social mobility in Scotland and how they relate to the 'Scottish myth' of egalitarianism. Facts may be 'chiels that winna ding', but how they are interpreted and used produces sociologically important results.

4

GETTING ON IN SCOTLAND

Few myths are more powerful and prevalent in and about Scotland than that it is a more egalitarian society than England, and that the commitment to 'getting on' is greater. This myth, often referred to as 'the Scottish myth', manifests itself in different ways. Consider, for example, the statement by the eminent Scottish historian, Gordon Donaldson:

> It is true to this day that Scotland is a more egalitarian country than England, but as a result of class consciousness horizontal divisions into classes have become ... more important than vertical divisions into nations.
>
> (1974: 117)

Historians are not alone in their belief about Scottish egalitarianism. The theme finds literary expression as well. Kurt Wittig makes it the central motif of his book *The Scottish Tradition in Literature*, as he charts its progress from the poetry of fourteenth and fifteenth century by writers such as Barbour, Henryson, and Lyndsay, through Burns and even Walter Scott, to the novelists of the nineteenth and twentieth century such as Lewis Grassic Gibbon and Neil Gunn. All make a virtue of the 'common folk'. Wittig describes their common theme:

> The democratic element in Scottish literature is one of its most striking characteristics. 'Democratic' is not really the correct word; it is rather a free manliness, a 'saeva indignatio' against oppression, a violent freedom, sometimes an aggressive spirit of independence and egalitarianism.
>
> (1958: 95)

Although the egalitarian myth is often to be found in accounts of the Scottish past, it is by no means dead, if only because history in the form of a reconstructed past is a potent social and political force in modern Scotland. Claims for Scotland's history frequently often have a legitimating function, not least on the radical side of the spectrum. Stephen Maxwell, a prominent Nationalist, points out the importance of versions of the myth, first, for Nationalists:

> The idea that Scottish society is egalitarian is central to the myth of Scottish Democracy. In its strong nationalist version, class division is held to be an alien importation from England. In the weaker version, it describes the wider opportunity for social mobility in Scotland as illustrated in the 'the lad o' pairts' tradition.
>
> (1976: 5)

The myth can take on a more radical guise for socialists: 'the myth that the Scottish working class has an instinct for radical if not revolutionary socialism [is] lacking in its Sassenach counterpart' (ibid.).

Even non-Scots are willing to help keep the egalitarian belief alive. Eric Hobsbawm (1969), for example, points up the different historical experiences of Wales and Scotland, and makes their commitment to political radicalism in Liberal then Labour voting a key feature of his opposition to independence for these nations. If nothing else, separation, he judges, would condemn the English to the folly of their own political conservatism.

The Scottish myth persists, and lends itself to a variety of usages and interpretations. In many ways, the ambiguity and ambivalence of the myth helps to explain its persistence. In various contexts it has continued to act as a partial interpreter of social reality and social change. And, as Allan MacLaren has pointed out,

> The belief that Scotland was an open society whose fundamental egalitarianism was gradually eroded, in part by contact with its more powerful neighbours is not just a piece of popular nationalism but has penetrated and been propounded by works of academic scholarship.
>
> (1976: 2)

Myths are notoriously difficult to examine. By their nature, they represent a collection of symbolic elements assembled to account for and validate a set of social institutions. In Mitchell's words myths operate 'to record and present the moral system whereby present attitudes and actions are ordered and validated' (1968: 122). 'Myth' here does not refer to something which is manifestly false, but to a perspective, a guide to help interpret social reality. As guides, myths are of little help in predicting or explaining actual features of the social structure.

Insofar as myths are drawn from the past, they are akin to traditions, and like traditions have an active, contemporary significance (Williams 1977: 115). Like traditions, myths connect with past realities. They do, however, draw selectively from the past, a process which involves selective exclusion as well as inclusion. In so doing, myth becomes a contemporary and an active force providing, in most instances, a reservoir of legitimation for belief and action.

In the Scottish myth, the central motif is the inherent egalitarianism of the Scots. This motif operates in different ways and at different levels. While there are social structural factors such as the system of education or forms of democracy which are judged to have contributed to the relatively open and democratic ethos of seventeenth-century Scotland, the myth of egalitarianism has at root an asociological, an almost mystical element. It is as if Scots are judged to be egalitarian by dint of racial characteristics, of deep social values. Man (or at least Scotsman) is judged to be primordially equal; inequality is man-made, created by the social structure he (for the myth is essentially male-centred) erects, or which are erected by others around him.

The myth is ambivalent, and it lends itself to two interpretations. The first, which might be called the activist interpretation, takes the co-existence of man-made inequality and primordial equality, and argues for an active resolution of this apparent anomally in favour of social equality. A second interpretation, which might be labelled 'idealist' adopts a more conservative response. If man is primordially equal, social structural inequalities do not matter, so nothing needs to be done. In this way, the egalitarian myth lends itself to conservative as well as radical interpretations.

These levels can be seen in at least two forms in Scots vernacular; the allusion to common humanity in 'we're a' Jock Tamson's bairns', and in Burns's poem 'For a' that and a' that'. The former phrase seems to have no precise origin in literature, whereas Burns's title so struck a chord in his own society that it entered immediately into the language (D. Craig 1961: ch. 4). 'Jock Tamson's bairns' has a curious and fascinating set of meanings associated with it. According to David Murison's authoritative *Scottish National Dictionary* (1986 vol. v: 337), the most common meaning is 'the human race; common humanity; also with less universal force, a group of people united by a common sentiment, interest or purpose' – innocuous enough, and fitting in with its usage by Presbyterian ministers to refer to 'God's children'. There are, however, other meanings: 'Jock Tamson' can also refer, jocularly, to whisky; more darkly, it is a Scottish version of 'John Thomas', which certainly conveys more force to the 'common humanity' reference.

In the same way that 'we're a' Jock Tamson's bairns' touches upon the essential common humanity, Burns's 'For a' that and a' that' seems to strip away the differences which are essentially social constructions. In spite of these (the 'a' that'), Burns is saying, people are equal. His meaning of equality is, however, ambiguous. He is calling not for a levelling down of riches, but for a proper, that is, moral appreciation of 'the man o' independent mind'. It is 'pith o' sense and pride o' worth' which matter, not the struttings and starings of 'yon birkie ca'd a lord'. The ambiguity of his message is retained to the last stanza – 'that man to man the world o'er shall brothers be for a' that' – an appeal to the virtues of fraternity rather than equality in its strict sense.

There are two inferences to be drawn from the myth. In the 'idealist' version, the objective facts of social inequality, status and poverty, melt into insignificance alongside the common humanity (and Scottishness) of people. In the 'activist' version, Burns is making a revolutionary appeal. In his own time, the French Revolution and the appeals for democracy gave a heady political flavour to such poetry, and in David Craig's opinion 'the significant Scottish literature of that time was popular, entirely so, and furthermore, the polite public tended to hold aloof from such work' (1961: 111). Burns may simply have adopted 'a man's a man . . .' from the vernacular, but there is no doubt that such works had an immediate popular impact, and found their way into popular parlance, and reinforced the imagery of egalitarianism.

Although egalitarianism was, in essence, a set of social values, a body of sacred truth, it has often connected with features of the social structure. 'Facts' about the social structure can provide prima-facie support for the myth, or, more likely, a set of data requiring interpretation. Nevertheless, myths do not depend on 'facts' to sustain them. Egalitarianism refers essentially to a set of social values, an ethos, a celebration of sacred beliefs; social inequality, on the other hand, is a characterisation of the social structure referring specifically to the distribution of resources, rewards and opportunities. In Scotland, the egalitarian myth has proved largely impervious to falsification, not because appropriate data are not always available, but because 'myth' in essence cannot be 'disproved'. Nor should myths be cast out as 'unscientific'. As Andrew McPherson has pointed out,

> The demythologiser is as likely to de-historicise, to discount the significance of the interplay over time of changing forms and ideas, as is the prisoner of myths who interprets present institutions as the unchanged expression of a timeless ideal.
>
> (1983: 217)

In a similar way, sociological evidence has made little impression on the American dream, the idea that hard work and ability will lead to achievement. Plainly, myths and legends of this sort could not be sustained if they had no connection whatsoever with what people recognised as reality. However, the Scottish myth and the American dream belong to the same realm as those 'truths we hold self-evident, that all men are created equal'. (It is interesting that there does not seem to be an equivalent English myth, for example.) The coexistence of egalitarian beliefs and socially created inequality need not be a contradiction in either society. The conservative may use it to justify the social order; the radical may seek to rectify the anomaly in political and economic ways.

The purpose of this chapter is two-fold: to examine the scientific evidence that Scotland was (and is) a society in which it is easier to 'get on' (the comparison is implicitly with England), namely, the evidence for social mobility; and to explain why the Scottish myth persists in such a way that it does not require evidence to support or refute it. Plainly, it is not enough to 'disprove' the myth in the expectation that it will simply wither and die. It is also necessary to ask why such beliefs persist in spite of contrary 'evidence'. What broader social and ideological purposes do they serve?

THE MYTH OF LITERACY

Using 'myth' here to refer to a self-evident belief rather than a falsehood, we find a widespread notion that Scots had a much higher level of literacy in pre-industrial Scotland, crucially higher than in England. Such literacy levels were a reflection, it was said, of a universal parish-school system post-Reformation which, according to Saunders's (1950) influential study, *Scottish Democracy*, 'created a community of values that made for an easily recognisable national character and outlook' (Houston 1985: 9). In his discussion of literacy in seventeenth- and eighteenth-century Scotland, Houston speaks of the 'legend' of literacy, pointing out that it has acquired the status of myth: 'a story which people tell themselves first, to explain the world, and second, to celebrate identity and to express values' (1985: 11).

Such a myth has grown within the nationalist tradition of the Scots language, inflamed by the standard Anglocentric view taken of British history. Taking as the usual measure the ability to sign one's name on a marriage register, a court deposition or taxation document, Houston argues that Scottish men only enjoyed superior literacy over their counterparts in northern England during the seventeenth century, and that improvements between this and the eighteenth century were largely confined to the middle ranks of Scottish society. The levels of literacy among women or in the Gaelic-speaking Highlands were significantly lower. To be sure, an ability to write one's name in English was not a culture-neutral characteristic, and Houston points out the continuing importance of oral over literate culture in the seventeenth and into the eighteenth centuries.

He also emphasises that the measurement of the distribution of literacy, while an indicator of education, reveals little about the uses to which the skill could be put. The central aim of early education was to ensure ideological conformity among the population especially for the church. The 'universal literacy' of lowland Scots lasted only as long as ecclesiastical hegemony. As Christopher Smout puts it,

> The system that gave rise to such self-congratulation had been inherited from the greatest days of church ascendency. Knox holding like Calvin and Luther the realistic view that children were born 'ignorant of godliness', and believing (the words are those of an eighteenth century presbytery) that the business of education was to prepare children 'for the business of life and the purpose of eternity', had laid down a programme of godly training. There were to be schools in every parish, schools in every burgh 'able at least to teach

grammar and the latin tongue', colleges teaching at least
logic, rhetoric and languages in every 'notable town'; every
child was to be made to attend, and money should be provided so that the poorest who went to the parish schools
should if they proved scholars eventually be able to go on
to college.

(1970: 450)

The assumption that literacy was 'a good thing' has to be tem-
pered, says Houston, with the knowledge of the narrow uses to
which it was put. Scottish education may have been more comprehensive and 'democratic' than its English counterpart but that was
not saying a lot in a European context. He argues that the idea
that Scotland had a superior education system originated in the
eighteenth century, and that it had an ideological function fostered
by the middle classes to justify their hegemony. The myth was
presented as a long-established, original and distinctive tradition,
and crucially, superior to that of Scotland's powerful southern
neighbour. Houston perceptively points out, echoing some of the
arguments of the previous chapter, the tendency 'to concentrate
on identifying cultural and economic differences as a means of
discovering particular attributes of Scottish and English society'
(1985: 262).

Nevertheless, the notion that Scotland (or, more precisely, men
in lowland Scotland) were educationally favoured was not inaccurate. Even by the mid-nineteenth century, Scotland seemed to hold
an advantage over England, according to the historian Cipolla.
Anderson (1983: 8) has cited the percentages of those who in 1855
could write their signature: in Scotland, males: 89 per cent,
females: 77 per cent; in England and Wales, males: 70 per cent,
females: 59 per cent.

If we were to exclude the Gaeltachd, the literacy levels in lowland Scotland would be even higher. It is also interesting to note
that while fewer females could sign their name in both Scotland
and England and Wales, the differentials in both cases are about
the same.

The extension of literacy reflected a 'parochial tradition' of
schools in every parish which in turn reflected the desire of the
Kirk to impose its vision on the population. Nevertheless, as
Callum Brown has pointed out, Presbyterianism came in large
part to represent plebeian culture: 'In the pre-industrial form of

religion, the church was the primary focus for community identity' (Brown 1987: 100), while, in the nineteenth-century industrial city, it had become 'increasingly a line of social demarcation' (1987: 135). By the nineteenth century, when Scotland's education system was palpably under threat of incorporation, John Knox and the *First Book of Discipline* (1560) came to be seen as a 'kind of expression of the Scottish Volkgeist' (Anderson 1983: 23). Significantly, just as the old order was passing, undergoing a threat of Anglicisation, so its origins and purpose became the stuff of legend. In Anderson's words, 'It has been characteristic to see the democratic virtues as in decline, part of a golden age of Scottish education located in the just-vanished past' (1983: 83).

THE LAD O' PAIRTS

The virtues of Scottish education carried their own personum, the lad o' pairts. The lad o' pairts was, in Murison's phrase, a 'talented youth', often the son of a crofter or peasant who had the ability but not the means to benefit from education. The term itself seems to have originated, according to Murison, in the late nineteenth century, and its first citing appears in the story 'Domsie' by the Kailyard novelist, known as Ian MacLaren. This story overtly describes the short life of George, a talented pupil who wins prize medals in Latin and Greek, ending up with a double first degree at university. The real 'hero' of the story is Domsie, the dominie or schoolteacher, whose task it is to spot likely talent, and who persuades the local farmer, Drumsheugh, to put up the money for the boy's fees at university. So successful was this village dominie that

> Seven ministers, four schoolteachers, four doctors, one professor and three civil service men had been sent out by the auld schule in Domsie's time, besides many that 'had given themselves to mercantile pursuits'.
>
> (1894: 8)

MacLaren's careful accounting of the 'professions' contrasted with his vagueness about the number going into trade (the quotation marks seem to withhold approval for such a career) indicates the social values being celebrated. Teaching, ministering and administering are the prime goals; Latin and Greek (with some maths and philosophy) plainly echo the old Scottish curriculum.

The teacher's obsessions are shared with the community, MacLaren leads us to believe:

> There was just a single ambition in those humble homes, to have one of its members at college, and if Domsie approved a lad, then his brothers and sisters would give their wages, and the family would live on skim milk and oat cake, to let him have his chance.

> (1894: 10)

The mawkish, sentimental tone comes into its own as MacLaren takes fourteen out of thirty-three pages to describe the final illness and death of Domsie's protégé. Domsie's importance in this Kailyard story is paramount:

> Domsie, as we called the schoolmaster, behind his back in Drumtochty, because we loved him, was true to the tradition of his kind, and had an unerring scent for 'pairts' in his laddies. He could detect a scholar in the egg, and prophesied Latinity from a boy that seemed only fit to be a cowherd.

> (1894: 8)

Kailyardism was a popular literary style from about 1880 until 1914 (Carter 1976; Campbell 1981), described by the *Penguin Guide to Literature* as consisting of 'minor writers who pursued Scottish country quaintness into whimsical middens'. In a splendidly splenetic characterisation of the Kailyard tradition, Tom Nairn has written,

> Kailyardism was the definition of Scotland as wholly consisting of small towns full of small-town 'characters' given to bucolic intrigue and wise sayings. At first the central figures were usually Ministers of the Kirk (as were most of the authors) but later on schoolteachers and doctors got into the act. Their housekeepers always have a shrewd insight into human nature. Offspring who leave for the big city frequently come to grief, and are glad to get home again (peching and hosting to hide their feelings).

> (1977: 158)

The Kailyard tradition which celebrates the lad o' pairts has been criticised by Nairn and others for laying down a distorting image of Scotland replete with pawky simplicities. In our analysis of Scottish culture in Chapter 7, we will assess whether the Kailyard tradition had the negative effect that its critics attributed to it. At this stage, it is enough to say that others, notably Willie Donaldson, have argued that this tradition was by no means as dominant in Scotland in the late nineteenth century, and took second place to a much more popular genre of writing in newspapers. Donaldson argues that the Kailyard was largely for export by the London-based book trade whereas the Scottish newspaper press was owned, written and circulating within Scotland (Donaldson 1986).

Whatever the merits and influences of the Kailyard tradition, the 'lad o' pairts' appears to have been a central image of late nineteenth and early twentieth century Scotland. However, the egalitarian element of the lad o' pairts had a precise meaning and specific sociological significance, for as Allan MacLaren has pointed out,

> the egalitarianism so often portrayed is not that emerging from an economic, social or even political equality; it is equality of *opportunity* which is exemplified. All men are not equal. What is implied is that all men are given the opportunity to be equal. Whatever the values attached to such a belief, if expressed today, it would be termed elitist not egalitarian.
>
> (1976: 2)

This 'opportunity' did not relate to equality of educational achievement or outcome for broad classes or collectivities. Instead it referred to formal opportunity afforded to an able pupil to proceed through the parish school to university. In this regard, it drew upon a meritocratic tradition rather than an egalitarian one. The lad o' pairts' path was smoothed by the local dominie who would bully, cajole and persuade affluent members of the parish, as in the case of Drumsheugh, the local farmer, to give a bursary to support his lad o' pairts.

It is interesting to note that the lad had no gender equivalent in a 'lass o' pairts'. Critics have pointed out that the egalitarian tradition in Scotland has hidden the gender inequalities in education (Fewell and Paterson 1990). A lass o' pairts, they argue, has no status at all in the Scottish educational tradition, and beliefs about the importance of domesticity have overwhelmed female education. One of the main problems we have with this debate about the lad o' pairts is that we have very little evidence as to whether or not it had an impact on ordinary people. In a fine piece of oral history derived from those who were schoolchildren in the early part of this century, Lynn Jamieson points out that while girls' and boys' experience of schooling has to be set in a gendered context, 'the reality for both boys and girls remained overwhelmingly one in which you left school as soon as possible' (1990: 37). Most pupils and their parents would have agreed with the character in William Alexander's novel set in the north-east in the late nineteenth century: 'there's little use for vreetin' [writing] aiven to loons; an' for lassies to hae ocht adee wi't's gaun clean oot o' reel' (quoted in Donaldson 1986: 17).

In eighteenth-century Scotland, however, the lad o' pairts system might work tolerably well, for a small, local elite was being catered for in a limited number of professions: education, law, the ministry, religion, and sometimes medicine. The failure of a talented lad to make it was rarely an indictment of the system itself because it seemed to rely on personal contacts and moral worth. Failure could result from a poorly connected dominie, or the imputed moral laxity of the candidate. Hence, the 'lad o' pairts' phenomenon seemed to have survived for much longer than it might otherwise have done, because, in Anderson's words

> The myth of the lad of parts [sic] became part of the ideology of 19th century individualism or meritocracy, in which a limited equality of opportunity was held to justify the reinforcing of structural inequalities.
>
> (1985: 84)

In many respects, egalitarianism was a key element in a conservative ideology which congratulated itself on the openness of Scottish (essentially rural and small town) society and its social institutions. What we have termed the 'idealist' version of egalitarianism was conservative, and in the 1960s was being mobilised to defend the existence of local authority fee-paying schools on the grounds that they, uniquely, afforded the lads o' pairts an educational and social opportunity not given in big city comprehensives. The lad o' pairts was an individual who escaped his working-class or peasant origins. Houston perceives the essentially conservative nature of the myth in his study of literacy. What is interesting to him is not simply the evidence for or against literacy in eighteenth-century Scotland, but why such an ideology should operate in the nineteenth. He concludes, 'The myth of equality of opportunity in education which purports to describe the social system actually helps to reproduce it by guiding perceptions and actions' (Houston 1985: 254).

Alongside the lad o' pairts stereotype sits a belief in the inherent democracy of Scottish society. In many ways these were connected because the Kirk, and its secular arm, the parish, lay at the heart of each. Presbyterianism was clearly a more democratic form of church government than Catholicism or Episcopalianism, and the doctrine of predestination, the essence of Calvinism, helped confirm the equality of this elect. Its association with national identity helped it retain its hold for longer than elsewhere. As Callum Brown points out,

> Scotland has been seen as one of a number of regions within European countries where the secularisation of religion has been held in check by the association of religion with a thwarted political nationalism.
>
> (1987: 9)

The more conservative side of Presbyterianism was able to translate its belief in character formation into a respect for modest money-making and enterprise. In his study of religion in nineteenth-century Aberdeen, Allan MacLaren showed how religion, education and economy were fused in the Presbyterian mind-set: 'Religion is beyond all comparison the most important part of education . . . when properly taught it includes every moral and social duty; and among others, industry, temperance and economy' (1974: 148).

The egalitarian myth is 'old' because it is premised upon the existence of a hierarchical social order, not a classless society. It described ideal conditions in the typical pre-capitalist and pre-industrial community, often rural. Says MacLaren,

> There is some evidence to suggest that the 'Scottish Myth' is a product of a former rural paternalism rather than an urban industrialism in which class identity and economic individualism overruled a declining concern for communal and parochial obligations.
>
> (1976: 9)

Social identity is one of community, not class. The commitment is to the parish, secular and religious, made up of sturdy and self-sustaining individuals. The social hierarchy of the parish is not questioned, and differences of economic and social power are taken for granted, rather than resented. Material rewards may even bring social or psychological disbenefits, if the social duties and obligations which wealth brings are not carried out. The unalloyed pursuit of profit offends the moral economy of the community (as the anti-Kailyard novels at the turn of this century by George Douglas Brown, *The House with the Green Shutters* (1901), and by J. McDougall Hay, *Gillespie* (1914), set out to show. In this regard, they share the scepticism of Kailyard writers such as Ian MacLaren with his suspicion of 'mercantile pursuits'). The political economy of the community inhabited by lads o' pairts is pre-capitalist. Money-making is judged to be too readily motivated by avarice and greed, rather than to be pursued in a rationalistic and emotionally neutral way. The locus of egalitarianism is the parish, in the country village or the small town. Such sentiments might well have chimed with the values of the Presbyterian bourgeoisie in the nineteenth century with its commitment to 'civic duty' (Walker and Gallagher 1990: 4). In this respect, the cult of the lad o' pairts fitted in well. As Anderson points out,

It suited the kind of stratified educational system thought appropriate for an industrial society, one in which a basic elementary education for the masses co-existed with a small secondary sector for the middle class; allowing a small number of talented children to cross the barrier satisfied the demand for merit to be rewarded, and was not incompatible with retaining a rather mediocre education for those who were not selected.

(1985: 86)

Can we simply dismiss the 'lad o' pairts' idea as an ideological figment of a traditional Scottish bourgeois imagination? Such a question cannot simply be answered in the affirmative. First, it runs the risk of avoiding an examination of the evidence for educational and social mobility, and second, such a debunking exercise fails to explain why such a myth should have such a firm hold on the imagination.

Robert Anderson's re-analysis of data from the 1860s Argyll Commission on Scottish education shows that as late as the third quarter of the nineteenth century many of working-class and peasant origin attended Scotland's universities. In a sample of 882 students (a quarter of the total) the commission showed that a half came from professional or business families, 127 were sons of farmers, 114 were from *petit bourgeois* backgrounds, but that 200 (23 per cent) could be described as 'working class'. They were largely the sons of skilled artisans (carpenters and joiners, masons, and shoemakers), or miners. Only two were the sons of crofters, three of shepherds, two of farm servants, one of a fisherman, and thirteen of labourers. He concludes, 'It was thus the skilled urban elite of the working class from which university students came rather than from the families of factory workers or the really poor' (1985: 92).

Working-class students in the late nineteenth century were usually mature men who had prepared themselves through private study, evening classes, and a few were qualified teachers. Although the Scottish system (1 in 1,000) had more university places than England (1 in 5,800) or Germany (1 in 2,600), it was based on the tradition of competitive individualism, or, in the term of Ralph Turner, 'contest mobility' (1960) in which individual failure or success maintained the system ideologically. Lasses o' pairts were barely recognised, and Catholics virtually non-existent in the universities (only two could be found in a sample of, 1,779 students between 1860 and 1900, although in 1891 Catholics numbered about 8.5 per cent of the Scottish population (Brown 1987)).

Nevertheless, both Aberdeen and Glasgow Universities had unusually large numbers of the 'disadvantaged'. While Aberdeen took in large proportions of students from agricultural backgrounds (16 per cent in 1860 and 20 per cent in 1910), Glasgow had a higher percentage of students from manual working-class backgrounds (19 per cent in 1860 and 24 per cent in 1910). Anderson qualifies these data appropriately. For Aberdeen,

> the majority of those who went to the university from a parish school were not poor boys but the sons of the rural middle class – of the minister, of the schoolmaster himself, of farmers, often described as prosperous although this category could cover different levels of wealth.
>
> (R. Anderson 1983: 124)

Glasgow, on the other hand, catered for the sons of skilled artisans. Nevertheless, 'by the eve of the First World War, the proportion of working class students was as high at Glasgow as it was later in the 20th century' (1983: 309). As the nineteenth century wore on, the proportion of university students from parish schools was in decline, while those from burgh schools increased. The traditional urban high schools catered for the professional and commercial classes, in which, says Anderson, 'both peer and peasant were conspicuous by their absence' (1983: 140). The idealisation of the rural parish school began in the 1890s (in the Kailyard literature, for instance), just as it was vanishing in practice, generating a rearguard defence of the institution and its culture, and lending validity to that version of the myth which sees it as a Scottish characteristic which has been eroded by Anglicisation (Davie 1961).

In his fine study of farm life in north-east Scotland, Ian Carter charts the decline of the peasant stock in the late nineteenth century, who were in many ways the ideal-type for the lad o' pairts. Leasing marginal land from landlords who were themselves sweirt to bring it into cultivation, the peasant class struggled to make a living until their labours were no longer required. However, says Carter,

> The crofter's son who stayed on the land might hope to climb some way up the farming ladder. His chances were not very good after the middle of the nineteenth century – it is clear that relatively few peasant farmers made it in these years into the ranks of the larger farmers – but the ideology of the lad o' pairts asserted the opposite and moulded the aspirations of the peasant children.
>
> (1979: 94)

As Anderson points out, myths do not survive and flourish unless they express some fundamental truths, unless they connect with realities of life. The Scottish myth of egalitarianism survived because it kept alive a sense of national identity as we shall show later in this chapter. In the shorter term, the lad o' pairts ideal survived because it was transposed on to social groups other than those for whom it had been intended. In Anderson's words,

> The lad of parts [sic] did exist, but they were drawn from the middle rather than the lower ranks; the children of ministers, teachers, farmers, shopkeepers and artisans enjoyed opportunities, especially for entry to the professions, which long had no equivalent in other countries, Scotland was also unusual in providing such opportunities even in remote areas, and it was the rurality as much as the social origins of the lad of parts which attracted attention.
>
> (1985: 100)

We should remind ourselves in dealing with the egalitarian myth that direct proof that people believed in it is hard to come by (Gray *et al.* 1984). However, its survival as a cultural construct depended perhaps less on what people actually believed and more on what institutional carriers were available. As we shall see, the Scottish educational system provided such a carrier, and we have evidence that its administrative elite gave voice to it right down to modern times (McPherson and Raab 1988).

The mythology of the lad o' pairts does appear to have survived well into the twentieth century, and in his re-analysis of the 1947 Scottish Mental Study, Keith Hope argues that the notion of educational opportunity – or 'meritelection' as he calls it – has some basis in fact. Recognising that 'the native tradition of merit-election, in which educational selection of the "lad o' pairts" was a recognised mode of social ascent of the poor [*sic*]' (1984: 19), Hope studied 590 males who were 11 years old in 1947 in order to find out the main determinants of their occupational position as 27–28 year olds in 1964. Using path-analytical techniques, he concluded that 'Scotland, as we would expect, is more meritelective than the United States' (1984: 30) even during this period when selective education was operating. Admitting that the concept 'equality of opportunity' has different meanings in each system, he is convinced that the Scottish system offered greater equality of opportunity in this period than its US counterpart. While the Scottish myth does seem to receive some confirmation in these studies (English data were not available to Hope), we will see that its survival does not rely on material confirmation, but on its capacity to provide a reinforcement of the Scottish identity.

EDUCATION AND THE SCOTTISH MYTH

One of the main carriers of that identity has been the education system. In this regard, the ideology has been kept alive by the experiences and beliefs of those who have led that system. Andrew McPherson has spoken of the 'Kirriemuir career', both moral and secular, and a 'symbolic world bounded by Angus, standing for the East and North and with Kirriemuir at its heart, by Dumfries in the South and, in the West by a Glasgow academy, perhaps The Academy' (1983: 228).

McPherson's analysis of the Scottish Advisory Council on Education between 1957 and 1961 shows that only four of the sixteen members came from the west of Scotland, and most articulated an image of Scotland 'as a nation of small towns, and implicitly therefore, a Protestant nation' (1983: 233). As many as nine of the sixteen held posts in independent, semi-independent or fee-paying schools, so the lad o' pairts ideology was mobilised in the late 1960s in the defence of the local authority fee-paying system. The debates about educational change in the 1960s took on a particular Scottish flavour with the publication in 1961 of George Davie's *The Democratic Intellect*, which, observed Andrew McPherson,

> served, in the context of English debates of the time about social class inequalities of access to educational opportunity in England, only to confirm to Scottish opinion the egalitarian pedigree of the national institution that Scotland had substituted for English gentility.
>
> (1983: 225–6)

Robert Anderson's work on the university system also adds some evidence that the myth had some backing in reality:

> The evidence suggests that the Welsh and Scottish 'democratic myths' had some substance, and that members of the British elite recruited there may have had broader social origins than their English colleagues.
>
> (1991: 12)

The Scottish education system seems to be less socially selective than the English one. In their analysis of social selection in European educational systems, Mueller and Karle (1990) show that the skilled working class in Scotland after 1945 had similar educational opportunities to mainland Europe whereas this class was noticeably at a disadvantage in England. Nor was this comparative advantage confined to the skilled working class. They point out, 'Scotland ... deviates from the cross-national average in another respect: the offspring of the petty bourgeoisie have much better opportunities to survive in the Scottish educational system than in any of the other countries' (1990: 22).

The Scottish myth, then, is kept alive not simply because people believe it to be founded in fact, but also because there are institutional mechanisms, like the education system and its ideology, which provide sufficient affirmation of its validity. Our next task is to broaden the argument beyond educational opportunity to wider patterns of social mobility in Scotland, and assess whether Scotland is an 'open society' in this sense.

SOCIAL MOBILITY IN SCOTLAND

The major evidence for social mobility in England and Wales comes from the study conducted at Nuffield College, Oxford, in the early 1970s by John Goldthorpe and his colleagues. It was not his purpose to examine mobility in Scotland, so a separate study was carried out at Aberdeen University in 1973, directed by Michael Carter, and then by Geoff Payne. Scotland was not included in Goldthorpe's study because a sampling frame based on population size (in proportion to England and Wales) would not have generated a big enough sample to make a separate analysis worthwhile. The Aberdeen sociologists sampled 4,887 males aged 20 to 64 residing in Scotland (excluding the Northern and Western Isles) in 1975.

The study of social mobility is a minefield and a battlefield rolled into one. Essentially, these related British studies focused on inter-generational occupational mobility, which involved comparing the occupations of respondents with the reported occupations of their fathers when they were 14 years of age. Secondly, women were excluded because social class is taken as deriving from the head of the household, the main bread-winner, who – it was argued – is usually male. Goldthorpe sought to justify the selection method as follows:

> despite the general tendency in modern societies for participation of married women in the labour market to increase, their employment still tends to be more intermittent than that of men, is less often full-time, and is only rarely such as to place them in what could be regarded as dominant class positions relative to their husbands.
>
> (1987: 281)

Not surprisingly, such a robust approach has drawn the fire of those who protest that women are thus rendered invisible in the class structure (see issues 2 and 4 of the journal *Sociology* vol. 18, 1984; and Crompton and Mann *Gender and Stratification* 1986). Goldthorpe's analysis of the 1972 data coupled with those from the 1983 British Election Survey argues that, in the main, 'wives themselves, and not just "sexist" sociologists, "derive" their class

positions from their husbands' employment rather than their own'
(1987: 296)

The Scottish Mobility Study (SMS), coming three years after
the one for England and Wales, was in large part constrained by
this methodology. Where it did depart from the southern one was
in its intention to focus on occupations rather than on social class,
and thus to devise its own occupational schema. Nevertheless,
Goldthorpe has re-analysed the Scottish data using his own classification system for England and Wales, and so we can make direct
comparison between social mobility – so defined – north and south
of the border. We should keep in mind, however, that any study
of social mobility in Scotland is likely to underrate the true rates
of mobility because of disproportionately high rates of out-
migration north of the border.

Nevertheless, Payne argues that we would expect Scottish patterns to be similar not just to England and Wales, but to most
other European countries insofar as it has a market economy, and
its social structure is founded on the nuclear family:

> these are all countries with similar forms of capitalism and
> a shared recent history. However, we would not expect pre-
> cisely the *same* patterns of mobility because Scotland has not
> shared an identical history. Its separate culture and histori-
> cally subordinate relationship to England mean that its
> employment opportunities have been distinctive.
>
> (Payne 1987: 2)

Clearly, there are resonances here of the debate about Scotland's
'dependency' on England, and the extent to which Scotland differs
in its employment structure. Nevertheless, as we have argued in
the previous chapter, this cannot be sustained in any meaningful
way by the evidence. While Payne acknowledges the tendency to
overemphasise the differences, he argues that the position of Kendrick *et al.* (1985) does attach

> an unusually high importance to the lack of difference
> between contemporary Scotland and England. By concentrat-
> ing on the similarities between Scotland and other industrial
> societies the reader may underestimate the extent to which
> Scotland does have a separate cultural and historical exist-
> ence.
>
> (1987: 10)

Of course, the reader would be mistaken, because denying 'difference' is no part of the Kendrick *et al.* thesis, merely that the significant (political and cultural) differences which do exist cannot be read off in a straightforward way from the employment structure of Scotland.

Payne's occupational schema is deliberately different from that of Goldthorpe, and is shown in Table 4.1.

Table 4.1 Occupational classification, Payne's schema

Class	Description	Census category	Percentage of total workforce
I	'upper middle class' professionals, large managers and proprietors, senior supervisory staff	1–4	13.5
II	semi-professionals, technicians, small managers and small proprietors	5–8	13.4
III	lower technicians, self-employed artisans, supervisors of manual workers	9–10; 12–13	13.4
IV	routine non-manual workers	14	7.7
V	skilled manual	11, 15–16	20.7
VI	semi-skilled manual	17–18	16.3
VII	unskilled manual	19–20	14.1

Payne's schema is impossible to compare with Goldthorpe's (shown in Table 4.2) because he allocates 'small proprietors' to class II, and self-employed artisans to class III, whereas Goldthorpe reserves class IV for what he terms the 'petty bourgeoisie'.

Goldthorpe provides the marginal distributions for England and Wales together, and Scotland, for fathers and sons, as set out in Table 4.3.

Payne and Goldthorpe employ similar ways of presenting data, namely, as 'inflow' and 'outflow' tables. The 'inflow' table (Table 4.4) focuses on the social origins (in terms of father's occupation) of respondents in a particular class. Similarly the 'outflow' table (Table 4.5) examines the destinations of respondents who had fathers in a particular class. Here we have used Goldthorpe's data

Table 4.2 Occupational classification, Goldthorpe's schema

Class	Description	Percentage of total workforce
I	'service class': all higher grade professionals, self-employed or salaried; higher grade administrators and officials in local and central government, and public and private enterprises; managers in large industrial establishments	9.8
II	'subaltern or cadet levels of service class': lower grade professionals and higher grade technicians; lower grade administrators and officials	11.9
III	'white collar labour force': routine non-manual employees in administration and commerce; sales personnel; other rank and file employees in services	9.1
IV	'petty bourgeoisie': small proprietors, inc. farmers and smallholders; self-employed artisans; all other own account workers except professionals	8.3
V	'blue collar elite': lower grade technicians (largely manual); supervisors of manual workers	11.2
VI	skilled manual workers	21.7
VII	semi- and unskilled and agricultural workers	28.1

Table 4.3 Occupational distributions, England and Wales, and Scotland

Class	Fathers (percentage)		Respondents (percentage)	
	England and Wales	Scotland	England and Wales	Scotland
I	7.3	5.2	13.6	9.8
II	5.9	4.9	11.5	11.9
III	7.3	7.4	9.2	9.1
IV	14.1	12.3	9.4	8.3
V	11.5	9.1	11.6	11.2
VI	27.5	29.7	21.2	21.7
VII	26.4	31.3	23.5	28.1

Source: Goldthorpe 1980: 44, 48, 289, 290

only because of the classification problems. Nevertheless, Payne and Goldthorpe come to similar conclusions about social mobility patterns north and south of the border.

Table 4.4 Inflow table: class composition by class of father at respondent's age 14. Data is percentaged by column (Scotland top line and England and Wales second line)

	I	II	III	Respondent's class IV	V	VI	VII	%
I	22.4	10.0	6.6	4.4	2.7	1.4	1.1	5.2
	24.2	12.0	9.1	6.0	3.0	1.9	2.0	7.3
II	11.0	12.3	7.8	2.1	4.4	2.2	1.9	4.9
	12.5	11.8	7.6	4.4	4.9	3.0	2.2	5.9
III	9.9	11.1	8.3	4.7	7.7	7.1	7.1	7.4
	10.0	10.0	10.2	6.1	8.2	5.4	5.3	7.3
IV	13.8	11.1	10.2	47.5	6.2	6.1	9.9	12.3
	13.0	13.9	12.2	36.5	10.6	9.6	12.3	14.1
V	10.1	12.5	8.0	7.0	13.3	8.0	7.5	9.1
	12.0	13.5	12.5	9.4	15.6	11.4	8.6	11.5
VI	16.4	22.8	27.7	13.2	29.9	42.4	32.8	29.7
	15.7	21.0	24.8	19.2	29.2	39.4	30.3	27.5
VII	16.4	20.3	31.4	21.0	35.8	32.8	41.1	31.3
	12.6	17.8	23.6	18.5	28.5	29.4	39.3	26.4
%	9.8	11.9	9.1	8.3	11.2	21.7	28.1	
	13.6	11.5	9.2	9.4	11.6	21.2	23.5	

There are a number of quite remarkable features in Table 4.4. First, with very few exceptions (cell IV/IV is the most obvious), the patterns of inflow mobility north and south of the border are very similar. A substantial proportion of the 'service class' is drawn from manual working-class backgrounds. If we treat classes VI and VII as working class, then one-third of respondents in class I had fathers who were manual workers. A similar pattern holds for class II, where the proportion from the manual working class is even higher (at 43 per cent). Second, if the top classes draw an unusual proportion from all parts of the social scale, the pattern among the manual classes is much more homogeneous. Hence, three out of every four skilled manual workers had fathers in manual trades, and a similar figure holds for semi- and unskilled manual workers. While, as we saw, there is a high degree of upward mobility into classes I and II, there is very little downward mobility into VI and VII, especially from the top classes. In other words, there is very little reciprocity, and this can be so because across this generation considerable changes have occurred in the occupational structure of Britain (and Scotland). Above all, while manual occupations have fallen in both absolute and relative terms, the number of non-manual occupations has grown, thereby allowing considerable upward social mobility without concomitant downward mobility. Those classes with the highest proportion of 'self-recruitment' are, in descending order, class IV (petty bourgeoisie), class VI (skilled manual), class VII (semi- and unskilled manual). The most 'heterogeneous' classes in these terms are class III (white collar), class II (cadet class), and class V (blue collar elite).

Looking at the pattern of recruitment as a whole, Payne's conclusion from his own analysis of the Scottish data still holds, north and south of the border: 'Although this is not to say that Scotland is an "open" or egalitarian society, it does show that direct inheritance of occupations is relatively rare' (Payne 1987: 65). These data do seem to confirm the relative openness of social mobility in Scotland (and in England and Wales, for that matter), and do not contradict the egalitarian myth in Scotland. (One might ask why there seems to be no such myth in England, as there is in Wales, as well as Scotland – but that is not our concern here.)

The significant changes in the employment structure of Scotland, Wales and England since 1945 have helped to create, at least in non-manual occupations, heterogeneous groupings drawn from across the social spectrum. We should bear in mind, however, that social opportunity is not by any means equally distributed. For example, while 22.4 per cent in the service class (I) had class I fathers, this group represented only 5.2 per cent of the population; hence, the opportunities for class I sons to 'self-recruit' was over four times greater than perfect mobility expectation (reflecting the raw marginal distribution), while the inflow into class I from classes VI and VII was only about half of what might be expected.

Finally, before we examine the 'outflow' – what happens to the sons of fathers in particular classes – we might comment on the very high degree of self-recruitment among the petty bourgeoisie (class IV). While the capacity of this class to reproduce itself by passing on modest amounts of property within the family is also to be found in the south, Goldthorpe's suggestion seems the most plausible. The 11-point disparity between Scotland and England and Wales, he suspects, results from there being a larger component of farmers and smallholders within class IV in Scotland than in England and Wales, and from these groupings showing an even greater tendency towards immobility, net of marginal effects, than do others within class IV.

(Goldthorpe 1980: 295)

We might recall here the finding by Mueller and Karle discussed above that the petty bourgeoisie in Scotland have made unusually effective use of educational opportunities in the post-1945 period. This differential between the different countries in respect of the petty bourgeoisie is carried over into Table 4.5, which calculates the data in such a way as to show the outcome of life chances, namely, the mobility expectations for the sons of fathers in a particular class.

Table 4.5 Outflow table: class distribution of respondents by class of father at respondent's age 14. Data is percentaged by row (Scotland top line and England and Wales second line)

| | Respondent's class | | | | | | | |
	I	II	III	IV	V	VI	VII	%
I	41.8	22.5	11.5	7.0	5.7	5.7	5.7	5.2
	45.2	18.9	11.5	7.7	4.8	5.4	6.5	7.3
II	21.8	29.7	14.4	3.5	10.0	9.6	10.9	4.9
	29.1	23.1	11.9	7.0	9.6	10.6	8.7	5.9
III	13.0	17.7	10.1	5.2	11.6	20.9	21.4	7.4
	18.4	15.7	12.8	7.8	12.8	15.6	16.9	7.3
IV	11.0	10.7	7.5	32.0	5.6	10.7	22.6	12.3
	12.6	11.4	8.0	24.4	8.7	14.4	20.5	14.1
V	10.8	16.3	8.0	6.4	16.3	19.1	23.1	9.1
	14.2	13.6	10.1	7.7	15.7	21.2	17.6	11.5
VI	5.4	9.1	8.5	3.7	11.2	31.0	31.0	29.7
	7.8	8.8	8.3	6.6	12.3	30.4	25.9	27.5
VII	5.2	7.7	9.1	5.6	12.8	22.7	36.9	31.3
	6.5	7.8	8.2	6.6	12.5	23.5	34.9	26.4
%	9.8	11.9	9.1	8.3	11.2	21.7	28.1	
	13.6	11.5	9.2	9.4	11.6	21.2	23.5	

Table 4.5 reinforces many of the conclusions of Table 4.4. It shows especially how successful class I is in reproducing itself, not

111

because it prevents upward mobility from below, but because it retains its sons in this class. In this 'outflow' table, the classes which have the largest proportion of self-recruitment are class I (41.8 per cent), class VII (36.9 per cent), class IV (32 per cent), and class VI (31 per cent). Conversely, the classes which are the most 'open', which show the least self-recruitment are, as we might expect, class III (white collar) with only 10.1 per cent, and class V (blue collar elite) with 16.3 per cent.

The dominant impression from this table is one of similarity between Scotland and the rest of Britain, rather than difference. The significant differences occur, once more, among the petty bourgeoisie (class IV), although it seems that fewer sons of class II fathers make it into I compared with England and Wales, and there is a higher degree of class retention in II. While one could speculate as to the reasons (the impact of a 'branch-plant economy', fewer headquarters in Scotland and so on), this remains a matter for conjecture and further research. Given the differences in employment structures north and south of the border, the similarities in social mobility patterns are what is striking, not the differences. Goldthorpe's remark in this respect seems sound:

> On the basis of such comparison, it would seem clear enough that, had our enquiry been extended to Scotland, no substantially different results would have been produced so far at least as the pattern of de facto intergenerational rates is concerned.
>
> (1980: 291)

He concludes that the mobility model for England and Wales has a tolerably good fit with the Scottish data, the model accounting for over 95 per cent of the association between class of origin and destination.

In the second edition of his social mobility study (1987), Goldthorpe sets the Scottish experience in the wider context of other industrial nations: England and Wales, France, West Germany, Republic of Ireland, Sweden, Hungary, and Poland. As regards *relative* rates of mobility:

> England and Wales, together with France, turn out to be the most central nations with the configuration that emerges. Scotland and Northern Ireland, along with Hungary, fall into the intermediate band, and it is Poland, Sweden, West

Germany and Ireland which, in that order, represent the most outlying cases.

(1987: 309)

As regards *absolute* rates of mobility (reflecting structural or exogenous factors), Scotland, England and Wales have common characteristics by virtue of early industrialisation and the demise of a peasantry. Hence, in terms of comparative inflow rates, Scotland has the highest percentage (49 per cent) in classes I and II who originate from manual working classes (England and Wales is next with 45 per cent, with Ireland at the bottom with 28 per cent), and the lowest recruitment from farm origins (a mere 4 per cent, like England and Wales). On the other hand, the UK nations show the highest proportions of self-recruitment into the manual working classes, with Poland and Hungary the lowest. These patterns are the result of a shared economic history of industrialisation. In Goldthorpe's words,

Britain's early industrialisation and the unique path that it followed can be rather clearly associated, first, with a service class recruited to an unusual degree from among the sons of blue collar workers, and secondly with a broadly defined industrial working class which is to an unusual degree self-recruited or which, one could alternatively say, is highly homogeneous in its composition in terms of its members' social origins.

(1987: 316)

Britain, he concludes, does not possess any kind of historical legacy or institutional barriers (reflected in these data) either to impede or to promote social fluidity. In this context, Scotland together with England and Wales are the nations in which the distributions of social origins and destinations differ least. On reflection, we should not be surprised at this finding, because Scotland, England and Wales have common features as industrialised countries. The similarities between these countries can be seen in Table 4.6.

Plainly, it would be perverse to conclude from these tables, or from the general data on social mobility, that Scotland had taken a different mobility route from the rest of the UK. Scotland has a slightly smaller middle class, and a slightly larger manual working class, but the processes of upward and downward social mobility which created these structures of opportunity are

113

Table 4.6 Distribution of class origins and destinations of men aged 20–64 (surveys in early to mid 1970s)

	Class of origin		Class of destination	
Class	England and Wales (%)	Scotland (%)	England and Wales (%)	Scotland (%)
I and II (service class)	13	10	26	21
III (routine non-manual)	7	7	9	9
IVab (petty bourgeoisie)	10	7	8	6
IVc (farmers)	5	5	2	3
V and VI (skilled workers)	39	39	33	33
VIIa (non-skilled workers)	23	26	22	25
VIIb (farm workers)	4	5	2	3

remarkably similar on both sides of the Tweed. We should stress, of course, that these social mobility studies are using categories such as social class which are theoretically derived rather than the products of people's own thinking. We might speculate, for example, that there might be a divergence between how sociologists think about class (as discrete categories) and how class is imagined in people's heads. One such study (Coxon *et al.* 1986) argued that most people envisaged a continuous rather than a discrete hierarchy of class categories, a model of class which might relate more closely to the ideology of the egalitarian myth. However, if a legend, a myth of opportunity, survives in Scotland as it seems to do, it does so essentially at an ideological rather than a material level. This is not to say that it has no basis in reality, because neither Scotland nor England and Wales are closed societies, and we cannot conclude that access to the upper occupational reaches are tightly controlled. The evidence on social mobility in Scotland does not contradict the egalitarian myth, although it is interesting that there is no obvious analogue south of the border.

THE EGALITARIAN MYTH IN SCOTLAND

Our earlier discussion pointed out that the myth was flexible, ambivalent and multi-stranded. It gave comfort to the conservative in persuading him or her that all was well with the world; to the nationalist in providing a vision of a past as well as a future Scotland, democratic and different; to the socialist, in confirming the radical predilections of the Scot. The flexibility of the myth derives from its neutrality; it is radical or conservative depending on its framing assumptions. Its egalitarianism is retrospective as well as prospective; it harks back to a putative golden age; it is old as well as new.

The myth persists in large part for three reasons: it is embedded in the Scottish identity, an identity crucially formed and recast by two socio-literary movements of the last two centuries, the Gaeltachd and the Kailyard; it is sustained by romantic retrospects particularly those of emigrants from Scotland throughout the last two centuries; and it receives its institutional expression in the structures of Scottish civil society, such as the educational and religious systems and the union movement.

The two main cultural carriers of the egalitarian myth, the

Gaeltachd and the Kailyard, are, to borrow the notion from Raymond Williams, 'cultural formations', that is

> effective movements and tendencies, in intellectual and artistic life, which have significant and sometimes decisive influence on the active development of a culture, and which have a variable and often oblique relation to formal institutions.
>
> (1977: 117)

The contribution of these cultural formations to Scottish culture will be analysed in full in Chapter 7. The task here is to outline briefly how they contained egalitarian assumptions. The Romantic quest after Gaelic culture and Highland mythology in the late eighteenth century, and the literature and culture of the late nineteenth century 'Kailyard', both emphasised egalitarianism. These cultural formations were crucial in the making of the modern Scottish identity.

The Gaeltachd

The late eighteenth century saw a rising interest in 'the Celts', and specifically the Scottish Gaels. The 'discovery' of the so-called Ossian poems with their imagery of the noble savage was essential to Romanticism. As Chapman says,

> In assisting at the birth of the Romantic movement, the Ossianic poems were defined in opposition to the English language classical tradition of the 17th and early 18th centuries, and owed their form far more to a reaction against this tradition than they did to the Gaelic verse tradition on which they were based. The reactions against the conventions of style and subject of classical verse took the form in Ossian and later Romantic verse of an assumed affinity with nature, simple and unaffected, a praise of the spontaneous rule of the emotions in human conduct, and later a *political radicalism*.
>
> (1987: 85, my emphasis)

This literary tradition lent itself to the idealist interpretation of the egalitarian myth, articulating with the Romanticism and idealism of late eighteenth century literary culture. Dubious dualities between 'Highland' and 'Lowland' culture were built into this socio-literary perspective. The Gaeltachd was credited with a symbolism, especially for Scots, out of all proportion to its actual significance. As Chapman points out, 'The use throughout Scotland of Highland symbolism is not mere theft, but part of a process whereby the social space that the Highlander occupies is defined' (1978: 131).

The Highlands were judged more mysterious, more interesting, because they appeared to have a different culture, one which, paradoxically, was seen as more authentically 'Scottish'. The irony was that whereas the Lowlands had connived in the destruction of this culture and society a few decades earlier, it now sought to use the Highlands as a vehicle for its own identity. The Highland way of life was believed to be egalitarian, a feature derived from the nexus of obligations and rights residing in the clan system. A sturdy communalism was woven around these social arrangements, and in the words of historians Caird and Moisley, 'Highland philosophy of the equality of all men is nowhere stronger than in the Hebrides' (1961: 21). Noted Gaelic scholars such as Derrick Thomson helped to give it credence by explaining the sturdy Gaelic folk-poetry tradition in terms of the clan system with its 'reduced class differences', and its 'egalitarian educational system' (Wittig 1958: 197).

If this version of egalitarianism had remained a Highland phenomenon, then its impact would have been minimal. Instead, the 'Gaelic vision' was incorporated into the image of Scotland. Henceforth, the Scottish face presented to the outside world was increasingly a Highland face. It was particularly potent in the late eighteenth century when economic and political changes were altering the face of Scotland. The incorporation of the country into the British state was sufficiently recent to make it susceptible to questioning and re-interpretation.

The Kailyard

The second cultural formation which helped to embed the egalitarian myth into the Scottish identity was the late nineteenth century Kailyard, which, as we have argued, had the 'lad o' pairts' ideal-type at the heart of its image of Scotland. The Kailyard celebrated egalitarianism at its most clannish and communal. The celebration of 'getting on', of the lad o' pairts, of social mobility through the parish school was always a fragile one. In many respects, democracy and egalitarianism were features of a bygone age, an age which, as Raymond Williams puts it, lies 'just back

... over the last hill' (Williams 1973: 9). By the time they were elevated into fiction, these ideals had already become anachronisms. The social and economic contexts of the closed communities had irrevocably altered. The egalitarianism bred of an attachment to peasant values and the social organisations of small towns was a nostalgic one.

The essence of 'Scotland' came to be located in this image of small, intimate communities, in much the same way as the Gaelic vision had provided an early image. Whereas the Gaeltachd emphasised egalitarianism born of primeval communalism, that of the Kailyard envisaged a society of sturdy peasants. In this utopia, egalitarianism extends to owners of property; those who sell their labour have no a priori claims to democratic participation. It is the egalitarianism of the *petite bourgeoisie*, the 'social credit' mentality translated into a societal ideal, one which radicals such as Hugh MacDiarmid paid considerable attention to (Bold 1990).

The Scottish self-image of egalitarianism is essentially set against English hierarchy and status consciousness. The egalitarian myth defines the boundary of 'Scottishness' in social and ideological terms; but its roots are firmly in the mythical past. It is largely unchallenged, because it lends itself to a variety of interpretations. To the exiled Scot, it evoked a nostalgia for a homely, rural past of the forefathers which 'produced the full Kailyard and "Canadian Boat Song" nostalgia, fixated on the auld hame, the wee hoose and the whaups crying on the moor' (Craig 1961: 148). The role of emigré Scots in sustaining this idealisation of the homeland is crucial. Some two million people have left Scotland this century (Lindsay 1991), and at least similar numbers did so in the previous century. In their acount of Scotland's population in the nineteenth century Anderson and Morse argue that

> not far short of 2m. people left Scotland for overseas destinations between 1830 and 1914. This probably placed Scotland in second place after Ireland in a European league table of the proportion of the population involved in emigration overseas, and it implies a gross emigration rate of around one and a half times that of England and Wales.
>
> (1990: 15)

Much of this emigration in the nineteenth century was to Canada, Australia, New Zealand and South Africa, but otherwise the United States was the predominant destination. Anderson and

Morse estimate that as much as a half of all emigrating Scots went to the USA between 1853 and 1914. The propensity of Scots to settle on the frontiers is reflected in naming of communities after their places of origin. For example, of ten 'Aberdeens', seven are in the United States (from California to Idaho to South Dakota to Washington); all seven 'Edinburghs' are in that country; and four out of five 'Glasgows' and the same number of 'Dundees' are in the USA. (As far as English place-names are concerned, there are four Birminghams, five Londons, seven Sheffields, but sixteen Manchesters.)

The propensity of Scots to 'get on' by 'getting out' in all probability grossly underestimates the true rates of social mobility which we outlined above. We know, for example, that those who left were usually people of some means, as this comment from *Scottish Population History* makes plain:

> Of adult male emigrants from Scotland in 1912 and 1913, 47% described themselves as of skilled trades (compared with only 36% from England and Wales), a proportion which rose to 55% in the early 1920s. A further 21% in 1912–13 (15% in 1921–4) came from the middle class categories of 'commerce, finance, insurance, professional and students'. Only 29% were described as labourers, and of these 19% came from agriculture. The proportions changed little in the 1930s despite the vast reduction in the numbers emigrating.
>
> (Flinn 1977: 453)

The social strata of skilled artisans and lower middle class were probably those to whom the Scottish egalitarian myth appealed most, and as such they appear to be the main makers and sustainers of the myth. For such people, 'social mobility' often meant 'geographic mobility', migrating to better opportunities with a reasonable chance of success, and sending back optimistic messages as well as encouragement for others to join them. For many Scots, then, as Bob Morris has put it, 'family was not home-sweet-home but the ballads of parting and the attempts to maintain contact by letter' (1990b: 2–3). Their accounts of life in the new country probably did much to promote ambitions of upward mobility, for the myths of being able to make it from a relatively humble background did not specify that you had to do it in Scotland, merely that you had to start from there.

While Scots emigrés helped to sustain and embellish the

egalitarian myth, institutional and social arrangements within Scotland cannot be ignored. We have seen how the educational system embodied and celebrated the myth, and provided some validity for the egalitarian view of Scottish culture and institutions. The influence of Presbyterianism on Scottish social institutions is important, for it provided the basis of a conception of 'civic duty' which emphasised communal values and social responsibility. Its attenuation into what, after Arthur Marwick (1985: 16), we might call 'secular presbyterianism' provided a civic doctrine which underpinned social relations long after the direct influence of the Kirk declined. Similarly, the emergence of the trade union movement reflected this strain of somewhat dour and puritanical egalitarianism which gave to the movement in Scotland a different set of traditions and perspectives from its southern counterpart (Harvie 1990).

The myth of egalitarianism is a flexible and ambivalent one. In its assumption of the primordial equality of Scots, it lends itself to radical and conservative interpretations. Certainly, the 'facts' about social inequality in contemporary Scotland offer support for the myth, and, as we have seen, the patterning of social mobility in Scotland is not all that different from that which operates in England and Wales. Essentially, the Scottish myth is not dependent on 'facts', because it represents a set of social, self-evident values, a social ethos, a celebration of sacred beliefs about what it is to be Scottish. It helped to underpin a social and cultural order which placed a premium on collective, co-operative and egalitarian commitments. It is an ideological device for marking off the Scots from the English, which seems to grow in importance the more the two societies grew similar. It becomes the essence of Scotland. The more Scotland lacks control, in economic, social and political terms, over her own affairs, so ideas about this essence hold fast to the imagery of Scotland. In the next chapter we will examine the extent of this control, and ask who has power in Scotland.

5

WHO RUNS SCOTLAND?

There is a prima-facie case for claiming that the last place one should look for an answer to this question is Scotland. After all, the argument might go, the Act of Union of 1707 removed all semblance of political decision-making from Scotland, and its Members of Parliament were always likely to be swamped by the numerically superior English. Further credence is given to this position by those who govern Scottish political institutions. When asked to explain how he managed to govern Scotland with only ten out of seventy-two of Scotland's MPs, the then Scottish Secretary of State replied, 'We do not have ten MPs, we have nearly 400' (*Scottish Eye*, Channel 4, 18 February 1989). The political incorporation of Scotland seems complete.

Economic processes, too, seem to mirror the political ones. In terms of private capital, the tale is one of virtually continuous decline in indigenous control. By the early 1990s, a mere five of the top fifty manufacturing companies were controlled from Scotland (*Glasgow Herald*, 15 January 1990). The shift of decision-making furth of Scotland has been a notable feature of the post-war economy. The trend towards external ownership, and hence, control, is especially noticeable among the major employers (STUC 1989). Takeovers have swallowed up the firms of Distillers, Britoil, Coats Patons, Govan Shipbuilders and Anderson Strathclyde, and threatened the major Scottish clearing banks. The problem is particularly acute among Scotland's major employers, although among companies operating in Scotland 61 per cent remain Scottish-owned independents. During 1985 and 1986 external takeovers cut the amount of capital controlled by Scottish-registered commercial and industrial companies from £4,672

121

million in 1985 to £2,278 million at the beginning of 1987 (STUC 1989).

The decline in manufacturing employment would have been undoubtedly much worse had it not been for the contribution of incoming multinationals, including Motorola, IBM, Hoover and NCR, and the efforts of government agencies such as Locate in Scotland and the Scottish Development Agency. The issue of external ownership and control became part of Scottish political discourse from the early 1970s, when John Firn's work on the 1973 data base showed that large and fast-growing enterprises operating in advanced sectors of manufacturing were more likely to have their headquarters outside Scotland, notably in England or North America. Since Firn carried out his work in 1973, the trend towards foreign investment has continued, and Scotland has taken on the characteristics of a branch-plant economy (Firn 1975). Work by the Scottish Office in the 1980s confirmed the trend (Taylor 1986). While in 1950 only 4 per cent of Scottish manufacturing employment was provided in overseas-owned plants, by 1985 it stood at 19 per cent (some 72,000 jobs in over 300 foreign-owned plants). Overseas ownership of Scotland's manufacturing base is compounded by ownership by British conglomerates controlled via the City of London, who control well over half of Scottish manufacturing capital. Given the policy of privatising major companies such as Yarrows, Scott Lithgows and Britoil, the share of manufacturing employment provided by Scottish-owned companies is less than 40 per cent (STUC 1989).

This loss of political and economic control furth of Scotland was reinforced, it has been argued, by cultural factors too. The Union of the Crowns in 1603 and of Parliaments in 1707 had transferred cultural as well as political power to England. Landowners in particular, as R. H. Campbell has pointed out, were particularly susceptible after the Union to cultural incorporation, based on

> the belief that intellectually and culturally Scotland could not offer the wider horizon for the life of an educated and cultured gentleman. It led as a direct consequence to the need to speak and write in a language more easily understood by cultured society, and that was not to be found in Scotland for many.

> (1988: 103)

Those opposed to the Union agreed that such processes of

Anglicisation were not confined to the Scottish landed gentry. Key institutions such as the legal and ecclesiastical systems, but above all, the education system, were deemed corrupted by English values. The Scottish universities came in for the most opprobrium in this regard, and the issue of 'Englishing' of the curriculum and the composition of the student body and academic staff are ones which make periodic headlines in the press as well as in academic works, notably those influenced by George Davie's magisterial *The Democratic Intellect* (1961). In this context, the terms 'sell-out' and 'betrayal' are not uncommonly used to describe acculturation of Scotland with England. Those with a liking for conspiracy theory seek out the appropriate parcel of rogues in the Scottish nation, whether they be leaders of the economic elite, the political establishment, or cultural institutions north of the border.

And yet there remains more than a suspicion that all is not what it seems. It becomes difficult to explain just why Scotland was permitted to retain distinctive institutions after the Union, why, in the nineteenth century when continental European middle classes were taking to nationalism, the Scots did not, and latterly, why there has been a reassertion of Scottish cultural and political identity in the last few decades of the twentieth century. This chapter will argue that Scotland's incorporation into greater Britain was always incomplete because Scotland's elites dealt in a process of negotiated compromise and institutional autonomy, which made the Union less of a once-and-for-all bargain, and more of continuously tested negotiation (Paterson 1991). Such a process allowed alternative social and political values to survive and develop. The survival of Scottish 'civil society' within the context of the British state was the result of limited autonomy being granted to powerful groups in Scotland as long as the political and military deal agreed upon in 1707 was not disrupted. The suppression of the Jacobites after 1745 stood as testimony to the power of the British state over those deemed to have taken the freedom of the Union too far.

This negotiated compromise between the two countries rather than the much simpler incorporation of Scotland by England (as had occurred in Wales and Ireland) has made it difficult to argue that Scotland had 'client' status. In their important account of Scottish history, Dickson and his colleagues recognise that 'client capitalism' has its limitations as a characterisation of Scottish economic processes. Their thesis is initially quite bold:

In relation to Britain as a whole, what were to emerge in Scotland were complementary rather than competitive forms of capitalism, their interdependence being regularised under the political domination of Westminster. Such were the roots of the dependent or client status of the Scottish bourgeoisie.

(1980: 90)

Nevertheless, the authors recognise that 'it is misleading to conceive of the political relations between England and Scotland in terms of one-sided domination' (1980: 102), and that 'Scotland's client position in relation to England guaranteed . . . a distinctively Scottish civil society' (1980: 130). While it is not clear, logically, why such a society should be guaranteed, in empirical and historical terms Dickson and his colleagues are surely correct in indicating the survival of Scotland within the United Kingdom.

The appeal of 'colonial' models and motifs in the 1970s has already been outlined in Chapters 2 and 3, and it is plain that similar sociological models have been applied to other 'advanced' capitalist countries, most notably Canada, which has an even higher level of external economic ownership than Scotland. Much of the empirical and historical work on Canadian elites has been informed by colonial models of development, most notably in the work of Wallace Clement (1975; 1983). Specifically, the Canadian elite is presented as divided, between an indigenous elite dependent for its economic wealth on finance, utilities and transportation, and on the other hand a *comprador* elite – literally, a purchasing elite (the term is taken from Third World models of underdevelopment) – who monopolise manufacturing and resource-based industries on behalf of foreign interests. However, attempts to characterise these elites in distinctive social and political ways have foundered, and by the 1980s there were signs that such models and concepts were losing their explanatory force. Extensive research by Carroll (1984), for example, concluded,

Our findings called into question Clement's notion of a 'continental financial–industrial axis' in which Canadian financial capital maintains only tenuous connections with indigenous industry, coalescing instead with foreign based multinationals . . . as in other advanced capitalist societies, at the centre of the Canadian corporate power structure – and at the apex of the Canadian bourgeoisie – we find groups of interlocked capitals who own or manage supra-corporate blocs of indigenous finance capital.

(1984: 265)

Attempts at applying models of dependency to advanced capitalist countries like Canada frequently do not work, and it is not surprising that few parallels can be applied to Scotland either. Certainly, an analysis of Scottish elites brings out their relative autonomy *vis-à-vis* their southern counterparts rather than their subordination to English power bases.

Like other advanced industrial countries, Scotland has undergone massive economic restructuring in the course of the twentieth century. As a consequence, its class structure has become more complex and opaque, reflecting changes in ownership and control of material assets and in the nature of occupations. The purpose of this chapter is to chart how the character of Scotland's elites has changed under economic, political and social pressures. In particular, we will argue that the elites have become more diverse, diffuse and defensive in the course of this century; that traditional forms of power based on land and local property have declined in favour of forms of ownership and control which are more impersonal, less concrete and more distant; that, nevertheless, Scottish 'civil society' has survived the centralising influences of both business and government to create a distinctive Scottish social and political agenda in the 1980s and 1990s; and that as Scotland approaches the twenty-first century, key groups in the Scottish class structure have dissented from the values of the Anglo-British state and of market liberalism to the extent that new political arrangements within that state grow increasingly likely.

The key players in this drama have been the gentry or landed aristocracy, the industrial and commercial bourgeoisie, the professional classes, the *petite bourgeoisie*, and the 'service class' – managers and administrators in both the public and private sectors. We will not assume these groups to be a 'ruling class' because their material and cultural interests are frequently quite diverse and unintegrated. Their rulership has been partial rather than hegemonic, relating to special spheres of influence and power which have waxed and waned over the course of the century. Neither is it possible to chart their changing fortunes in a rigorously statistical way, because the available data are not precise enough, even in occupational terms, over the course of the century.

Quite apart from the fundamental assumptions which have to be made about how social class is operationalised, there are considerable difficulties and risks in using what appear to be straightforward statistical data. The problems of constructing time-series, for example, based on the census and showing shifts in occupations are considerable. It was not until 1961 that occupations were shaped into 'socio-economic groups' by the Registrar-General, and before that 'classes' referred to simple classifications of occupations. Further, even if we knew how an occupational title was classified in, say, 1921, we cannot assume that it has the same social meaning and economic significance in 1981.

CLASS AND POWER IN TWENTIETH CENTURY SCOTLAND

The turn of the century marked a new maturity in the Scottish economy, one which sought new commercial opportunities overseas and in England. At home, the Forth Bridge, completed in 1890, stood as a monument to technological progress and the industrial bourgeoisie which had made it, much as the Eiffel Tower, completed one year previously, had for the French counterpart. Overseas investment was also important. In 1900 it stood at £300 million, and by the outbreak of the Great War it had reached £500 million. Scottish money found its way into Australia, Canada and New Zealand, into the rebuilding of Chicago, into American ranches and real estate. The jute masters of Dundee had helped to create the investment trust as a vehicle for surplus profit, and lawyers channelled small and large funds into overseas opportunities. None of this was deemed unpatriotic, and as Lenman says: 'It was a commonplace of late Victorian comment that Scotland invested abroad on a scale per head with no parallel among the other nations of the United Kingdom' (1977: 192). Clearly, these levels of overseas investment by Scots related to the extent of Scottish migration abroad and their key roles in developing new territories.

By the outbreak of the Great War, Scotland was firmly locked into the international division of labour. It is commonplace to describe Scotland's economy as over-specialised at this time, too dependent on the staple trades of textiles, coalmining, shipbuilding and heavy engineering. If this was so, it was because Britain's industrial and trade structure itself had adapted to international opportunities. The above trades accounted for approximately 50 per cent of net industrial output and employed 25 per cent of the working population. Continental Europe remained a key market for Scottish as for British goods; other important export markets were to be found in the British empire, South America and Asia (Kirby 1981). In this regard, Scottish entrepreneurs were no different from their British counterparts. In David Marquand's words,

> British entrepreneurs failed to compete with the Germans and Americans in the new technologies of the late 19th and early 20th century because, in the short term, they could survive and prosper by selling more of their existing products in their traditional markets in Latin America and the Colonies. Meanwhile, capital which might have been invested in modernising British industry flowed abroad instead.
>
> (1988: 9)

The landed gentry

While Scotland in 1900 continued to share in the prosperity of imperial Britain, so also could its elites afford to assert their power and influence in most spheres of Scottish life. At the top of the Scottish social hierarchy in the early years of this century stood, in Sidney and Olive Checkland's apposite phrase, the 'mighty magnates': men (rarely women) heading the great houses of Buccleuch, Argyll, Bute, Atholl and Sutherland, who owned huge tracts of the Scottish countryside, and not a little urban space as well (Checkland 1984). This was a *rentier* class which made its money from its substantial stake in land, and which retained control over key social institutions. As Ian Levitt has pointed out,

> The administration of nineteenth-century welfare in Scotland was dominated not by new forces, the new wealth, the industrial capitalist that ruthlessly exploited the natural and labour resources around them, but by an older set, one that looked back to an earlier, seemingly golden period. Scottish government meant the laird, who as was said by Skelton, sought the quietness of country life, but instead 'lamented the encroachment of Morningside suburbia' (*Scots Pictorial*, 1897: 434).
>
> (1989: 121)

The gentry were marked off from the industrial and commercial bourgeoisie by their commitment to the country rather than the city. Culturally too, they were distinct. These lairds and nobles had for long diluted their Scottishness by sending their sons to English public schools, a feature which marked them apart from the Scottish bourgeoisie which had set up their own Scottish independent schools, and who, by and large, spoke with Scottish accents and affected such manners and life-styles as were compatible with their new-won wealth.

In religion too the classes were divided. Many of the gentry had retained a commitment to Episcopalianism, and a few, like the Marquess of Lothian, were Catholics. Many probably retained an attachment to the aristocratic ethos of the 'old society', and its social ideal of harmonious, organic values. Those who had access to the trappings of a more ancient Highland culture, with its patina of tradition and romantic *noblesse oblige*, could play the clan chief. As late as the 1960s, for example, the Duchess of Erroll could write,

> In too many countries the great historic families are separated from the mass of the people, but in Scotland we have been fortunate in that pride of Name has never depended on wealth and rank, and in that the clan tradition has always prevented class barriers from arising to divide our proud nation . . . We are all one family of Scots, the branches of that family being the clans and Names, and the Chief of Chiefs our Queen.
>
> (Bain 1968: 7)

The possession of country estates, or access to those of friends or family, allowed the Scottish gentry to forge a distinctive life-style with pastoral and sporting pursuits. Hunting and shooting were the pastimes of the great magnates like Buccleuch, the largest landowner in Britain, and Roxburghe, his near neighbour.

The bourgeoisie

Alongside these landed families, stood the industrial and commercial bourgeoisie. The owners of both land and capital in Scotland were powerful and self-confident, and as a result, in the words of the Checklands, 'Scotland became endowed with great commercial and industrial families, taking their place alongside the landed nobility, and to some extent linked together by marriage' (1984: 175). The new commercial dynasties were often assimilated to the older landed ones in this way. The alliance was also political. The lords and lairds had provided leadership for the Conservative Party in Scotland, and indeed, helped to give it its somewhat reactionary image right down to the 1890s. In the intake of MPs following the 1895 election, nine Conservative MPs were landowners, seven were businessmen and one came from the professions. This was in contrast to the Liberal-Unionists who had broken away from the Liberal Party over Irish Home Rule in the 1880s. Nine Liberal-Unionists were businessmen, two were professionals, and only three described themselves as landowners. Such was the power of this Unionism that, unlike the English case, it was able to absorb the ideologically weaker Conservatism. It drew its strength from the burgeoning, imperialist-inclined capitalist class concentrated in west-central Scotland. As Michael Fry pointed out, 'It was Unionist because imperialist; it was imperialist because its prosperity was bound up with Empire' (1987: 110).

This Unionism was assertive and resilient, and carried all before it, at the general election of 1900 making a clean sweep of Glasgow's seats. Although its fortunes ebbed in 1906 and 1910, it retained the capacity to mobilise its coalition of bourgeoisie and Protestant workers. As a result of this burgeoning power, Toryism, hitherto regarded, in Hutchison's words, as the creed of 'lairds and law agents' (1986: 200) had to accommodate to this new Unionism. Gradually, Conservatism moved from its reactionary position of the 1890s to a degree of commitment to progressive reform. Above all, however, as the Checklands observe, the Liberal-Unionists acted as 'a bridge over which middle class man could pass from Liberalism to Toryism without suffering any sense of betrayal' (1984: 85).

'Calvinistic inheritance', as the Checklands put it, of Scottish capitalists generated an image of Presbyterian reserve coupled with tightfistedness, sanctimoniousness, 'and a liking for whisky' (1984: 4). This new elite were not averse to criticising the landed interest for its inefficiency and laxity, such a critique drawing upon 'the harsh realism of political economy' (1984: 85). The Checklands provide a neat summary:

> By 1900, Scotland had produced a breed of major industrialists whose actions and prestige dominated the economic

scene. They included such names as Colville, Baird, Yarrow, Tennant, Lorimer, Elder, Pearce, Neilson and Beardmore. These were the magnates of shipbuilding, heavy engineering, iron and steel and coal. They were autocrats, their decisions were made, conveyed and not discussed. They had a strong desire to keep everything in their hands.

(1984: 178–9)

The cousins and the brothers of these industrialists entered the professions, to become the lawyers, doctors and churchmen of Edwardian Scotland. Crucially, the professions were Scottish, educated at fee-paying and Merchant Company schools in Edinburgh and Glasgow, and at Scottish universities. The traditional bourgeoisie, big as well as small, was nothing if not Scottish. Since the Treaty of Union in 1707, it had dominated Scottish civil society, its institutions and its mores. This was not some pliant agent of southern power, but a class with its roots deep in Scottish culture and tradition. Not only did it speak with a Scottish accent, it immersed itself in the folklore and literature of its native land. It spoke the poetry of Burns, it knew the novels of Scott, and it took pride in the folk memories of Wallace, Bruce and the Covenant. Its Kirk had long seen itself as one of the few institutions left to speak for Scotland, although its capacity to do so had been fatally weakened in the Disruption of 1843. It celebrated its distinctive values of thrift, hard work and personal achievement. 'Getting on' was an unspoken but vital aim in life, as well as a moral duty.

In these respects, egalitarianism was a key element in a conservative ideology which congratulated itself on the openness of Scottish society and its social institutions. This egalitarianism was, as we have seen, of a qualified kind: equality of opportunity, which was not incompatible with the liberal economic order. It also had the virtue of appealing to sections of the skilled working class when that political and cultural moment required it. Such an ideology of social opportunity also helped to unite the Scottish middle class, its *haute bourgeoisie*, with its reliance on substantial capital, its professions with their hold on credentials allowing them to dominate much of Scottish life, and at the margins of this class, the *petite bourgeoisie* whose hold on middle-class status was so much more fragile.

The petite bourgeoisie

In the late nineteenth and early twentieth centuries, the *petite bourgeoisie* came to dominate much of the economy and polity of Scotland's towns and cities, for most forms of enterprise were small-scale and local. This economic base gave the wherewithal to dominate the political life of Scotland's towns. In late nineteenth-century Edinburgh, for example, the lawyers and professional men withdrew from local political affairs, leaving the town council to be run by small landlords and shopkeepers. The kind of politics they indulged in were largely negative and defensive. Because local revenues were raised by property taxes – 'the rates' – many small property owners got themselves elected to the local council in order to control the level of public spending. Much as in the rest of Britain, Scotland's small business class owed its position to the ownership of petty property: small parcels of houses, flats and shops (McCrone and Elliott 1989). Out of these, a modest living could be had as long as economic and political conditions remained stable. Landlordism provided for many a means of livelihood, particularly as some insurance against business failure, and to provide for women and children should they outlive the owner himself. These petty property owners were *rentiers*, depending on letting out a few small flats to working class tenants, which supplemented other modest returns from business enterprise. Often they themselves lived close by their investments, in 'superior' tenements built to a higher standard than those they let out, or in villas in the growing suburbs of the cities.

Both politically and geographically, the small business stratum had limited horizons. Rarely did they own property outside their communities, seeing it as stone and lime, something they could go and see. Above all, they dominated town politics for much of the twentieth century. By the 1920s the challenge from Labour persuaded them out of their 'Independent' labels and into loose coalitions variously described as 'Progressive' (in Edinburgh, Aberdeen and Dundee) and 'Moderate' in Glasgow. Claiming that 'politics had nothing to do with local government', that local men were the best guardians of the public purse, they maintained their hold on politics until the 1930s (in Glasgow), until the 1950s in Aberdeen and Dundee, and in Edinburgh, right down until the 1970s. If bigger capital and the professions were content to let small capitalists run the towns and cities, they did so as long as no serious challenge came from Labour.

In the countryside the lairds kept a firm grasp of local politics until the reorganisation of local government in 1974 (Morris, A. 1989). The Duke of Buccleuch and the Duke of Roxburghe between them held the convenorship of Roxburgh County Council for forty-three of the years between 1900 and 1975. The great Border landowners were able to exercise influence directly in this way, but also indirectly through the offices of Sheriff Depute, and Commissioners of Supply. They were, in addition, Lord-Lieutenants of the counties, and Commissioners of Peace. In 1918 the convener of Roxburgh County Council was the Duke of Roxburghe; his vice-convener was the Duke of Buccleuch; Lord Ellesmere was a fellow council member. In 1975, before the county council was abolished, the convener was the Duke of Roxburghe; the Duke of Buccleuch and Baroness Elliot were also on the council. Little had apparently changed.

For much of the century, the traditional elites of Scotland continued to dominate the economic, social and political life of the country. Only the small business stratum was marginalised as the state, after the social unrest in 1915, placed restrictions on the rent levels of 'small dwelling houses' or tenement flats. The barrier between this stratum and the skilled artisans had always been a weak one, and after this defeat, the *petite bourgeoisie* became steadily detached from the bigger bourgeoisie.

At its upper reaches, the industrial and commercial bourgeoisie merged into the ranks of the gentry, marrying into their families, and purchasing landed estates on the fringes of Glasgow and Edinburgh. Those who remained in the cities symbolised in stone their superior status. As Smout has put it,

> Their finest monuments were their own homes – the sweeping terraces of Glasgow's West End, with gleaming stained glass and art nouveau decoration, and the stolid villas, with their ample gardens of lilac and laburnum, in Edinburgh's southern suburbs.
>
> (1987: 112)

The bourgeoisie were Presbyterian by religion and individualistic by inclination. In their heyday before the Great War, they maintained a firm hold over their fellow-countrymen and women. In Lenman's words,

The main achievement of the great self-confident Victorian bourgeoisie which dominated Scotland before 1914 was to maintain their own ascendancy within a society which tolerated, nay, positively encouraged enormous inequalities of income, without provoking any serious challenge to their position.

(1977: 203)

How was this ascendancy lost?

THE CHANGING CHARACTER OF SCOTTISH BUSINESS

The first and most important reason is that Scottish capitalism altered significantly. In a remarkable but neglected piece of research, John Scott and Michael Hughes (1980) analysed the structure of Scottish capital for specific time-points: 1904/5, 1920/1, 1937/8, 1955/6, and 1973/4. They charted the radical transformations in Scottish business this century, from a self-confident, locally controlled economy, to a weakened, externally dependent one. At the outset of their research, Scott and Hughes sought to apply explicit models of colonialism to Scotland. In a paper published in the 1970s, they borrowed directly from Gunder Frank: 'We are arguing that London is both political centre and economic metropolis whilst Scotland is a peripheral satellite' (Scott and Hughes 1976: 171). By the time their *The Anatomy of Scottish Capital* was published in 1980, however, they argued, 'We see Scottish capital as a distinct system with its own characteristics and which follows a distinct pattern of development' (1980: 15).

Their analysis of the structure of business in 1904/5 reveals the importance of the railway companies, and their inter-connections with coal, steel and engineering. Regional clusters were important, no more so than in Dundee where the jute barons of Cox, Baxter and the Flemings held sway. Similarly, there appeared to be a clear distinction between Edinburgh clusters – centred on the banks and the North British railway – and the Glasgow segment, focused on Tennants' companies, the Caledonian railway, and the Clydesdale Bank. Central to the business inter-connections were the banks and the financial system generally, a system in which the landed gentry played a leading part. The Marquess of Linlithgow, for example, was a director of the Bank of Scotland, and

133

Standard Life; the Duke of Buccleuch, of the Royal Bank, Standard Life, and Scottish Equitable; the Earl of Mansfield, of the National Bank, and Scottish Equitable; and the Marquess of Tweeddale, of the Commercial Bank, Edinburgh Life, and Scottish Widows.

This complex web of interlocking ownerships and directorates within Scottish dynasties helped the Scottish economy to remain fairly independent from England, although the take-over of indigenous companies by those from the south had been noticeable as early as 1900. That Scottish business by the outbreak of war in 1914 still bore the signs of its origins as family concerns was both its strength and weakness. There had been few attempts at financial or technical reorganisation on the lines of American or German business, and little signs of a managerial revolution in this period. The capacity of Scottish business leaders to wield personal control did not bode well for the future. After the Great War the expansion of the Scottish banks and the development of insurance companies led not only to a more interlocked system, but one in which Scottish capital had less autonomy. Family control remained relatively strong, despite the fact that more resources and power had flowed away from Scotland in the inter-war period, a feature which was to become even more marked after the Second World War.

Just as Scotland had benefited from being part of 'the world island', 'the centre of an informal network of trading relationships and capital movements, of which her formal empire was merely a part' (Marquand 1988: 8), so it suffered from general British decline. Marquand comments,

> What is special about Britain . . . is not that she abandoned market-led adjustment. It is that, after abandoning it, she failed to become a developmental state on the pattern of her more successful competitors on the European mainland and in the Far East.
>
> (1988: 113)

Although Scotland, as part of this unitary British state, could not escape its downturn, moves were afoot in the 1930s to restructure its economy, moves which were not to come to fruition until after 1945 when economic diversification became even more necessary. In the inter-war period, the regrouping of the civil service, the designation of Scotland as a separate area for industrial development, and the creation of the Scottish Economic Committee seemed to indicate the makings of a corporate state. Foster and Woolfson observe,

> State planning was now presented as a key vehicle for the fulfilment of national development. The character of the planning was statist, corporativist [*sic*] and paternalist, owing at least something to the Presbyterian heritage of previous centuries.

> (1986: 92)

Foster and Woolfson point out that the eclipse of the old-style Tories in 1940 ushered in new corporatist initiatives, and as a result 'the wedding of pre-war directive statism with the mixed economy concepts of Keynes, left a lasting legacy within the Scottish establishment' (1986: 97). While the old dynastic families retained their hold on traditional industry, foreign and English capital began to play a much greater role in Scottish economic affairs. Scotland's earlier prosperity had reflected its rapid adaptation to the market opportunities of empire, a pattern which was to prove very difficult to break in the twentieth century. Because the fortunes of the Colvilles, the Tennants, the Beardmores and others like them had rested upon the earlier opportunities of steel, coal, and engineering, the cold winds of economic change in the 1920s and 1930s left the social and political order which they had built up cruelly exposed. The Second World War had given a belated boost to those Unionist interests which remained on condition they accepted an extension of state power. Nevertheless, demise was not far off, and as Fry has put it, post-war saw the 'decline of the Scottish capitalist class, from the self-made local businessmen, to the dynasties of the Clyde' (1987: 193).

What had happened to the structure of Scottish business in this period? The dominant force in Scottish heavy industry in the 1930s, the Colville–Lithgow–Nimmo complex based on coal, iron and steel had disappeared with nationalisation, and the links between financial companies became a more pronounced part of the business network which, according to Scott and Hughes,

> was a mixture of family firms and firms controlled by financial interests. It was the financiers and members of the dominant families who welded these companies together into a densely connected system in which, nevertheless, certain spheres of influence could be identified.

> (1980: 153)

By the mid 1950s there was still little evidence of a 'managerial revolution', although new family dynasties were created which shared control with older interests. The late 1960s, however, 'seem to mark a period in which Scottish capital, the traditionally dominant dynastic families, were encountering a major crisis of confidence and direction' (1976: 114). By the 1970s, while companies subject to family control had a predominantly Scottish character, those companies – growing in importance – which were controlled by corporate interests had much lower levels of Scottish participation. The network of Scottish business interests was increasingly held together by the three banks, the Bank of Scotland, the Royal Bank of Scotland, and the Clydesdale Bank, each with its own cluster of related companies and spheres of influence. In spite of the fact that Scottish companies formed less and less of a distinct and autonomous entity in the face of external take-overs and amalgamations, 'family control remained a potent element in Scottish capital'. 'The major characteristic of the period studied [1904/5 to 1973/4]', they conclude, 'has not been a managerial revolution, but a managerial reorganisation of the propertied class' (1980: 153). Hence there emerged a small corps of multiple directors who manage the business system as a whole in Scotland. The same names, said one critic, crop up again and again. In the summer of 1989 the Secretary of State for Defence in the Conservative Government, George Younger, announced that he was resigning from politics to take up a directorship with the Royal Bank of Scotland. His family name is indeed one of those which 'crops up again and again' in the upper echelons of Scottish business.

The surviving importance of kinship in Scottish business has to be set alongside the growing significance of foreign and English capital in Scottish business. Scottish dynasties may continue to wield influence but in a diminishing sector of Scottish business. The problems of rapid industrial decline in the last fifty years forced the state, both national and local, to play a more active role in diversifying the Scottish economy. Hence the government induced merchant capital to fund the building of a steel strip mill at Ravenscraig in the late 1950s, the Rootes Car Company to relocate at Linwood, and new timber and aluminium plants to be set up at Fort William and Invergordon. The influx of foreign-owned plants began to generate concern over Scotland becoming a 'branch-plant economy' (Firn 1975; Young 1984). Since the mid 1980s the following major Scottish companies have been subject to take-over: Distillers (by Guinness), Coats Paton (by Viyella), House of Fraser, Yarrow (Trafalgar House), Bell's (by Guinness). Further unsuccessful raids were carried out on the Royal Bank of Scotland (by Standard Chartered Bank) and on Scottish and Newcastle Brewers (by Elders of Australia).

CREATING A SCOTTISH AGENDA

What are the implications of these major transformations in Scottish business for the structuring of power and control in Scottish society? First, it is plain that an indigenous business elite continues to exist in the financial sector, although in recent years it has found its control of these key institutions under attack. Second, the state at different levels has played a significant role in economic affairs, and state officials are a larger and more important part of Scotland's bourgeoisie. Third, the phenomenon of the 'branch plant economy' has reduced the number of native capitalists and swollen the number of officials and managers in key sectors. Fourth, Scotland is more of a corporate society, given the role of what the late John P. Mackintosh described as the 'non-democratic elite' – bureaucrats, businessmen, politicians – who have, in the absence of devolved political power, had the task of 'modernising' Scotland's economy. The structure of economic power in Scotland, then, is an amalgam of old and new wealth, the individual and the corporate, the indigenous and the foreign, the private and the public. One journalist was drawn to comment in the late 1970s that Scotland's elites 'all know each other – a tight circle of politicians, businessmen, civil servants, lawyers, trade unionists, churchmen, academics, and a nostalgic sprinkling of titled gentry. They fix the nation's agenda' (C. Baur, *The Scotsman*, 18 September 1978).

The point was reinforced by research by Moore and Booth (1989) which suggested that, while in strict terms Scotland cannot be called a corporatist state, if only because it is not a separate political system, it does contain a 'pattern of policy networks' in which the values and culture of decision-making elites sustain a distinctive set of institutions and relationships which influence bargaining and policy outcomes. Scotland, said Moore and Booth, is a 'close-knit community where a high level of individual contact is possible' (1989: 29). Central to this policy network are bodies such as the CBI in Scotland, the Scottish Trades Union Congress

(STUC), the Scottish Council (Development and Industry), and the Scottish Development Agency–Scottish Enterprise. The authors argue that Scotland represents a 'negotiated order' operating somewhere between corporatism and free-market pluralism, that the 'Scottish policy community' mediated through the Scottish Office represents a 'meso-level of the British state' (1989: 150).

While some writers like James Kellas have argued for a distinctive Scottish political system (1989), others disclaim a Scottish version of corporatism, and prefer to see it as a sub-set of the British administrative system, as a Scottish political arena (Midwinter *et al.*):

> The Scottish Office lacks the power to come to binding agreements of this [corporatist] sort and tends to follow policy leads elsewhere. The smaller scale of the Scottish arena and the degree of personal acquaintance, however, may permit detailed matters of policy and administration to be resolved in a more consensual mode.
>
> (1991: 91)

In certain fields of administration, most notably education, there is an identifiable policy community made up of a 'community of individuals who mattered; it was also the forum in which the interests of groups were represented, reconciled or rebuffed' (McPherson and Raab 1988: 433). Such a community stretches across government and outside groups who are involved in the implementation of policy, and while there is no single 'policy community' covering Scotland, the scale and administrative history of the country has made this form of governance particularly apt. It also helps to explain why the Thatcherite strategy of cutting down the state and asserting the primacy of the market has proved to be less than popular among the governing classes of Scotland, as well as among the population more generally.

In this context, we can begin to see the underlying political and economic reasons for the divergence between the Scottish and English political agendas which has been so striking in the 1980s, and which we will analyse in the following chapter.

THE CHANGING CLASS STRUCTURE

These shifting agendas are linked to the changing class structure in Scotland. Here we are dependent upon census data, which carry risks as well as opportunities. Bearing this in mind, we are indebted to the researchers who carried out the Scottish Mobility Study in the 1970s for reclassifying occupational titles between 1921 and 1971 to provide a valid time series (see Table 5.1) (Payne 1977).

Table 5.1 Socio-economic groups 1 to 12 (non-farm, non-armed forces), 1921–71, each shown as a percentage of the total

Socio-economic groups	1921	1931	1951	1961	1971
1 and 2 Employers and managers	6.1	5.6	6.2	6.8	8.0
3 Professional self-employed	0.6	0.4	0.4	0.7	0.7
4 Professional employees	1.3	1.1	1.6	1.8	2.8
5 Intermediate non-manual	3.1	3.1	4.4	6.1	8.2
6 Junior non-manual	14.7	15.9	19.5	21.9	21.6
7 Personal service	7.7	8.9	5.7	4.7	5.7
8 Foremen and supervisors	1.4	1.5	1.9	2.5	2.6
9 Skilled manual	35.3	31.3	29.0	28.2	24.3
10 Semi-skilled manual	15.4	14.1	14.9	15.8	13.9
11 Unskilled manual	10.3	13.9	13.8	9.6	10.3
12 Own account workers	3.9	4.2	2.5	1.9	2.0

Source: Censuses (Scotland) 1921 to 1971, economic activity tables

These series show a continuing decline in the proportion of skilled manual workers in the labour force, and second, a continuous rise in non-manual employment. The major proportional increases over this fifty-year period are among professional employees, intermediate non-manual workers (occupations ancillary to professions), and junior non-manual workers (eg clerical, sales). The major decreases are to be found among skilled and semi-skilled manual workers. The overall percentage of manual workers (categories 9, 10 and 11) has fallen from 61 per cent in 1921 to 48.5 per cent in 1971.

Major revisions of occupational categories make it very difficult to compare 1981 data with the above, but the general distributions are similar (Kendrick 1986). For the purposes of this paper, the categories have been grouped together (see Table 5.2).

Between 1961 and 1981, there have been major proportional increases among managers and administrators, professional employees, and intermediate non-manual workers. On the other

Table 5.2 Social class in modern Scotland, 1981

Class	Percentage of total
'Propertied' class (employers, self-employed professionals, farmers, own account workers)	6.5
'Service' class (1), upper (managers and administrators, professional employees, intermediate non-manual)	21.9
'Service' class (2), lower (junior non-manual, personal service)	27.3
Manual, 'working class' (foremen and supervisors, skilled, semi-skilled, unskilled, and agricultural workers)	42.4
Other	1.7

Source: adapted from 1981 Census, Scotland, Economic activity (10% sample), table 18b

hand, the biggest proportional fall has occurred among skilled manual workers. There are, of course, major gender differences in employment patterns. Whereas skilled and semi-skilled manual occupations account for 43 per cent of men's employment, most women are to be found in junior non-manual jobs (38.2 per cent), followed by intermediate non-manual (16.6 per cent) and personal service work (13.7 per cent) (Kendrick 1986: 246–7).

What evidence is there that Scotland's historical trajectory has affected the distribution of its occupations? As we saw in Chapter 3, traditionally Scotland has had a higher proportion of manual workers than the UK as a whole, and a lower one of non-manual workers. Scotland shows a shortfall among non-manual workers compared with England and Wales, but this is almost wholly accounted for by the shortfall of managers and administrators in the private sector, suggesting that Scotland's status as a 'branch plant' economy has eroded the apparatus of decision-making within its boundaries. Similarly, there is a proportional shortfall in own-account workers in Scotland – broadly speaking, the self-employed. Scotland's dependence on the state since the 1960s shows up insofar as the rapid expansion of the state service sector almost wholly explains the increase in intermediate non-manual workers. Thus the expansion in employment in the state sector virtually accounts for the boom among non-manual employment right up until the 1980s.

We can conclude, therefore, that Scotland's recent economic history has given a distinctive profile to its occupational structure, even although the broad trends – the decline in the proportion of manual workers, and the increase in non-manual – reflect those of other advanced industrial countries. The broad shaping of its occupational structure reveals that there are now more workers in the service class than in the manual working class, for the first time in Scotland's history. However, as the percentage of people doing non-manual work has grown, so it is likely that Scotland's middle class (however we choose to define it) has grown too, and in the process has become more fragmentary and diverse.

As we discussed in the previous chapter, such has been the rate of occupational and social change in Britain, especially since the war, that social classes are fluid and open to the extent that 'at all levels a majority of sons enter other classes, and in all classes, the incomers outnumber those whose fathers were in the same class' (Payne 1987: 89–90). The implication of these findings for this chapter are far-reaching, namely, that Scotland's middle classes have not only grown in size, but have become much more varied in their social origins, and hence life-styles, social values and even political attitudes. Far less than before are we able to read off the politics of class interests from occupational position. At the turn of the century it was possible to identify a fairly self-contained professional class, a class of bourgeois owners of capital, together with a minuscule but powerful landed aristocracy, as Scotland's 'ruling class'; in the late twentieth century such an exercise becomes much more difficult. It seems the case that the operations of this power have become much more opaque, and that forms of ownership and control have become more impersonal, distant and less concrete.

TOWARDS A 'PRINCIPLED SOCIETY'

At this stage we can gather together some of the strands that have made up our account of Scotland's class structure, and see how they sustain the argument that in terms of its moral economy, Scotland is (to adapt Marquand's phrase) a 'principled society'. Marquand's important thesis is that while Britain abandoned its market-led adjustment of the nineteenth century, it failed to become a 'developmental state' in the twentieth on the pattern of its more successful economic competitors. He argues,

> My central thesis is that the roots of Britain's problems are to be found in a coherent, though often unconscious, set of attitudes to policies and political man – to the relationship between man and society, between individual purposes and social purposes, and to the political dimension of these relationships – and in the reductionist model of human nature which lies behind them.
>
> (1988: 213)

The collapse of Keynesian social democracy in the 1970s ushered in a radical assertion of reductionist individualism with the election of the Thatcher government of 1979, which, by the early 1990s, had run its course. In Marquand's view, Britain's adjustment problems have as much to do with politics as with economics, notably the intellectual and moral vacuum at the heart of the political economy. The emergence of a distinctive political economic agenda in Scotland over the past thirty years seems in large part to reflect the fact that Scotland has moved significantly towards such economic developmentalism. The curious character of the British state adds to this growing divergence. In Marquand's (Anglocentric) words,

> We cannot speak of a 'British state' in the way that one speaks of a 'French state' or, in modern times, of a 'German state'. The UK is not a state in the Continental sense. It is a bundle of lands . . . acquired at different times by the English crown [sic], and governed in different ways. Its inhabitants are not citizens of a state, with defined rights of citizenship. They are subjects of a monarch, enjoying 'liberties' which their ancestors won from previous monarchs.
>
> (1988: 152)

Westminster governments are not held in high esteem by Scots. For example, in a poll conducted by MORI for *The Scotsman* in 1989, only 11 per cent of Scots questioned agreed or strongly agreed with the statement that the Westminster Parliament works for Scottish interests (49 per cent disagreed or strongly disagreed); and only 12 per cent agreed or strongly agreed that decisions made by UK ministers worked in Scotland's interests (60 per cent disgreed or strongly disagreed) (MORI, *The Scotsman*, 1989). We have, of course, no way of knowing whether the other peoples of the UK have equally low opinions of their rulers. The disparity between public opinion in Scotland and elsewhere in Britain, however, is reflected in these data from the British Election Survey for 1987. While only 26 per cent of Scots named the monarchy as the main source of 'pride in Britain' (compared with 37 per cent for the rest of Great Britain), the largest number of Scots (28 per cent) named the health and welfare systems (compared with only 16 per cent for the rest of Great Britain) (Paterson 1991).

Given the semi-autonomous nature of Scottish civil society within the British state, it is not difficult for significant strata within Scotland to assert their distinctive voice. Thus Scotland's traditional upper class, while educated at English public schools, might well retain a degree of commitment to 'Scottish' values if only because it has taken on the patina of aristocratic historic culture. Further, we might surmise that its aristocracy and gentry retain a commitment to the aristocratic ethos of the 'old society', and its ideal of harmonious, organic values. Similarly, the most likely social carriers of neo-liberal, free-market values – the indigenous bourgeoisie – have not only been caught up in 'corporatist' activity from the 1930s, but are the class which has suffered most from the process of economic restructuring which has occurred since 1945.

Scotland's professional classes – lawyers, doctors, teachers, churchmen – while socially conservative, embody the institutional survival of a distinctive Scottish 'civil society', and can be considered as keepers of native institutions, and hence incipient 'nationalists', resistant to further Anglicisation. The 'service class', in broad terms the managers and administrators, especially those working in public institutions, who operate within a managerial ethos, are likely to be supportive of a proto-corporatist, interventionist political economy.

At the same time, Scotland's working class is to date thirled to a 'labourist' tradition, at least since the 1930s, which places high value on corporatist activities in its quest for economic prosperity. The close links between organised labour and Scottish economic agendas which encompass collectivist or community values have a long pedigree north of the border (Keating and Bleiman 1979).

CONCLUSION

In a decade short of the twenty-first century, the role of the Scottish elites has changed significantly. At the turn of the century, they were more self-confident in their own economic abilities and capacity to map out a new direction for Scotland. The political leaders of this society saw their future and that of their country firmly within the United Kingdom. That was what it meant to be Unionist. It meant economic self-confidence and social control, linked by imperial interests, and cemented by a robust Protestantism which brought many working class Scots into the Unionist fold. By the late 1980s Unionism as a political creed had grown thrawn and defensive, and reduced to its most simple meaning of doing Westminster's bidding. It no longer provided a game-plan for a country and its leading classes.

Nevertheless, it is plain that Scottish elites cannot be simply subsumed into those of the British state or capital. The process of negotiated compromise since the Union of 1707 has afforded elites north of the border a degree of limited autonomy over Scottish institutions to such an extent that no outright demand for political independence for the country as a whole was deemed necessary by them. Nevertheless, in the last three or four decades, Scotland has moved steadily away from the ethos of market liberalism, and the reductionist model of human nature which underpinned it.

This shift has occurred, firstly, for economic reasons insofar as the collapse of the Scottish economy from the 1930s ushered in a more 'developmentalist' strategy for the state in Scotland. Secondly, Scotland has developed a political 'negotiated order' of decision-making, which has sought to establish a consensus. This order was in place by the time Thatcherism, with its neo-liberal, anti-state ethos, emerged. The attack on the state in Scotland came to be viewed in large part as an attack on the country itself. Finally, changes in the composition of Scotland's class structure weakened the social interests attracted to the ideology of neo-liberalism, and strengthened social strata sympathetic to collectivist and 'organic' principles. Diverse social groups, from the aristocratic upper class through to organised labour were not hostile to the 'developmental' state.

There is irony in the fact that the culture which spawned Adam Smith has, in the 1980s, decisively rejected the crude reworking by the New Right of his views. The diverse agencies of the state, together with sections of Scotland's industrial and commercial elite have helped to frame a set of principles, albeit incomplete, for the development of modern Scotland. Such principles were founded on a growing sense of common purpose, a vision of society and a set of moral precepts, reinforced by nationalism, which were deeply at odds with the tenets of Thatcherism and the Anglo-British state. In the next chapter, we will explore how this alternative political agenda emerged, and the changing political sociology which lay behind it.

6

POLITICS IN A COLD COUNTRY

The major changes which have occurred in the Scottish political agenda during this century have had only a limited impact on the analysis of politics north of the border. The dominant wisdom in political science has emphasised the political homogeneity of British political behaviour, reflecting in large measure the influence of a centralised, unitary state. Hence Scotland's politics have been described in an influential textbook (McAllister and Rose 1984) as 'British with a difference' insofar as the vast majority of Scots vote for ostensibly British political parties. If there are differences in electoral behaviour between Scotland and England, the orthodox explanation is that Scotland shares a political economy with other declining industrial regions of the UK (such as the north of England, and Wales). So, any electoral differences are judged merely to reflect an antiquated social and economic structure which has historically been resistant to change, often because political interest groups such as the Labour Party in these 'regions') have undue influence.

Such an analysis, however, ignores the different histories and agenda of political parties in Scotland. This chapter will examine the diverging trends in political behaviour north and south of the border, and will argue that Scottish politics are increasingly concerned with an alternative agenda. However, it is important not to leap to the opposite conclusion, that Scotland is 'essentially' and historically different from England (treating it largely as undifferentiated internally). For much of the nineteenth century, Scotland behaved in electoral terms quite differently from England. For example, from the 1840s until the 1880s, the Liberals notched up disproportionate majorities north of the border, especially in 1847 when 81.7 per cent of Scots voted Liberal compared with

57.2 per cent in England, and again in 1865 when the figures were 85.4 per cent and 59 per cent respectively. By the mid-1880s, however, largely as a reflection of the Liberal crisis over Irish home rule, the differential between Scotland and England in the Liberal vote began to diminish. After 1945 the deviations between the two countries as regards voting for the three main British political parties were small, and major differences in voting behaviour north and south of the border only emerged in the 1960s. The focus of this chapter will be on Scottish politics in the crucial thirty years since then.

The view that Scotland has always been historically and essentially different from its southern neighbour has political currency in Scotland, emphasising as it does strongly radical and nationalist traditions such as the 'Scottish insurrection' of the eighteenth century (Ellis and Mac A'Ghobhain 1970), the Highland 'land wars' of the late nineteenth century, and the unrest on 'Red Clyde' in early twentieth-century Scotland (Young 1979, and Melling 1983). These events have an undeniable importance but they should not be shifted out of context and imbued with a significance out of all proportion to their historic meaning. The argument in this chapter will be that in the last thirty years or so Scotland has diverged markedly from England, and that this divergence cannot simply be attributed to quite different social and economic forces impacting on Scotland, but rather their differential political impact north of the border. In most respects, as has been argued in previous chapters, Scotland has undergone quite similar social changes to the rest of the UK (and, indeed, to other advanced industrial countries). These changes are, however, refracted through diverging political agenda, and hence, the political outcomes of these social changes tend to be different. It will be an important part of this argument that different forms of political behaviour do no necessarily require quite different sets of social changes to be in operation, merely their different expression in political culture. In this regard, we can see again the power of myths to mediate social change.

The first task is to document political trends in Scotland as measured by electoral behaviour at general elections (Table 6.1). For the sake of completeness, all elections since 1832 have been included.

A number of preliminary observations can be made. For much of the nineteenth century, Scotland was Liberal territory to an extent that even Labour failed to match in the twentieth. Indeed,

Table 6.1 Votes and Seats in Scotland, general elections, 1832–1987

	Labour	Conservative	Liberal	SNP	Other	Turnout	Number of seats uncontested	Total number of seats
		Percentage of vote, no. of seats in parentheses						
1832		21.0 (10)	79.0 (43)			85.0	15	53
1835		37.2 (15)	62.8 (38)			70.9	23	53
1837		46.0 (20)	54.0 (33)			68.0	22	53
1841		38.3 (22)	60.8 (31)		0.9	62.2	29	53
1847		18.3 (20)	81.7 (33)			51.1	37	53
1852		27.4 (20)	72.6 (33)			45.5	33	53
1857		15.3 (14)	84.7 (39)			66.3	38	53
1859		33.6 (13)	66.4 (40)			65.6	45	53
1865		14.6 (11)	85.4 (42)			70.7	37	53
Extension of franchise to all male householders and tenants								
1868		17.5 (7)	82.5 (51)			74.1	26	58
1874		31.6 (18)	68.4 (40)			70.9	22	58
1880		29.9 (6)	70.1 (52)			80.0	12	58
Extension of franchise to all male occupiers								
1885		34.3 (8)	53.3 (51)		12.4 (11)	82.0	5	70
1886		46.4 (27)	53.6 (43)			72.3	9	70
1892		44.4 (19)	53.9 (51)		1.7	78.3	0	70
1895		47.4 (31)	51.7 (39)		0.9	76.3	5	70
1900		49.0 (36)	50.2 (34)		0.8	75.3	3	70
1906	2.3 (2)	38.2 (10)	56.4 (58)		3.1	80.9	1	70
1910 Jan.	5.1 (2)	39.6 (9)	54.2 (58)		1.1 (1)	84.7	0	70
1910 Dec.	3.6 (3)	42.6 (9)	53.6 (58)		0.2	81.8	12	70

Table 6.1 (cont.)

Year								
			Extension of franchise to all men over 21, most women over 30					
1918	22.9 (6)	32.8 (30)	19.1 (25) coalition / 15.0 (8) non-coalition		10.2 (2)	55.1	8	71
1922	32.2 (29)	25.1 (13)	17.7 (12) Nat. Lib. / 21.5 (15) Lib.		3.5 (2)	70.4	3	71
1923	35.9 (34)	31.6 (14)	28.4 (22)		4.1 (1)	67.9	4	71
1924	41.1 (26)	40.7 (36)	16.6 (8)		1.6 (1)	75.1	3	71
			Extension of franchise to all women over 21					
1929	42.3 (36)	35.9 (20)	18.1 (13)	0.2	3.5 (2)	73.5	0	71
1931	32.6 (7)	49.5 (48)	13.5 (15)	1.0	4.4 (1)	77.4	8	71
1935	36.8 (20) / 5.0 (4) ILP	42.0 (35)	6.7 (3) / 6.7 (7) Nat. Lib.	1.1	1.8 (2)	72.6	1	71
1945	47.6 (37) / 1.8 (3) ILP	41.1 (27)	5.0	1.2	3.3 (4)	69.0	0	71
1950	46.2 (37)	44.8 (32)	6.6 (2)	0.4	1.6	80.9	0	71
1951	47.9 (35)	48.6 (35)	2.7 (1)	0.3	0.5	81.2	0	71
1955	46.7 (34)	50.1 (36)	1.9 (1)	0.5	0.8	75.1	0	71
1959	46.7 (38)	47.2 (31)	4.1 (1)	0.5	1.2	78.1	0	71
1964	48.7 (43)	40.6 (24)	7.6 (4)	2.4	0.7	77.6	0	71
1966	49.9 (46)	37.7 (20)	6.8 (5)	5.0	0.6	76.0	0	71
1970	44.5 (44)	38.0 (23)	5.5 (3)	11.4	0.6	74.1	0	71
1974 Feb.	36.6 (40)	32.9 (21)	8.0 (3)	21.9 (7)	0.6	79.0	0	71
1974 Oct.	36.3 (41)	24.7 (16)	8.3 (3)	30.4 (11)	0.3	74.8	0	71
1979	41.5 (44)	31.4 (22)	9.0 (3)	17.3 (2)	0.8	76.8	0	71
1983	35.1 (41)	28.4 (21)	24.5 (8)	11.7 (2)	0.3	72.7	0	72
1987	42.4 (50)	24.0 (10)	19.2 (9)	14.0 (3)	0.3	74.3	0	72

Sources: Parry 1988: 2–3; Craig 1981
Note: ILP–Independent Labour Party (MPs joined Labour, 1947); Scottish Universities seat (abolished 1948) excluded

the Liberal Party won a majority of Scottish seats at every election between 1832 and 1910, excepting 1900. Second, the Conservative Party was the most popular party in Scotland between the Great War and the mid-1950s, winning 37 per cent of all the Scottish seats contested at the eleven elections in that period. The Labour Party and its allies (the ILP) won 35 per cent of seats during this time. The third preliminary observation is that it is only since the 1950s that Labour has been the dominant party, and that it has been challenged for the anti-Tory vote by the Liberals, who made a modest comeback in this period, and above all, by the rise of the Scottish National Party.

In many respects, Scotland has been less radical than other parts of the UK, notably Wales. The latter returned Liberal or Labour MPs for 70 per cent of seats fought between 1868 and 1983, whereas Scotland returned 58 per cent. Punnett's work on the 'Anglo-Celtic' divide (Punnett 1985) shows that the images of 'Tory England' and 'radical Scotland' are broadly accurate, but need qualification. Wales and the north of England have averaged, since 1945, a higher percentage of Left seats than Scotland, and Labour's success north of the border has come belatedly since the late 1950s, and that only partially. If anything, Punnett concluded, polarisation between England and Celtic Britain was more pronounced before 1914 (Conservative versus Liberal) than in the modern period between Tories and Labour. Further, there was little evidence up to 1983 of the Tory south of England, despite its population, imposing its political will on the Celtic periphery. Punnett points out, 'The supposedly dominant south of England has been on the winning side less often than has Scotland (and less often than the North and Midlands of England)' (1985: 2). Nevertheless, since 1979 Britain has become politically divided not simply between England and the Celtic countries, but between north and south Britain in which a marked north-south political slope has developed. Punnett concludes, 'Over the post-war period as a whole, the North-South Britain divide has replaced the Anglo-Celtic divide as the most conspicuous regional electoral cleavage within Great Britain' (1985: 28).

In Scotland there are two broad and interrelated trends in postwar electoral behaviour – the rise of the Scottish National Party, and the growing divergence in the electoral performance of the Conservative and Labour parties north and south of the border.

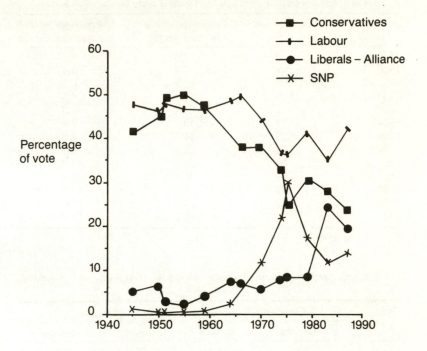

Figure 6.1   General elections in Scotland, 1945–87

The trends in Scottish voting behaviour since 1945 are outlined in Figure 6.1.

Both of these trends are separate but inter-connected insofar as they reflect social change in Scotland over the past three decades. Much of the focus of political attention has been on the rise of the SNP since the late 1960s, although the party's advance up until 1970 was concentrated on fighting more seats in Scotland rather than increasing its share of the vote.

Table 6.2 shows that, while the SNP's rising electoral support began in the 1950s rather than the 1960s, it was not until the 1970 election that it could be considered a national party fighting virtually all Scottish seats. The electoral appeal of the Nationalists will be examined later in this chapter, but it is now necessary to outline the second major trend in Scottish politics, the growing divergence between Scotland and England in terms of support for the Conservative and Labour parties.

Table 6.2 Trends in Scottish National Party voting, 1945–87

	Seats fought	Percentage of vote in seats fought	Percentage of total vote
1945	8	7.6	1.2
1950	3	7.4	0.4
1951	2	12.2	0.3
1955	2	14.5	0.5
1959	5	11.4	0.8
1964	15	10.7	2.4
1966	23	14.1	5.0
1970	65	12.2	11.4
Feb. 1974	70	22.1	21.9
Oct. 1974	71	30.4	30.4
1979	71	17.3	17.3
1983	72	11.6	11.6
1987	71	14.2	14.0

Source: Craig 1989

Table 6.3 Conservative and Labour voting in England and Scotland, 1945–87

Year	Conservative*, as %		Labour, as %	
	England	Scotland	England	Scotland
1945	40.2	41.1	48.5	47.6
1950	43.8	44.8	46.2	46.2
1951	48.8	48.6	48.8	47.9
1955	50.4	50.1	46.8	46.7
1959	49.9	47.2	43.6	46.7
1964	44.1	40.6	43.5	48.7
1966	42.7	37.7	48.0	49.9
1970	48.3	38.0	43.4	44.5
Feb. 74	40.2	32.9	37.6	36.6
Oct. 74	38.9	24.7	40.1	36.3
1979	47.2	31.4	36.7	41.6
1983	46.0	28.4	26.9	35.1
1987	46.2	24.0	29.5	42.4

Source: Craig 1989
Note: *'Conservative' includes 'National' and 'National Liberal' between 1945 and 1966.

Table 6.3 reveals the extent to which the fortunes of the major parties have diverged in these two nations of the UK. Whereas the Conservative vote in England held up, in Scotland it was virtually halved between 1955 and 1987, as Figure 6.2 makes plain.

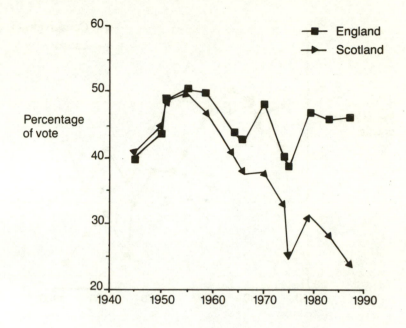

Figure 6.2 Conservative vote, England and Scotland

The only marked improvement in the Conservative vote in Scotland came between October 1974 and 1979, being a partial recovery of the vote in February 1974. Labour's share of the vote in Scotland and England provides no such clear-cut contrast. The trends in Labour support are close between 1945 and 1955, and again between 1964 and February 1974. Labour is vulnerable to the SNP in the 1970s, but since 1979, when the Nationalist threat recedes, it has been much more successful than its southern counterpart, although it does not regain the level of its post-war support. Figure 6.3 compares the Conservative and Labour votes in Scotland since 1945.

The systematic swing away from the Conservatives and towards Labour in Scotland, excepting the period of SNP success between 1966 and 1974, can best be gauged by focusing on the 'combined gap' between Labour and Conservative voting in Scotland and England. Such a measure is simply constructed by adding the

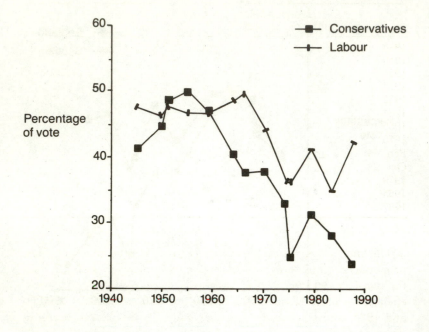

Figure 6.3 Conservative and Labour voting in Scotland

Labour gap – the Labour share in Scotland minus the Labour share in England – to the Conservative gap – the Conservative share in England minus the Conservative share in Scotland.

Table 6.4 shows that there has been a systematic swing away from the Conservatives and towards Labour in Scotland, excepting the period of the SNP upsurge – from 1966 through to the mid-1970s. Despite Liberal successes in the north and south of Scotland, the party has done less well in Scotland than in England in the last fifty years. Only at the 1951 election did the Liberals perform marginally better in Scotland than in England. When the SNP was at its peak in the two 1974 elections, the Liberals were taking only around 8 per cent of the vote compared with over 20 per cent in England. By the 1980s, the gap in Liberal performance in the two countries had fallen to a few percentage points (1.8 in 1983, and 3.2 in 1987).

Table 6.4 Differences in Labour and Conservative performances in Scotland and England

	Labour advantage in Scotland	Conservative shortfall in Scotland	Combined gap
1945	−0.9	−0.9	−1.8
1950	0.0	−1.0	−1.0
1951	−0.9	0.2	−0.7
1955	−0.1	0.3	0.2
1959	3.1	2.7	5.8
1964	5.2	3.5	8.7
1966	1.9	5.0	6.9
1970	1.1	10.3	11.4
Feb. 74	−1.0	7.3	6.3
Oct. 74	−3.8	14.2	10.4
1979	4.9	15.8	20.7
1983	8.2	17.6	25.8
1987	12.9	22.2	35.1

The move away from the Conservatives has been much more pronounced and more consistent than the swing to Labour, and the non-Conservative parties have at different times been the beneficiaries – first Labour in the mid-1960s, then the SNP in 1970 and 1974, and since 1979, Labour again. To be precise, much of the growing divergence between Scotland and England is the result of long-run decline in support for the Conservative Party in Scotland, rather than sustained electoral popularity for Labour. Further, the decline in the Conservative vote has occurred since the mid-1950s, for in the decade after the war the 'combined gap' in Labour and Conservative performances in Scotland and England was negligible. The first task in constructing a political sociology of modern Scotland, then, is to explain the rise and fall of support for the Conservative Party north of the border.

THE RISE AND FALL OF SCOTTISH CONSERVATISM

In the last chapter, we argued that Unionism – that brand of Scottish Conservatism which flourished in the first half of the twentieth century – had a particular appeal to local Scottish capital. Scottish Unionism had deep roots in Scotland, and the Conservatives are by far the oldest political party north of the border. At a relatively low ebb for much of the nineteenth century, the party polled between fifteen and twenty percentage points less in

Scotland than in England, much as it was to do in the late twentieth century. Its political strength among the landed classes kept it penned into the rural areas, until the Liberals began to fragment over the issue of Irish home rule after 1886. That year, the Liberal Unionists broke away from the Liberal Party, and strengthened the connection between Protestantism and Conservatism. In 1900, the Liberals for the first time did not win a majority of Scottish seats, their 34 being beaten by a combination of 19 Tories and 17 Liberal Unionists. In that election, the Liberals took 15 of the 31 burgh seats in Scotland, while the Conservatives and Liberal Unionists took the other 16. Similarly, there was little difference between the two political blocks insofar as both took the same proportion of burgh and of county seats. The right-wing grouping took all 7 of the Glasgow burgh seats, while the Edinburgh seats were shared, with the Liberals winning the 2 Aberdeen and the 2 Dundee seats. The rural predominance of Liberal voting did not occur until after the First World War (and the débâcle over Irish Independence).

The rise of Labour, the extension of the franchise, and the granting of home rule in Ireland in 1922 allowed the bulk of the Scottish Catholic working class to support Labour. Partly as a response, the middle-class vote swung increasingly behind the 'Unionists'. As James Kellas pointed out in the 1970s, 'The Conservative Party in Scotland has until recently derived its strength in the industrial west from the remnants of this Liberal-Unionist vote' (1973: 109). By the 1920s the Conservatives and their allies had overtaken the Liberals in Scotland, and while they never managed to perform as well as their counterparts in England, they were – culminating in 1955 – the most successful party electorally north of the border.

What made this achievement even more remarkable was the fact that, in terms of social structural factors, Scotland was not fertile soil for Conservatism. The party's performance after 1945 is surprising when one considers that in social class and housing tenure, variables traditionally linked to political behaviour, the Conservatives were at a disadvantage, for both manual workers and council tenants were more likely to vote Labour. Since Scotland had more of each social category, the performance of the Conservatives in matching Labour was unusual. Miller's assessment (Miller 1981) of the 'normal' Scottish–English difference in social class alone (involving the Tories doing 4 per cent worse in

Scotland and Labour doing 4 per cent better) implies that in the 1950s when there was actually rough parity in voting, the Tories were doing 8 per cent better than they should have done. In this regard, then, the question becomes 'Why was the Conservative Party doing so much better in the 1950s than it should have done (in terms of the social structure of Scotland at the time)?'

The success of the Conservatives nationally was all the more remarkable given that they did not operate at the level of local politics for much of the twentieth century. They had put up candidates at municipal elections in the early part of the century, but by the 1930s they had all but disappeared, to be replaced by a coalition of Tories, Liberals and Independents gathered under 'non-political' labels such as 'Progressives' (in Edinburgh) or 'Moderates' (in Glasgow). These fairly loose coalitions kept alive the belief that local government was essentially a non-political business in which individuals were elected on their merits. As we pointed out in the previous chapter, the appeal of the Progressives and Moderates was particularly to small local businessmen who believed in apolitical administration by knowledgeable, essentially local, people like themselves.

At the same time as these new coalitions were put together, militant Protestantism became a feature of local politics in the large cities. In Edinburgh, Protestant Action operated an informal electoral pact with the right-wing Progressive Association in the 1930s, and was a presence on the city streets right until the 1950s. In Glasgow, there is irony in the fact that the intervention of the Scottish Protestant League in 1933 gave Labour control of the city for the first time (Gallagher 1987a).

Although Conservatism as such did not intervene in Scottish local politics in modern times until the late 1960s, it is likely that Conservatives were able to mobilise, at the national level, a similar set of social and religious beliefs. Religion has always mattered in Scottish politics, and it dominated nineteenth-century cleavages to a remarkable extent. These influences were carried into this century in a potent form. While direct and systematic evidence on the middle years of this century is hard to come by, survey data from the 1950s and 1960s suggest that strong religious connotations were present in Scottish politics. National and local surveys (Budge and Urwin 1966; Bochel and Denver 1970) show that 'one important influence – religion – does seem to carry a different and stronger weight among Scottish electors when they are compared to English electors' (Budge and Urwin 1966: 71). Bochel and Denver, on the basis of a survey carried out in Dundee in 1968, found, if anything, a closer tie between religion and voting. Of Church of Scotland manual workers, 39.5 per cent voted Conservative compared with only 6 per cent of Roman Catholic manual workers.

These surveys were carried out in the 1960s when many of the social mechanisms underlying Catholic-Labour and Conservative-Protestant voting associations were losing their force, but they do testify to the power of Unionism to mobilise an older – essentially Protestant – sense of what it meant to be Scottish. As Callum Brown has pointed out, even as late as 1986, 45 per cent of Kirk members claimed to vote Tory (and only 17 per cent Labour) (Brown 1990: 82). This identity consisted of a complex of inter-related elements of Protestantism and Unionism welded together by a strong sense of British national and imperial identity, and symbolised by the Union Jack (still an emblem of Glasgow Rangers football club). This version of Scottishness was not at odds with Conservative rhetoric about British national and imperial identity, given the powerful strand of militarism which ran through Scottish society in the late nineteenth and early twentieth centuries. The mobilisation of men for war during the later imperial period and on through two World Wars helped to fit together Scottish and British identities. The connection was reinforced by the religious factor, which in turn received emotional resonance and respectability from the national and imperial elements of the complex.

While there is little by way of direct empirical proof that this ideological complex underpinned the relative success of the Conservatives in Scotland in the middle of this century, it is an explanation which links Conservative success to some of the most powerful and deep-rooted strands of Scottish popular consciousness. It is important to point out, however, that this version of Toryism laid stress on civic duty and social responsibility rather than on reductionist individualism. If anything, the political ideology of neo-liberal Thatcherism moved away from its social and ideological base in Scotland rather than vice versa.

Alternative versions of political Scottishness, associated with the SNP and nationalist elements in the Labour Party, emphasise the gulf between Scottish and British national consciousness, rather than their continuity. The ending of empire, of military conscription, together with forty years without world wars, coupled with the extensive secularisation of Scotland and Britain, have eroded and enfeebled the connection between Conservatism, Protestantism and British national identity. As the native leaders of Scottish capital, the local businessmen and great Clydeside dynasties, found their influence slipping away, Conservatism fell once more in the hands of 'lairds and law agents'. By 1964 the 'Unionist' label was dropped in favour of the Anglicised 'Conservative' one. The native social base of Scottish Unionism was eroded, and with it its power to mobilise the Scottish Protestant working class. As the previous chapter argued, this particular version of the Scottish identity, centred on religion and patriotism, was relegated to history.

By the 1970s wider social changes were sweeping through Scottish society and politics. Rapid social change, coupled with increased social and geographical mobility, were detaching many from their traditional allegiances. As we shall see later in this chapter, the Scottish National Party became one of the main beneficiaries of these changes, appealing as it did to the young and the socially semi-detached in particular. The capacity of the SNP to destabilise party politics in Scotland in large part reflected an increasingly volatile electorate. Scottish Conservatism, on the other hand, had lost its traditional social leadership among Scotland's bourgeoisie at a time when national differences between Scotland and England became more salient. In many ways, there simply was not a sufficient social base left in Scotland in which to naturalise the Conservative message. Instead, new versions of Scottish national consciousness began to emerge in the 1960s which were more amenable to political mobilisation.

NATIONALISM, IDENTITY AND THE STATE

Most analyses of nationalism, including the Scottish variety, tend to explain the phenomenon in 'internal' terms, that is, in terms of the specificities and peculiarities of the society in question. Such a view tends to ignore the fact that virtually all modern societies are nationalist, although nationalism, practised successfully, often remains implicit. As Raymond Williams has pointed out, 'It is as if a really secure nationalism, already in possession of its own nation-state, can fail to see itself as "nationalist" at all' (1983: 183).

Modern societies are indubitably, if implicitly, nationalist. Ernest Gellner has argued that the size, scale and complexity of

159

these societies require an explicit sense of loyalty and identification on the part of the population, an explicit binding of citizenship to the state. This requirement becomes all the more imperative because of the elaborate division of labour, coupled with rapid rates of social change. The modern social system makes an assumption ('a kind of null hypothesis', according to Gellner) of social equality based on equality of citizenship, and the modern industrial economy stimulates this aspiration to equality. Gellner does not deny the extent or salience of economic inequality in capitalist society, but argues that it does create problems of legitimacy. So one of the reasons why nationalism is a feature of modern societies is that equality of status and a shared culture are preconditions for the functioning of complex industrial societies. These societies do not tolerate 'cultural fissures' within them that can become correlates of inequality and 'which thereby become frozen, aggravated, visible and offensive' (Gellner 1978: 108).

In the modern state, national identification becomes a *sine qua non* of citizenship. Social inequality in modern industrial societies is a precarious phenomenon. The assumption of equality of citizenship laid down by the state makes conspicuous inequality a more problematic issue; it has to be justified. Similarly, citizens have to be bound legally and culturally to the modern state in a way which was not required of its pre-industrial counterpart. As Poggi says, 'The modern state is not bestowed upon a people as a gift of God, its own Geist or blind historical forces; it is a "made" historical reality' (Poggi 1978: 95). Because it is a 'purposively constructed, functionally specific machine' (1978: 101), the modern state has to mobilise commitment to it through 'national' ideology. The modern state is faced continuously with legitimating itself before its citizens. The importance of citizenship, the guaranteeing by the state of civil, political and social rights (Marshall 1963) ultimately makes nationalism more, not less, important. Nationalism appeals to the 'national interest'; it is applied as an ideological balm to societies with many centripetal tendencies.

Since the Second World War, the search for legitimacy has become a problem for states, for they have been drawn more and more into full participation in the economic and social life of societies. The political historian Keith Middlemas (1979; 1986) has even argued that a 'corporate bias' was introduced into Britain as early as the second decade of this century, and that it flourished after 1945, before falling into disrepute in the 1970s. Corporatism, despite its association with fascism, was a system in implicit use after the war, partly because in western societies the conditions of war had led to a considerable degree of central control. The need to co-ordinate production efforts and to resolve differences of interest between employers and employees laid many of the foundations for corporatist structures. The state, through its civil servants, mobilised groups on the basis of 'the national interest'. Middlemas pointed out that 'those who aspire to and are able to compete at the "altruistic" level of the national interest enter the environs of the state' (1986: 10). Those who remained outside the invisible boundary were defined as self-interested lobbies or pressure groups.

The focus on the 'national interest' provided the political legitimacy for corporatism. As Winckler pointed out in a seminal article in 1976, nationalism is one of the central elements of corporatism:

> It is a collectivist system, not an individualist one. The collectivity on which concern focuses is the nation, not the class, the family, religion, caste or ethnic group. The aim is national economic well-being, not personal affluence or mobility. The general welfare has moral primacy over individual preferences or rights. 'Individualism' is a label for stigmatising recalcitrance, not eulogising freedom.
>
> (1976: 107)

Winckler has been criticised for simplifying and stereotyping corporatism, but he is correct to identify nationalism as one of the focuses of corporatism.

Almost regardless of political ideology, the state in the post-war period has intervened in economic processes, and played a more central role in directing economic resources. It is seen as the appropriate instrument for guaranteeing the individual life chances of its citizens, and ironing out social inequalities. In the post-war period, the state has endeavoured to hitch its star to the quest for economic growth. In Poggi's words,

> The state found a new and different response to the legitimacy problems; increasingly it treated industrial growth per se as possessing intrinsic and commanding political significance, as constituting a necessary and sufficient standard of each state's performance, and thus as justifying further displacement of the state/society line.
>
> (Poggi 1978: 133)

In this respect, Britain was not an exception in the post-war years. Throughout the 1950s and 1960s there existed an agenda and a set of rules for the political game shared by both the main British political parties, sometimes referred to as 'Butskellism', or 'consensus politics'. The government took explicit responsibility for employment, prices, the balance of payments and economic growth. The Second World War, and the inception of the Welfare State (a counter to Hitler's 'Warfare State' (Marwick 1986: 49)) ushered in a new social contract between the state and its citizens, a post-war settlement which was underpinned by the economic boom of the post-war period.

The longer-term economic decline of Britain since 1945 has thrown these problems into harsh relief. Successive governments have sought to appropriate 'the national interest' to justify their actions and policies. Appeals to nationalism and patriotism, the stock in trade of parties and governments in all countries, are made by the parties of the Right and the Left. Politics becomes the struggle for the 'national soul'. Nevertheless, this nationalism has remained largely implicit, and politics have been defined as about the delivery of economic benefits by means of economic management of the national economy. However, nationalism has become more, not less, necessary in societies characterised by 'mobile privatisation'. 'National statism', says Williams, helps to preserve a coherent domestic social order, to regulate and contain what would otherwise be intolerable divisions and confusions.

The failure of policies to promote economic growth at a fast enough rate has destabilised the political arrangements of the United Kingdom. The attack by the Left on corporatism was less incisive than that by the Right in the 1970s, led by the radical Right and Mrs Thatcher. Even the centrist academic Anthony King, writing a tract in 1976 called 'The Problem of Overload', concluded,

> Governments have tried to play God. They have failed. But they go on trying. How can they be made to stop? Perhaps over the next few years they should be more concerned with how the number of tasks that government has come to perform can be reduced.

> (1976: 29)

The thesis of 'state overload' chimed nicely with the separate critiques from both Left and Right. Nevertheless, as we shall see later in this chapter, the radical successor to 'consensus politics' – Thatcherism – involved the re-mobilisation of nationalism. A different piper played a new variation on a old tune.

How does Scotland fit into this analysis? The disintegration of the post-war settlement occurred at a crucial conjuncture in Scotland's history. Briefly put, Scotland, as we have argued in the previous chapter, underwent its own version of economic planning. The lessons of Keynesian economic management had been applied to Scotland by the Scottish Office, that 'semi-state' which had acquired administrative power from Whitehall since 1885 when it was founded (Kellas 1989: 32–3). Given the collapse of indigenous industry after the war, the Scottish Office had played a more directive role in restructuring the economy by means of direct employment, and by offering inducements to foreign capital to locate in Scotland. Like other declining regions of the UK, it relied more heavily on public initiative than on private enterprise. In its desire to act as the midwife of economic regeneration, the state devolved a significant part of its administrative resources to Scotland. In the absence of devolved government, the Scottish Office provided a powerful administrative apparatus, or 'negotiated order' in the phrase of Moore and Booth, whose work we introduced in the previous chapter. In their words, 'We are not arguing that Scotland can be seen as a separate political system, but that there is a degree of decision-making and administrative autonomy in certain sectors, and over certain issues a Scottish interest emerges' (1989: 15). Hence, there operates in Scotland a set of 'policy communities', in which the values and culture of decision-making elites help to sustain a distinctive set of institutions and relationships which influence bargaining and policy outcomes.

The late 1950s and early 1960s saw the transmission of the idea of Scotland as a unit of economic management to the mass electorate, via the Labour Party in Scotland, and especially via the Scottish media, in particular television. Labour's strategy in this period was, according to Keating and Bleiman, largely pragmatic:

> Labour's attitude to the Scottish question was based upon the assumptions that the basis of any discontent was economic, and that the electorate were more concerned about the economic goods which they received than with the constitutional mechanism by which they were delivered.
>
> (1979: 151)

The perception of Scotland as a separate unit of political and economic management coincided with the arrival of North Sea oil, which opened up the political possibility of an alternative Scottish future, and which the SNP was to exploit brilliantly. The postwar belief in 'equal citizenship' was mobilised as equal citizenship for Scots within the UK in such a way that the (British) nationalist assumptions built into the Welfare State could be transferred easily in the rhetorical form of Scottish nationalism. Certainly, the ability to transfer from one form of nationalism (British) to another (Scottish) occurred at the right moment for the Nationalist party, as well as for many Scots.

The SNP was in the right place at the right time, making explicit the 'national' dimension of the post-war consensus, and providing a political alternative when the British settlement began to fail. Both the Conservative and Labour Parties paid the electoral price, the former more profoundly than the latter. Labour's early success was based on a view of the state as a generator of economic growth. As Labour was seen to fail to deliver the economic goods, the SNP became increasingly the beneficiary. Ironically, when the next major ideological battle occurred in the late 1970s – between the radical Right with its anti-state project, and the defenders of the post-war settlement – Labour in Scotland was in a much better position than the Nationalists to switch the terms of the struggle on to a Left/Right dimension. Nevertheless, the SNP acted as an electoral catalyst for change, and provided a political home for the socially mobile and the young, in search of a new political identity in a rapidly changing Scotland. It is in the systematic swing away from the Conservatives, however, that we have the most coherent manifestation of the emerging Scottish political system, a system increasingly incompatible with the ideology of that party's role as the British or English national party.

SOCIAL CHANGE AND SCOTTISH NATIONALISM

What was the social base of nationalism? We can accept this characterisation by James Kellas:

At all times, it seems to have attracted defectors equally from all parties, although this varies from constituency to constituency. Up to 1974 it seems to have appealed to first-time voters or previous abstainers. Its declining support after

1978 was particularly marked among young voters and New Town voters, many of whom had consistently supported the party since the late 1960s.

(1989: 141)

The appeal of the party to such social groups was reflected in the volatility and unexpectedness of its successes and failures. Its first major by-election victory in modern times was at Hamilton in 1967, when Winnie Ewing took the seat with 49 per cent of the vote. In the local government elections of the following year it held its support at 30 per cent nationally, allowing it to maintain the balance of power in Glasgow. However, at the Glasgow Gorbals by-election in 1969 it could muster only 25 per cent. The volatile appeal of the SNP to the young, the socially and geographically mobile, was reinforced by the absence of a significant class base. Hence, it performed consistently well (or badly) across all social classes. The October 1974 election in which the SNP had 30 per cent of electoral support in Scotland proved to be the party's best performance to date. At that election, the SNP did well across all classes, but especially among skilled manual and routine non-manual workers, those groups who had become electorally detached from traditional social bases. Further evidence (Davis 1979) suggests that the party's appeal was stronger among the 'new' working class – technicians and craftsmen – than it was among 'traditional' manual workers – steelworkers and miners. The Scottish Election Survey for October 1974 indicates the 'classless' appeal of the SNP, which proved to be both its strength and its weakness. Table 6.5 indicates the broad appeal of the SNP in the October 1974 election.

Table 6.5 Percentage of each socio-economic group voting SNP in October 1974

Employers and managers	27
Professionals	30
Intermediate	40
Junior non-manual	26
Foremen and supervisors	18
Skilled manual	35
Semi-skilled manual	23
Unskilled manual	23

Source: Scottish Election Survey, October 1974

165

In contrast to its broad-based class appeal, the SNP attracted the young in high proportions. As Kendrick (1983) points out, the age structure of SNP support was virtually the mirror image of Conservative strength. Thus, whereas the SNP captured 42 per cent of electors aged 18 to 24 (Conservatives took 10 per cent of this age group), they managed only 16 per cent of those aged 65 and over (Conservatives, 38 per cent). Kendrick's analysis is among the most detailed and most persuasive we have, and his results allow us to identify further and with more confidence the social base of Nationalism in the mid-1970s. For example, he points out that intergenerational social mobility is a major discriminating variable. While 24 per cent of SNP voters in non-manual jobs had fathers who were also in non-manual jobs, 32 per cent of similar voters had fathers who had been in manual work. Hence, non-manual workers who had been upwardly socially mobile from the working class were especially susceptible to the appeal of the SNP. Similarly, Kendrick showed that this relationship holds even when controlling for age, as indicated in Table 6.6.

Table 6.6 Percentage voting SNP among higher non-manual workers by age and father's socio-economic group

	Father's occupational position	
Age of respondent	Percentage of non-manual	Percentage of manual
Under 35	31	42
35–54	29	39
55+	21	36

Source: Scottish Election Survey, 1974

In other words, at the high point of its political success in 1974, there was a distinct differential as regards father's social background for each different age group, suggesting that social origins, as well as age, were crucial social variables relating to SNP voting. Similarly, there was a fairly consistent 'mortgage effect' insofar as the SNP did especially well among those buying a house (younger people, in the main) rather than outright owners of houses (who tended to be older). Since then, of course, a new generation of voters has appeared, notably the children of those who were socially mobile in the 1960s. It remains to be seen whether they are influenced by their parents' mobility. The fact that there is now a substantial history of SNP voting, and that the party stands at a higher base than in the early 1970s might suggest a more secure platform for the SNP in the 1990s.

Drawing upon a variety of sociological studies, Kendrick argued that the SNP were beneficiaries of key social changes in Scotland in the 1960s and 1970s, notably rising affluence, full employment and upward social mobility. Groups who became less reliant on the support of kin as well as more home-centred – Scotland's analogues of the classic 'affluent workers' studied in England – found themselves drawn to the Nationalists less for reasons of political ideology than because of their social detachment. A study in the 1970s at Peterhead, a town where the SNP made an early and lasting impact, and which it won in 1987 as part of the Banff and Buchan constituency, pointed to this important Nationalist social base: 'The SNP was most successful in winning affiliations from the upwardly aspirant who were renouncing the class of their homes while not yet entering the middle class' (Bealey and Sewel 1981: 160).

The precise lack of class connotations in the SNP was perhaps the key appeal to this socially mobile group. Such people were susceptible to alternative frameworks of perceptions, said Kendrick, insofar as their traditional forms of social (and political) identity were weakening. In this context, television came into its own as a political frame of reference rather than kin and workmates, as in traditional working-class communities. Television served a mobile and privatised way of life because it provided a more appropriate frame of political and social reference. Kendrick argued that the SNP benefited from the development of a new kind of ideological field created out of what Raymond Williams called 'mobile privatisation', high rates of social mobility, and an increasing influence of the media (especially television) on views of social reality.

To be sure, Scotland differed little from the rest of the UK with regard to these social changes, but from the late 1960s 'Scotland' was an ideological category in terms of which the political world could increasingly be interpreted. Crucially, the SNP was a political party which could more easily capture this 'Scottish' label, because it was a taken-for-granted reference very like the 'national' identity implicitly assumed by the Conservative Party in England. In another important respect the SNP was a 'media' party, well suited to an increasingly volatile electorate, and one which did not need to make the 'long march' through the political undergrowth as the Labour Party had to do at the turn of the century. Just as the SNP came to rapid prominence through the media, so it fell from electoral grace at a later stage. Kendrick concluded that the party was in the right place at the right time, making an appeal to the right people. In many ways, its Scottishness was almost incidental, but yet vital:

> It has been profound changes at all levels of social develop-ment which Scotland has shared with England, and indeed with much of the advanced industrial world, which, in their mutual interactions and in their differing reactions with the national level, have given political dynamism to the sense of Scottish national identity, and are exposing the anachronism of Scotland's present constitutional status.

(1989: 89)

Kendrick's analysis brought together different levels in explaining the rise of the SNP in the late 1960s and early 1970s: the level of everyday life (mobile privatism), the level of communications media (the arrival of television), and the level of state activity (the Scottish growth project). The SNP captured the generation enter-ing the electorate in the 1960s and 1970s who, in England, might have tended towards the Conservatives or the Liberals. The role of television was crucial in the political socialisation of this gener-ation. We have no direct evidence of the actual impact of television on consumers, but the case to be made is circumstantially plausible nonetheless.

The collapse of the SNP in the late 1970s left the bulk of its support nowhere to go but to Labour. Insofar as the SNP shared in the general optimism about the state's capacity for economic intervention, so it was ill-prepared for the waning of public faith in the state. By the late 1970s the Scottish stage was set for a new – yet more traditional – battle over the role of the state, between Labour and Conservative, which the latter were singularly ill-equipped to fight. This is the final key element in the process of political divergence between Scotland and England. As Figure 6.1 makes clear, the slippage in Conservative support began well before 1979 and the election of the first Thatcher government. But as the data also make plain, the 1980s drove a considerable wedge between the electoral performances of the two nations.

Mrs Thatcher may not have created the divergence, but she gave it a flavour all her own.

THATCHERISM IN A COLD CLIMATE

Throughout the 1950s and 1960s the role of an interventionist state was not a politically contentious issue. Both major parties might place different emphasis on the state's role, but they shared similar assumptions about the Welfare State, public housing and the mixed economy. Under Thatcherism, the consensus was shattered, and all areas of state activity were thoroughly politicised, and in this respect Scotland had more to lose than England. Scotland had a greater share of its population living in publicly rented housing (between 18 and 25 percentage points higher between 1961 and 1981). Whereas in the 1950s and 1960s there was considerable bipartisanship between Labour and Conservative over public housing, by the late 1970s adversarial politics over housing re-emerged, and as a consequence, it is likely that there was an increase in the political effects of housing tenure.

The housing issue was one strand in a broader process to politicise the role of the state, and the social structure of Scotland was much more 'state oriented' than England's. As we argued in Chapter 3, Scotland's occupational structure has more of a collectivist bias than has England and Wales. First, the self-employed in Scotland (socio-economic group 12, non-professional self-employed without employees), amount to only 2.4 per cent of the workforce compared with 4.3 per cent south of the border (1981 figures). Second, Scotland's relative shortfall in non-manual workers consists almost entirely of fewer managers and administrators in the private sector, reflecting in large part the location of headquarters outwith Scotland. Third, the higher proportion of employment in health and education in Scotland has boosted intermediate non-manual state employment, primarily for teachers and nurses. Of these factors, only the last one generates a significantly large numerical difference to explain political divergence. To what extent is the political divergence between Scotland and England, then, simply the result of these 'material' – socio-economic – differences?

The most systematic attempt to assess the role of social class and housing tenure differences in explaining these voting differences is that by Heath, Jowell and Curtice (1985). Using the 1983 British Election Survey, they compared actual differences in vote between

Scotland, Wales, the north, Midlands and south of England with those that could be predicted simply from differences in class structure and housing tenure. For example, the actual Conservative vote in Scotland was 22 per cent in the Election Survey, and in the South of England, 53 per cent, a gap of 31 per cent. On the basis of class and housing structures, however, the predicted Conservative vote in Scotland was 36 per cent, and in the south of England 47 per cent, a gap of 11 per cent. Hence, there is a difference of 20 per cent which is left unexplained by these social structural factors. If, on the other hand, we compare Scotland and the north of England, which have remarkably similar class structures, we find that there is a significantly lower Conservative vote in Scotland in 1983 (22 per cent compared with 39 per cent in the North of England). Heath and his colleagues estimate that 8 of the 17 percentage point difference can be attributed to different housing structures. The remaining difference (around 9 per cent) seems to be attributable to a genuine national effect or to social structural factors other than class and housing.

Further evidence for the growing importance of regional effects has come from British election surveys. In an analysis of elections between 1964 and 1987 Heath and his colleagues identify significant regional effects which are net of social structural differences such as social origins, trade union membership and housing tenure, at least for the manual working class (1991: 109). Among the 'salariat' too, regional differences have grown in importance as discriminators of electoral behaviour (1991: 97). Further support for regional effects in voting behaviour comes from the Social Change and Economic Life studies of six labour markets in Britain carried out in the mid-1980s. In a comprehensive examination of social structural factors including tenure, class, age, gender, social origins, income, employment sector and trade union membership, the two Scottish areas of Aberdeen and Kirkcaldy show patterns of voting behaviour which cannot be explained by these variables, suggesting the presence of a national or cultural effect north and south of the border (McCrone and Bechhofer 1991). Support for this view comes from a related study of political and social attitudes derived from the same data set. Gallie and Vogler concluded that 'there appears to be a distinct Scottish effect – with the level of collectivism substantially higher among the secure higher paid in Aberdeen and Kirkcaldy than in any of the other labour markets' (1990: 104–5).

Outlining material differences, then, cannot simply account for the growing political divergence between the two countries. We must also deal with the particular ideological appeal of the political parties. Historically, the relationship between the Conservative Party and 'the nation' has been a close one, and the Tories have deployed the politics of 'the nation' to counteract the politics of class, with considerable success (Gamble 1974). As Gamble later pointed out,

> The Conservatives have always viewed the British state as their state. There may be a Whig history of England, but there is also a Tory history, the history of the nation-state, its expansion within the British Isles and throughout the world. The success of the British state in avoiding both internal overthrow and external defeat for so many centuries has ensured that most of the national myths are Tory myths, and most of the rituals and institutions of the state are Tory rituals and institutions.
>
> (1988: 170)

As long as the Scottish political dimension remained latent, it was perfectly possible for generalised Conservative rhetoric about the nation to coexist with the everyday reality of Scottishness. And, of course, for much of the twentieth century the presence of an ideological affinity between Conservatism, Unionism and Protestantism was useful to the party. Latterly, however, alternative dimensions of Scottishness have emerged, making Scotland as an ideological category incompatible with Conservative Anglo-British rhetoric. Nothing did more to make explicit this Conservative nationalism than the election of Mrs Thatcher in 1979.

A large part of Thatcher's success south of the border derived from harnessing conservative motifs. Stuart Hall described her Thatcherite populism as 'a particularly rich mix. It combines the rich themes of organic Toryism – nation, family, duty, authority, standards, traditionalism – with the aggressive themes of a revived neo-liberalism – self-interest, competitive individualism, anti-statism' (1983: 29).

Much of the explanation for the rise of Thatcherism focused on the latter – neo-liberal – ideas of extending market power, but alongside these lay a powerful stream of ideas which were quite distinct. Its neo-conservative motif was authority, not freedom: the desire to re-establish and extend the power of the state over many aspects of social, political and even personal life. If the notion of the 'citizen' derived from liberal ideas of the state, then the conservative idea of the 'subject' was drawn from an allegiance to the nation. Earlier in this chapter, we argued that in post-war societies politics operated by claiming the legitimacy of the 'national interest'. Clearly, Thatcherism represented a radical break with this consensual, corporatist style of government. Nevertheless, nationalism – a key element in this discredited system – was remobilised by the radical Right in the new cause of Thatcherism. What Britain saw after 1979 was the re-assertion of nationalism under a new set of political and economic ideas. And it was a nationalism which was distinctly at odds with the new alternative variety north of the border. While the older Unionist one was quite compatible with Anglo-British nationalism, the newer post-1979 version was not. Thatcher's unpopularity in Scotland was the down-side of her electoral support in England. In Gamble's words,

Thatcherism has reinvigorated it [the old Tory state-authority], and restored the confidence of the party in its basic appeal to the English. This is not Unionism. The Scots, Welsh and Irish are increasingly detached; but then so too are the former colonies of Greater Britain. There can be no return to the dreams of Empire.

(1988: 172)

In Scotland, the attack on state institutions – the nationalised industries, the education system, local government, the public sector generally, even the church, institutions which carried much of Scotland's identity – was easily perceived as an attack on 'Scotland' itself. Essential to current Conservative appeal south of the border was an appeal to 'the nation' on whose behalf politicians and the state act. But Scots had a nation of their own, and the vision of recreating bourgeois England was out of kilter not only with Scottish material interests, but with this alternative sense of national identity.

The Englishing of the modern Conservative Party has clearly played a part. Since 1979 the Tory benches in the House of Commons have been significantly more 'southern' than before. As Malcolm Punnett (1985) pointed out, in 1979 the winning party achieved a majority of seats in just two of the six political regions of the UK, the first time this had happened since 1982. In all, less than 10 per cent of Conservative MPs elected in 1979 and 1983 came from Scottish and Welsh seats, the smallest proportion since the 1920s, and only 16 per cent from the north of England (the smallest proportion for over a hundred years). Modern Conservatism spoke overwhelmingly with a southern English voice. The populist, nationalist, anti-state appeal which sustained Thatcher in England for the whole of the 1980s had distinctively negative resonances north of the border. It is hard to envisage a political message more at odds with what had gone before, or one that would run more counter to the grain of Scottish civil society.

CONCLUSION

This chapter has analysed political trends in Scotland, and has argued that in the second half of the twentieth century distinctive political agenda emerged north of the border. Important social changes – the decline of an indigenous class of Scottish capitalists, new opportunities for social and geographical mobility, the development of state employment – compounded the problems for the Conservative Party in Scotland, wedded as it has been to an attack on the state and to an Anglo-British national identity. The Scottish National Party found itself the recipient of a cohort of new electors in the late 1960s and early 1970s who, south of the border, would have tended towards the Conservatives.

The emerging Scottish frame of reference fixed a new dimension in politics, and when the SNP began to falter in the late 1970s, the Labour Party inherited the new electoral cohort, and with it the neo-nationalist mantle. Faced with a hostile Conservative government, Labour found itself playing the nationalist card in the defence of Scottish interests. At the time of writing, the Conservative Party in Scotland has been reduced to nine out of seventy-two MPs, and its performance at the next election in Scotland is almost irrelevant. Whether it wins five or fifteen MPs at the next election has taken second place to major shifts in the agenda of Scottish politics. In an important sense, we are all nationalists now. However, the emergence of a nationalist agenda brought into focus the problematic character of Scottish culture. Oddly and unusually, there was no simple correspondence between cultural and political nationalism. Politics and culture had grown apart.

7

SCOTTISH CULTURE
Images and Icons

Unlike many forms of nationalism, the cultural content of the Scottish variety is relatively weak. Compared to Welsh, Irish, Catalan, Breton or Quebec nationalism, it is less ready to call up the ancient ghosts of the nation, its symbols and motifs, in its quest for independence (Brand 1978; Webb 1978). There is, of course, less to call up, for the lack of linguistic, religious or similar cultural markers in Scotland forces nationalists to conjure up an alternative 'imagined community' (Anderson, B. 1983). And in this regard, the modern model for an independent Scotland has been, at least since the sixties, the Scandinavian countries rather than Ireland, perhaps a more obvious comparator. There is a reluctance among many Scottish Nationalists today to mobilise simply around the signs and motifs bequeathed from the Scottish past. This tendency within Scottish nationalism to look sideways rather than backwards has much to do with a wider characterisation of this Scottish past. It is deemed to be dominated by negative motifs; it is deformed and distorted.

This chapter examines the view that Scottish culture has been dominated by the two mythic structures of tartanry and Kailyard (Craig 1983) to such an extent that they seem to offer only negative representations of Scotland, reflecting the political and cultural developments since the Union of 1707. This view has been so predominant among Scottish intellectuals that their contribution to the development of neo-nationalism in Scotland has been negative and critical. Their analysis itself represents a dominant discourse which itself has to be examined critically. The argument here is not that Scottish culture is necessarily deformed – that Scottish culture contains nothing but distorted motifs – for that would be to accept what is highly problematic. We are not arguing here that Scottish culture consists of tartanry and the Kailyard and of nothing else, but that these have represented the dominant discourses on Scottish culture. There is, of course, more to Scottish culture than these sets of images, but the search for a distinctive culture has been so dominated by them that they cannot be avoided. The argument of this chapter will be that they are far less dominant than is made out, nor is their influence quite as unproblematic and pernicious. Indeed, it will be argued that the variety and eclecticism of Scottish culture today corresponds to world conditions in the late twentieth century rather than the distorting legacy of these 'mythic structures'.

To describe tartanry and Kailyard as mythic structures is not to imply that they are false, to be driven out of Scottish culture by wholesome reality. Deconstructing myths in an anthropological sense is to identify the social and cultural forces which keep them alive, for they often serve key legitimatory purposes. As Bruce and Yearley pointed out in their analysis of the royal portraiture in Holyrood Palace in Edinburgh, 'To paraphrase W. I. Thomas, just as we must actively define every present situation, so too every past which is called into the present must be defined' (Bruce and Yearley 1989: 186). If myths and legends are kept alive and embellished, even invented, it is not enough to show that this is so; it is necessary to ask why some are retained and others disappear. As Tom Nairn points out in his study of the British monarchy (Nairn 1988a), it is easy to show up the discontinuities and inventions in this supposed unbroken lineage; seeking to show why it retains its 'glamour' (a word he uses in its older Scottish sense – its magic, its enchantment) in the late twentieth century is quite another matter.

The most powerful and dominant analysis of Scottish culture remains Tom Nairn's *The Break-Up of Britain* first published in 1977, the most perceptive and critical account we have. Nairn has established the terms of the debate about Scottish culture while sceptics may still be waiting for Britain to 'break up'. Nairn characterises Scottish culture as being split, divided, deformed. This not unfamiliar view of Scottish culture, epitomised in Walter Scott, is that Scotland is divided between the 'heart' (representing the past, romance, 'civil society') and the 'head' (the present and future, reason, and, by dint of that, the British state). The 'Caledonian Antisyzygy' (Nairn 1977: 150) – this personality split between the Scottish heart and the British head – is perhaps the most common characterisation of Scotland.

The image of Scotland as a divided and unhealthy society is a common one in Scottish literature, which has acted as a key carrier of Scottish identity. In Douglas Gifford's words,

> Through recurrent patterns of a relationship such as father versus son, brother versus brother, or variants, a recurrent and shared symbolism states overwhelmingly the same theme; that in lowland Scotland, aridity of repressive orthodoxy, religious and behavioural, tied to an exaggerated work ethic and distorted notions of social responsibility, have stifled and repressed vital creative processes of imaginative and emotional expression, to the point where it too often has become, individually and collectively, self-indulgent, morbid and unbalanced.
>
> (1988: 244)

Nairn's view of Scotland is similar. It suffers, he claims, from 'subnational deformation', or 'neurosis' (and psychiatric disorders are a Scottish speciality here). 'Cultural sub-nationalism' is a favourite phrase of Nairn's in representing Scotland:

> It was cultural because of course it could not be political; on the other hand, this culture could not be straightforwardly nationalist either – a direct substitute for political action, like, for example, so much Polish literature of the 19th century. It could only be 'sub-nationalist' in the sense of venting its national content in various crooked [*sic*] ways – *neurotically*, so to speak, rather than directly.
>
> (1977: 156)

It is interesting, in passing, to note where Nairn borrows this resonant phrase 'cultural sub-nationalism' from. In a footnote (1977: 156) Nairn acknowledges that he gets it from a Third World context, in this case, eastern Nigeria. It seems that it refers to instances where the culture of a region develops into a nationalism proper. This seems an odd phrase to borrow because it implies almost the opposite in Scotland – that a hitherto national culture became subverted into a sub-national variety, rather than the other way round, which seems to be the original allusion. Still, the meaning which Nairn has given it seems to have stuck in a Scottish context.

176

The 'sub-nationalism' is, according to Nairn, a poor thing. While Scottish civil society survived in the bosom of the British state, the Scottish 'heart' was split from the British 'head'; the 'national' with its over-emphasis on the past, was separated from the 'practical' with its emphasis on the present and future. This came about because, by the late eighteenth and early nineteenth centuries, the intelligentsia was 'deprived of its historic nationalist' role. Says Nairn, 'there was no call for its usual services' (1977: 154) of leading the nation to the threshold of political independence. Intellectuals after the Union migrated, if not in body at least in spirit, to the bigger, more rounded culture of Anglo-Britain, leaving a stunted residue of intellectual life in Scotland (at least so it seems to Nairn). In this context, then, it is easy to explain the Scottish Enlightenment of the late eighteenth century, an otherwise awkward phenomenon to arise in a 'deformed' culture. In essence, says Nairn, it wasn't Scottish at all, or rather it represented the belated intellectual fruits of the Union. Operating on a much bigger stage before a larger and more sophisticated audience, it was 'strikingly non-nationalist – so detached from the People, so intellectual and universalising in its assumptions, so Olympian in its attitudes' (1977: 140).

Smith, Hume, the Mills, Robertson, Adam and its other luminaries, Nairn argues, may have been Scots by birth and education, but they were universal men, and certainly 'British' in orientation. The cultural void in Scotland was created largely by the migration of Scots intellectuals to the richer pastures of England. Macaulay, Carlyle, Ruskin, Gladstone and many more were not even thought of as Scots at all. England, says Nairn, was a 'mature, all-round thought-world': 'It was an organic or "rooted" national-romantic culture in which literature – from Coleridge and Carlyle up to F. R. Leavis and E. P. Thompson – has consistently played a major role' (1977: 156–7).

THE KAILYARD CULTURE

Contrasted with this rich, southern feast of culture, what Scotland got (quite literally) was 'cauld kail'. The Kailyard, or 'cabbage-patch' tradition flourished, with its petty obsessions and mean-minded parochial jealousies. Kailyardism is usually described as a popular literary style celebrating Scottish rural quaintness, and lasting from about 1880 until 1914 (Anderson, E. 1979). It helped, as we pointed out in Chapter 4, to give cultural expression to the 'lad o' pairts', the boy of academic talent but little financial means, which became an ideal-type in Scottish educational ideology. The term 'Kailyard' is usually attributed to the critic George Blake, who described its essential elements as domesticity, rusticity, humour, humility, modesty, decency, piety and poverty (Shepherd 1988). Its key writers were 'Ian Maclaren' (John Watson) (1850–1907), S. R. Crockett (1860–1914) and J. M. Barrie (1860–1937). Shepherd points out that not all late nineteenth and early twentieth century writers belonged to the Kailyard school (R. L. Stevenson, G. D. Brown, and W. Alexander were obvious exceptions), nor did all Kailyard works conform to the 'formula' which involved an omniscient narrator, a rural setting, imprecise chronology and episodic format, and key roles for the minister and the schoolmaster.

The conventional wisdom has been to see the Kailyard as a cultural formation well suited to its age. Scotland in the late nineteenth century was an industrialised society, occupying a place in the sun of Victorian prosperity. In social and political terms, the latter decades of the century brought special anxieties. The mid-century destruction of the unity of the Kirk, the removal of the last vestiges of the old Scottish administration betrayed anxieties about national identity. Mass migration into towns and cities from the Highlands and the Lowlands, and from Ireland, reflected unprecedented social change. In rural areas as Ian Carter (1979) points out, the penetration of peasant agriculture by agrarian capitalism was undercutting the social and economic organisation which had supported peasant culture and values. In this respect, the Kailyard with its homely celebration of, and panegyric for, the virtues of independence, hard work, and 'getting on', became a celebration of a doomed culture and way of life. The parish, the community, was no longer the typical locus of social existence; the industrialised and anonymous city was now dominant. In this environment, the lad o' pairts was no longer an appropriate social model.

Although the Kailyard school probably failed to survive the Great War, its influence on Scottish culture has been adjudged to be long-lasting and malevolent. The latter-day manifestations of this 'sub-cultural Scotchery' (Nairn 1977: 158) include *Dr Finlay's Casebook*, *Sutherland's Law*, *Take the High Road*, and above all, those *bêtes noires* of the Left, the *Sunday Post*, the *People's Friend*, their publisher D. C. Thomson and all his works and pomps. Nairn argues that much of the Kailyard's output was produced by Scottish emigrés with rosy, romantic memories of the simple Scotland they had left behind for richer pickings in the south. Nairn's argument is that their pawky simplicities had a ready market in Scotland, and while kitsch was in no way unique to Scotland, it took on the character of a national popular tradition. At this point we may note in passing the implication of what Nairn is saying. Scottish culture became overwhelmingly the Kailyard, and as a result, a proper 'mature, all-round thought-world' (as in England) could not be Scottish.

In recent years, however, the notion that the Kailyard dominated literary and cultural representations of Scotland has been questioned. T. D. Knowles (1983) was critical of the view which explains the Kailyard entirely within a Scottish historical context and literary tradition. The output of writers like Maclaren, Crockett and Barrie, he argued, was geared to a wider British, and even American, market with its vogue for religious fiction and sentimental retrospection. The editor of the Nonconformist *British Weekly*, W. R. Nicoll, encouraged such writers to address this growing political-religious market in the UK, as well as the demand for 'local-colour' writing in the USA (where the Scottish-American audience was sufficiently large and influential to adopt highly-coloured tales from home). The key role of the emigré both as producer and consumer was vital. Knowles points out that Maclaren was Essex-born, and based in Liverpool, while he describes Barrie as the 'classic emigré' (1983: 22). All in all, the Kailyard writers had significance furth of Scotland:

> Their work contained British Victorian elements as well as Scottish; they were regionalists, and there is influence from the gothic novel, the fairy tale, 18th century sentimentalism, and the Victorian penchant for dying and death.
>
> (1983: 64)

Such a revisionist view of the Kailyard is not only echoed but developed by Willie Donaldson (1986) who argues for a clear distinction between book-publishing (which carried the Kailyard novels) and the popular Scottish press in the late nineteenth century. Notably, he points out, it was the weekly press (at the end of the century there were over 200 weekly titles all over Scotland) which had much greater impact than the London-centred book-trade. This press was much more willing to use vernacular Scots, and to address major issues of social change in both urban and rural Scotland. He concludes,

> On the whole, popular fiction in Victorian Scotland is not overwhelmingly backward-looking; it is not obsessed by rural themes; it does not shrink from urbanisation or its problems; it is not idyllic in its approach; it does not treat the common people as comic or quaint. The second half of the 19th century is not a period of creative trauma or linguistic decline; it is one of the richest and most vital episodes in the history of Scottish popular culture.
>
> (1986: 149)

Writers like William Alexander, Donaldson argues, had a realistic appreciation of social change and its impact in north-east Scotland, quite distinct from the narrow and distorting imagery and 'pietistic fiction' of bourgeois Kailyard writers addressing the British and American bourgeois book-markets.

These revisionist accounts by Knowles and Donaldson help to undermine the view that Scottish culture was overly dependent on Kailyard themes and values, which in turn were deemed largely responsible in the twentieth century for a deformed and distorted sense of Scottishness.

THE FALL AND RISE OF TARTANRY

Welded on to this Kailyard tradition, in this characterisation, is an older, altogether wilder tradition of 'tartanry', what Nairn calls the 'tartan monster' (note the sub-Freudian motif of fear, nightmare, neurosis here, of Scotland as a psychiatric condition, not forgetting the 'real' monster in Loch Ness). Tartanry is never treated as seriously as the Kailyard by Scottish intellectuals; perhaps it is too unspeakable to be worthy of their analysis, although they are often linked conceptually together, as in this comment by Christopher Harvie: 'tartanry attained its fullest extent in the shrewd marketing of the Kailyard authors in the 1890s' (1988: 27).

Tartanry was not a literary movement, but a set of garish symbols appropriated by lowland Scotland at a safe distance from 1745, and turned into a music-hall joke (Harry Lauder represented the fusion of both tartanry and Kailyard – the jokes and mores from the latter, the wrapping from the former). The appropriation of Highland motifs by lowland Scotland has been described elsewhere (Chapman 1978; McCrone *et al.* 1982) but tartanry has come to stand for tourist knick-knackery, visits to Wembley, and the Edinburgh Tattoo. Oddly, no serious analysis of tartanry, the set of symbols and images, has been carried out by Scottish intellectuals, although there are a number of studies of the history of tartan (Telfer-Dunbar 1962, 1981; Hesketh 1972; Adam 1980; Stewart and Thompson 1980). Instead, it has been left to the English historian, Hugh Trevor-Roper. In a knock-about piece in Hobsbawm and Ranger's collection *The Invention of Tradition*, Dacre attempts a demolition job on tartanry. Not only does it have no basis in history, it was invented, he claims, by an *Englishman* who did Highlanders a favour:

> We may thus conclude that the kilt is a purely modern costume, first designed and first worn by an English Quaker industrialist, and that it was bestowed by him on the Highlanders in order not to preserve their traditional way of life but to ease their transformation: to bring them out of the heather and into the factory.
>
> (1984: 22)

It has to be said that Trevor-Roper's interpretation is thoroughly contentious, and Telfer-Dunbar, the major historian of tartan, dismissed similar views (1981: 69–70). He concluded, 'One cannot help wondering if any of this argument would have arisen if it had been claimed that the kilt was invented in the early 18th century by a Highlander' (1981: 72).

Other parts of the tartan story are fairly well known, and less contentious. The Proscription Act of 1747 forbade the wearing of tartan until 1782. The Act enacted

> That from and after the first day of August . . . one thousand seven hundred and forty seven no man or boy within that part of Great Britain called Scotland, *other than shall be employed as Officers and Soldiers in his Majesty's Forces* [my emphasis], shall on any pretext whatsoever, wear or put on the clothes commonly called Highland clothes (that is to say) the Plaid, Philabeg or little Kilt, Trowse, Shoulderbelts, or any part whatsoever of what peculiarly belongs to Highland garb.

This Act helps to question the myth that tartan was invented by

Rawlinson, the English Quaker industrialist referred to by Trevor-Roper. Quite simply, if a lone Englishman could effect such a change in Highland fashion, why was it deemed necessary for such an Act of Parliament to be passed, given that it brought seven years transportation to the wearer? Why a legal sledgehammer to crack such a puny nut?

Sumptuary laws to curb extravagances in dress had been passed in many European countries for centuries, and the English King Henry VIII had passed a Proscription Act in Ireland in 1539. Henry seemed to have understood the political and ethnic symbolism of dress. Once the Scottish Proscription Act was passed in 1747, the kilt and tartan were appropriated by the British army in its colonial wars – quite literally stealing the enemy's clothes – and it set about with gusto inventing new tartans, in notably darker shades of green, brown, blue, and black as more suited to camouflage in the northern hemisphere. The Proscription Act itself was not repealed until 1782, under lobbying from the London Highland Society which had such establishment members as General Fraser of Lovat, Lord Chief Baron MacDonald, the Earl of Seaforth, Colonel Macpherson of Cluny, and MP John Graham, Duke of Montrose. It was a measure of the incorporation of Highland landed aristocracy into the British elite that they were able to effect such a change. In this respect, Trevor-Roper is correct to say that the development of (modern) tartans originated 'more often in the officers' mess than in the straths and glens of Scotland' (1984: 29).

The 'gentrification' of tartan was aided considerably by Walter Scott, who, as impresario, persuaded George IV, a large man by all accounts and with a poor command of English, to visit Edinburgh in 1822, and worse, to wear a kilt set off fetchingly by pink tights. Despite, or perhaps because of this, tartan became an instant fashion, and polite society members clamoured to have their own. The weaving company, William Wilson of Bannockburn, duly obliged, and was not averse to allocating the same tartan to more than one clan label. Wilsons seem to have developed its list of tartans in an opportunistic way without worrying overmuch about the authenticity of the design, as we can see from this selection from a 1794 list of patterns:

black and red tartan
red and white tartan
42nd sett

red and white drumluthy sett
blanket tartan green ground plaids
McDonalds sett
common kilt
Bruce sett
blue and green
blue and green with red stripes
Gordon
Gordon with silk

By 1800 Wilson had, according to Telfer-Dunbar, brought his repertoire of patterns up to eighty, including 'the Aberdeen sett, the Atholl pattern, the Perth sett, and the Caledonian'. The colonial market was booming, and slave owners in the West Indies and the southern states had found it a useful uniform for identifying their human property in a crowd.

Queen Victoria's acquisition of Balmoral in 1848 gave the royal seal of approval to the tartan enterprise, and she and Albert had one of their very own designed. The royal association, begun by 'German Geordie', helped to guarantee commercial success. Behind all this was a considerable 'heritage' industry bent on authenticating the ancient designs for an anxious world eager to believe. The picture was completed by the Allen brothers, who so fell in love with the mythology of tartan that they changed their names to the Sobieski Stuarts, claiming to be the grandsons of the Young Pretender. There is little doubt that they fabricated their most famous work, the *Vestiarium Scoticum*, published in 1842 in Edinburgh, supposedly from a manuscript dated 1721 and claimed to have been compiled in 1842. This was soon to be denounced as a forgery (Stewart and Thompson 1980), but seemed to do nothing to dampen the desire to accept the authenticity of tartan. Trevor-Roper describes the Sobieski Stuarts' *The Costume of the Clans* of 1844 as 'shot through with fantasy and bare-faced forgery'. Telfer-Dunbar is more relaxed in his assessment:

[It] is, without doubt, one of the foundation stones on which any history of Highland dress is built. It cannot be ignored, and it is surprising how little it has been consulted by writers on the subject. We can think what we like about the ancestral claims of the Stuart brothers, but this does not reduce the value of their monumental books.

(1962: 111)

What are we to make of the claims and counter-claims as to the authenticity of tartan? Its survival and development occurred because a number of factors came together at an opportune time: the Romantic search for the 'noble savage', and the 'discovery' of the Ossian poems by Macpherson in the 1760s; the raising of Highland regiments after 1745 was a master-stroke by the British state in incorporating the symbols of its enemies into its own identity; and by the nineteenth century, the climate was right for Walter Scott's romantic tales to become bestsellers, the king acting as literary agent by visiting Edinburgh in 1822. The Sobieski Stuarts simply took the whole thing to its logical extremes. Wilsons of Bannockburn added the commercial element, and gave material expression to this fantasy.

This, in brief, is the tartan story. A form of dress and design which had some real but haphazard significance in the Highlands of Scotland was taken over by a lowland population anxious to claim some distinctive aspect of culture at a time – the late nineteenth century – when its economic, social and cultural identity was ebbing away. It may have taken a High Tory English historian, master of Peterhouse – home of neo-conservative ideologues – to put the critique together, but few left-liberal Scottish intellectuals would have dissented much from it.

ICONS NEW AND OLD

What, of course, this critique does not do is explain why Nairn's 'tartan monster' survives to be a symbol of Scotland, whether at Wembley or at more douce occasions such as family weddings and university graduations. Nairn has little doubt: 'Tartanry will not wither away, if only because it possesses the force of its own vulgarity – immunity from doubt and higher culture' (1977: 165).

This is rather an unsatisfactory explanation in many ways, because we are still left to wonder why it remains immune. Nairn argues that it results from the separation of 'high' and 'low' culture, and the fact that the latter remains unintellectualised for the reasons spelled out earlier. Scottish culture is schizophrenic; its low culture is a bastard product, partly indigenous and partly maintained by British imperialist mechanisms (the Scottish solider is the obvious example (Wood 1987)). This sense of separation, of fragmentation, runs throughout much intellectual analysis of Scotland. The historian Chris Harvie (1975), for example, argued

184

that this schizophrenia – Scotland's split personality again – has taken a social form: between the 'red' Scots – those who leave in search of new opportunities, the outward-bound strain of 'Scot on the make', unspeakable or otherwise – and the 'black' Scots – those who stay to nourish the home culture, the Kailyard and the tartan monsters. These are social, even psychological, types and little sociological evidence is proffered for their existence, but it is a typology which fits into the conventional intellectual wisdom of Scotland. It is interesting that both Nairn and Harvie belong to the 'red' variety (nothing to do with politics in this instance). It seems that only if you have lived in the 'wider' culture – the 'mature, all-round thought-world' of England perhaps – the 'real world' – are you immune for the insidious psychological effects of Scottish culture. Indeed, at its extreme, this strain of criticism seems to imply that even to *think* about Scotland is proof of 'neurosis', thereby seeming to lock us into a pessimistic Catch 22. Indeed, to be 'normal' (un-neurotic) you'd be advised not to think of Scotland at all. The language of this critique is certainly sub-Freudian. It is replete with 'monsters', with 'neuroses', with 'split personalities'. And it was, after all, a Scotsman, Robert Louis Stevenson, who invented Dr Jekyll and Mr Hyde.

This chapter has focused on Nairn's analysis of Scottish culture because it is the most comprehensive, and the one which has marked out the agenda for the debate subsequently. We now turn to its later manifestations, particularly those associated with the Scottish literary intelligentsia. The pages of the literary magazine *Cencrastus* is a good hunting ground in this respect. Much of the discussion has focused on deconstructing the 'Scotch myths' of tartanry and Kailyard (see, for instance, 'The politics of tartanry', in *Bulletin of Scottish Politics*, 1981). The exhibition mounted by Barbara and Murray Grigor at the 1981 Edinburgh Festival was a key event. This exhibition had gathered together representations of Scotland, from postcards to orange box labels from California to representations of Scotland in film and television, and aimed to generate discussion of Scotland's 'deformed' culture. In 1982 the Edinburgh Film Festival held a showing of *Scotch Reels*, the film of the exhibition, as it were, together with a three-day discussion event about a collection of essays (1982), edited by Colin McArthur. The remit was clear. In McArthur's own words, 'Clearly the traditions of Kailyard and tartanry have to be exposed and deconstructed, and more politically progressive representations constructed, circulated and discussed' (1981: 25).

Borrowing Althusser's idea of 'interpellation', McArthur argued that these Scotch myths have had hegemony over Scots' perceptions of themselves to such an extent that they have a 'systemic' quality:

> Having had two centuries to develop, it [*note that the two have become focused – my comment*] now constitutes a durable and hegemonic system, the representation of one part of which can dredge up into consciousness the system as a whole, and, of course, the complex articulation of attitudes to history, to nationhood and to political decisions in the here and now which it is *its objective function to serve*.
>
> (1981: 22, my emphasis)

This is powerful stuff. Two disparate cultural formations have combined into a hegemonic system which locks Scots into a sense of their own inferiority in the face of a powerful Anglo-British culture. Much of the evidence is based on graphic representations in film, television and what its proponents call the 'sign media' generally. The semiotics of Scotland, they argue, are regressive in cultural terms, and in their political manifestations lock us into subordination and dependency. Tartanry and Kailyard maintain cultural hegemony over Scotland's sense of itself. In the words of McArthur, 'a limited number of discourses have been deployed in the cinema to construct Scotland and the Scots, and to give an impression that no other constructions are possible' (1982: 69).

There are, according to this analysis, other discourses which are healthier, and indigenous to Scotland. 'Clydesidism' is one such which is spoken of with approval by some of the critics. It is 'extremely refreshing in the Scottish context', says McArthur, it is not a 'pernicious discourse'. He contrasts the comedy of Billy Connolly (good) with that of Harry Lauder (bad). What Clydesidism has in its favour is that it is constructed from 'real' images of working-class life, from the discourse of class, and from naturalism. Says John Caughie, the tradition is 'based on working class experiences which, since the twenties, have seemed to offer the only real and consistent basis for *a Scottish national culture* (1982: 121, my emphasis).

And that is it. The search is for a national culture which will speak to people in their own terms, an integrated discourse which will connect with political and social realities in Scotland. The problem, however, with Clydesidism as a discourse is not simply that it is resonant of socialist realism (heroic workers and all – 'Stakhanovite political iconography', says McArthur, 1983: 3). As Cairns Craig (1983) has pointed out, it is itself becoming a 'historic discourse' even in its heartland of west central Scotland in the late twentieth century. Its language is redolent of early twentieth-century Clydeside, with its appeal to the 'industrial masses' and to masculine culture. And as Eleanor Gordon and Esther Breitenbach observe, 'skill' is a social construct which is 'saturated with male bias' (1990: 6).

It is fine, says Cairns Craig, to break out of the mental traps of the historic myths of tartanry and Kailyard, to imagine a future, even a revolutionary future, through which to overcome the static quality of the dominant myths, but we risk embracing another myth based on a fast-disappearing working-class culture. Says Craig, 'What is worrying in the contemporary situation is the way that the death throes of industrial West-Central Scotland have become the touchstone of authenticity for our culture.' And he continues, 'if we make the victims of that decline the carriers of our essential identity, we merely perpetuate the cultural alienation in which we negate the on-going struggle of our experience by freezing its real meaning in a particular defeat' (1983: 9).

This is a more fundamental criticism, and much more to the point. We search in vain for the 'true' image because none such exists, nor indeed should we be looking for it in the late twentieth century. Indeed, if our argument is correct that, far from being dependent on or subservient to England since 1707, Scotland has operated with a considerable degree of civil autonomy, then it follows that its cultural formations and expressions reflected that. Those who point out that nineteenth-century Kailyard was not the simple expression of a deformed culture, but one manifestation of a developing international literature, have their analogue in those who attribute the popularity of tartanry to the development of music hall and vaudeville in the twentieth century. In practice, the anti-tartanry, anti-Kailyard obsessions of writers in the 1970s have not only been questioned as historically inaccurate, but many of the symbols themselves have been mobilised as icons of opposition against current political arrangements.

To take McArthur's comment, and play it back on his own analysis: 'a limited number of discourses have been deployed . . . to give an impression that no other constructions are possible'. Not only are tartanry and Kailyard such discourses, along with Clydesidism, but so is this radical discourse itself. And its problem is that it asks a particular question: What is (distinctive about) Scottish culture? And why should a limited set of discourses have dominated the debate about Scottish culture?

THE ECLIPSE OF SCOTTISH CULTURE?

One familiar answer, presented in its starkest form by Beveridge and Turnbull (1989), is to argue that Scottish culture has undergone an eclipse as a result of its cultural subordination to England. Drawing on notions of dependency, and its cultural correlate, 'inferiorism' (derived from a Third World context by Franz Fanon), they argue that, so overwhelming has been the application of 'metropolitan ways' that it is believed that Scotland has ceased to produce important thinkers. These authors argue that it is the power of the *belief* that causes intellectuals to devalue their own culture, and there is good evidence, particularly in the fields of philosophy and theology, that Scotland has in fact produced important and original thinkers. They argue that 'the inferiorist view is as false as it is powerful' (1989: 3).

Their starting point, then, is quite similar to that expressed in this chapter, namely, that a narrow set of discourses – crucially tartanry and Kailyardism – have been employed in the cultural analysis of Scotland, and the end result is a fairly pessimistic and misleading account of Scottish culture. This analysis has political overtones:

> Suspicious of concepts like 'tradition' and 'identity', many tough-minded, left-wing nationalists were even prepared to abandon the cultural argument entirely. Scottish nationalism's cultural-intellectual base was therefore altogether too narrow for the nationalist challenge to be sustained over any extended period.
>
> (1984: 4)

Beveridge and Turnbull, on the other hand, promote as the central task of cultural nationalism 'the recovery of Scottish cultural practices', which have to be rescued from the metropolitan-influenced analysis of Scotland. Intellectuals such as Tom Nairn are accused of a 'deep aversion to everything native and local' (1989: 59), which in turn derives from long-standing processes of 'cultural colonisation'. Such processes inflict a Manichaean view on Scottish culture. 'In Nairn's description, there are no shades or contours; everything stands condemned' (1989: 58). Fundamentally, they continue, Nairn is essentially a unionist not a nationalist; the nationalist project is suborned to the cause of socialism: 'Restated, the meaning of Scottish nationalism for Nairn is as a moment in the development of British socialism. His commitment to nationalism is pragmatic and conditional rather than principled' (1989: 60).

The authors argue that Nairn was converted to nationalism as a way out of the crisis of the British Left in the late 1970s, and that, fundamentally, he 'exemplifies the adoption by Scottish intellectuals of metropolitan perspectives' (1989: 61). In contrast, Beveridge and Turnbull set themselves the task of identifying and promoting Scottish cultural traditions, untainted by the 'Anglicised traditions' of the universities in Scotland (which are not, of course, in their view, 'Scottish universities').

This critique of the analysis of Scottish culture is not without force. In this chapter we have outlined the limited discourses adopted by Scottish intellectuals in their analysis of culture. Beveridge and Turnbull make the valid point that those who argue that tartanry and Kailyardism are hegemonic in their effects fail to acknowledge that meanings are never passively consumed, but always subject to selection and adjustment to other discourses. Consumers' responses to tartanry, therefore, are 'not uncritical assimilation, but a complex negotiation dependent on the beliefs and values which are bound up with those of other concerns' (1989: 14). Much of the attack on tartanry and Kailyard has depended on an uncritical assumption that their impact has been comprehensive and homogeneous.

The essence of Beveridge and Turnbull's argument is that there is an unwarranted focus on the 'deformity' of Scottish culture among intellectuals, and that this focus arises from 'inferiorism', a form of cultural dependency on the metropolitan, English, power. Here, we can see that they draw on the powerful paradigm of dependency which illuminates much research on Scottish social structure, discussed in previous chapters. They present us with its cultural correlate; cultural dependency is the result of employing limited discourses. In crucial respects, however, they make one central assumption, that Scottish national culture exists, and remains to be uncovered and rescued from intellectual pessimism. Thus,

> If a *national culture* is to remain alive, its history too must live in some distinctive way and must be perceived as integral to the lives of those who share it. This helps to define their sense of collective identity, gives them their confidence, lets them know where they are.
>
> (1989: 16, my emphasis)

THE SEARCH FOR SCOTTISH CULTURE

We might, however, ask an altogether more radical set of questions: Why should there be an obsessive search to find a national identity? Why is the question even framed in this way? Where does it come from? The answer is that it derives from an older, essentially nationalist assumption that all societies worthy of the name should have a distinctive culture. Despite the fairly critical stances taken against political Nationalism by Scottish intellectuals, this perspective seems to echo its assumption that Scotland has (or had) a 'national' culture waiting to be discovered. This is essentially an idea traceable back to the eighteenth-century Enlightenment notion of sovereignty, embodied in the culture of a nation waiting to be brought to its political realisation.

The role of intellectuals in this context has been to identify the 'essential character' of a people, and to give it political expression. Such a modernist project involved seeking out the essence of national culture, and presenting it as distinctive and self-contained. This process required that the contradictions and the paradoxes were smoothed out so that national identities were clear-cut and paramount. Above all, these identities were gendered, relegating women to walk-on parts, and to their role as keepers of the moral and family values of the nation. It is, then, no coincidence that those identities diagnosed as archetypically Scottish by friend and foe alike – the Kailyard, tartanry and Clydesidism – have little place for women. As we pointed out in Chapter 4, there is no analogous 'lass o' pairts'; the image of tartanry is a male-military image (and kilts were not a female form of dress); and the Clydeside icon was a skilled, male worker who was man enough to 'care' for his womenfolk. Even the opponents of these identities took them over into their own images of social life. Jenni Calder

190

has pointed out that in George Douglas Brown's anti-Kailyard novel *The House with the Green Shutters* (1901), women are uncompromisingly relegated: 'Not only do they have no rights, they have no personalities beyond what is interpreted by husband, father and son. With the two men dead, they have no alternative but to die also' (1988: 271).

Similarly, those who wish to inject a class-based national identity into the contemporary Scottish context run the risk of adopting the 'big man' myth. More radically, we might argue that the search for a single carrier of national identity is doomed to ignore the pluralism and complexity of identities in the late twentieth century. The search for such a single identity in contemporary nationalism seems increasingly time-bound and anachronistic. Why, after all, should any country have a distinctive 'national' culture, when we know that many of these 'nations' were constructed with very little cultural straw? Gellner's rather terse dismissal 'nationalism is not the awakening of nations to self-consciousness; it invents nations where they do not exist' (Gellner 1983: 168) does seem rather sweeping, but has more than a kernel of truth to it. We shall see in the final chapter that it is a convenient but distorted truth of nationalism that the nation is 'natural', that every nation deserves a state. Max Weber, for example, echoing Hegel, believed that a nation was 'a community of sentiment which would find its adequate expression only in a state of its own, and which thus normally strives to create one' (Beetham 1974: 122). Gellner's argument, on the other hand, is that national sentiment of this sort is not a given, but is historically constructed and mobilised by social interests (most notably by national bourgeoisies in nineteenth-century Europe). We should not, in other words, take the existence of a prior 'national' culture as a given.

How does this view connect with the analysis put forward by critics of tartanry and Kailyard? In some fundamental ways the critique of this 'mythic structure' as a discourse is not radical enough. It is premised upon the previous existence or at least the future possibility of a rounded, mature national culture. As Cairns Craig pointed out, the problem of identity is precisely the one we should not be trying to solve, because 'the "identity" we construct will be an essentialising, an idealising, a reduction to paradigmatic features, of Scotland as *home*, a counterbalance to the 'home counties' as core of English/British culture' (1983: 8).

So, applying tartanry and Kailyard as the essentials of our

191

national culture, albeit negative ones, is to simplify and freeze them. This process will also predispose us to look for what we have lost, to reduce culture to a series of tragic failures (in which Scotland is not lacking) – the 'Ally McLeod syndrome', with its devastating combination of 'if only' and 'we wuz robbed'. Once the issue is set up in this negative way, we can find any number of contradictory 'explanations' for the national condition. So it results from too little independence, or too much (insufficient incorporation into British civil society); it results from too little industrial capitalism (failure to have a thoroughgoing capitalist revolution), or too much; from too little Calvinism (the Catholic legacy) or too much. All seem plausible if we define the problem as a failure of a 'Scottish national culture' to develop. The point here is that once we frame the problem in this way, we imply the uniqueness of the Scottish problem; we look inside for the explanation. The assumption that certain forms of kitsch are uniquely Scottish cannot be true in a comparative context. And Scotland did not invent the soap opera.

A considerable amount of effort has gone into discovering the 'real' Scottish culture, especially in the pre-industrial past. Lying behind the deformed images is a sense of the 'golden age', pre-independence, when society and the state were one, when it was possible to argue that this 'Scottish culture' was a communal culture, reflected in the sturdy vernacular literature of the Makars, of Henryson, Dunbar, Barbour, then Ramsay, Fergusson, and Robert Burns (David Craig 1961; Kurt Wittig 1958). This search for a truly Scottish culture is inevitably retrospective and romantic, a celebration of the past, and helps to explain Scottish history's obsession with what has ended, as Marinell Ash's trenchant critique makes plain. This 'strange death' of Scottish history in the nineteenth century reflected real political and economic changes:

> The time that Scotland was ceasing to be distinctively and confidently herself was also the period when there grew an increasing emphasis on the emotional trappings of the Scottish past . . . its symbols are bonnie Scotland of the bens and glens and misty shieling, the Jacobites, Mary Queen of Scots, tartan mania, and the raising of historical statuary.
>
> (Ash 1980: 10)

So the search into the past for a distinctive and un-neurotic Scottish culture is doomed to reproduce a new set of myths about what Scotland was like. Instead, it is argued here that we have to look not simply into the future, but at what is going on in other societies. It seems that nation-states themselves are losing their political, economic and cultural integrity in a rapidly changing world (Beetham 1984). Scotland may be striving to attain something which is going out of fashion. Similarly, the quest for Scottish cultural independence from a culturally suffocating and homogeneous Anglo-British one ignores the fact that, as Cairns Craig has perceptively pointed out, the latter has fragmented. The post-1918 period saw the collapse, he argues, of the English cultural imperium, and subsequently, 'English culture' could no longer be equated with 'the culture of England'. In most English-speaking countries, there was a burgeoning of indigenous literature: in Canada, Australia, South Africa, New Zealand, the United States, and Ireland.

The Scottish literary renaissance of the 1920s expressed itself in the work of MacDiarmid, Grassic Gibbon, Linklater, MacColla, Muir, Bridie, as well as Violet Jacob and Naomi Mitchison (Harvie 1981). These socio-cultural developments were rooted in a pluralistic cultural system in Scotland – in Gaelic (Sorley MacLean), in Scots (notably, MacDiarmid and Gibbon) and even in standard English (Muriel Spark). These traditions have survived and prospered, and have ceased to be simply literary forms. Spoken language through radio and television has also contributed to a varied culture which cannot in any serious way be reduced to the discourses of tartanry and Kailyard. The point is that only rarely do they seek to address the Scottish condition as such, although it is the implicit starting point for much of it. The aim, it seems, is not to identify the unique Scottish experience, but to address the universal condition through day-to-day (Scottish) reality. The search for new images which express these experiences are no longer simply literary but artistic and cultural in the widest sense. The folk music which has become a key carrier of Scottish culture is cross-fertilised in its styles, tunes and instruments. What is 'traditional' can no longer be taken as predating the nineteenth century, or confined to oral conventions (Munro 1984).

These ways of expressing Scottish culture are inclusive rather than exclusive, building on the erstwhile alternative ways of being 'Scottish' – Lowland and Highland, Protestant and Catholic, male and female, black and white. This involves borrowing and adapting what is available. Who would care, for example, to categorise

193

the award-winning BBC television series *Tutti Frutti* in simple (Scottish) terms? In Cairns Craig's words,

> The fragmentation and division which made Scotland seem abnormal to an earlier part of the 20th century came to be the norm for much of the world's population. Bilingualism, biculturalism and the inheritance of a diversity of fragmented traditions were to be the source of creativity rather than its inhibition in the second half of the 20th, and Scotland ceased to have to measure itself against the false 'norm', psychological as well as cultural, of the unified national tradition.
>
> (1990: 7)

These cultural developments are seeking to make sense of shared social, economic and political experiences – of urban living, or working or not working, of living in a capitalist society, a society in which our own ability to control even limited political power is severely constrained. The obsession with a unified Scottish national culture has its parallel in the assertion that, in order to explain Scotland's political divergence from England, its industrial and occupational structures must be different from those south of the border. When this turns out not to be the case, we worry about the fact that it is not, in case it denies Scotland's right to exist. Hence, there is intellectual pressure to assert the premise because we desire the conclusion. Similarly, if we set out to look for what is distinctive in Scotland, we run the risk of focusing on the trivial and epiphenomenal, which will be found only in the past and in the museum. To argue that the essential features of any society are those which it shares with other societies is not to imply that they have no differentiating features, that the United States and Britain are identical, for example. However, focusing merely on those elements of difference as the defining ones runs the risk of imbalancing any social analysis. The problem is that Scotland's right to exist as a separate society has too often seemed to depend on the unusual characteristic, as if in allowing similarity to a high degree, we undermine Scotland's very existence.

Identities as well as societies can co-exist. If Scots were 'Scottish' for certain purposes and 'British' for other purposes as John Mackintosh pointed out, then they were simply recognising the complex pluralities of modern life. 'This sense of a dual consciousness or loyalty is true of most periods and most people in Scottish life.

194

Again, to say so is neither to praise, to blame nor to recommend, it is simply a fact' (Mackintosh 1982: 148).

Similarly, being black, Glaswegian and female can all characterise one person's culture and social inheritance without one aspect of that identity being paramount (except in terms of self-identification). What is on offer in the late twentieth century is what we might call 'pick 'n mix' identity, in which we wear our identities lightly, and change them according to circumstances. Those who would argue for the paramountcy or even the exclusivity of a single identity have a hard time of it in the late twentieth century. The question to ask is not how best do cultural forms reflect an essential national identity, but how do cultural forms actually help to construct and shape identity, or rather, identities – for there is less need to reconcile or prioritise these. Hence, national identity does not take precedence over class or gender identities (or, indeed, vice versa) except insofar as these are subjectively ordered. These identities themselves, in turn, cannot be defined except with reference to the cultural forms which give them shape and meaning.

The argument in this chapter has been that the critique of tartanry and Kailyard as the hegemonic discourse in Scottish culture arises from an essentially 'internalist' account of Scotland, that it ignores major cultural and social changes in the world generally. It arises because it sets out to address the issue of Scottish national culture, a hunting of a Scottish snark. The search for a distinct identity is likely to degenerate into a pessimistic conclusion that none is possible because we are prevented from seeing it by the power of the regressive 'Scotch myths', rather than because in modern, pluralistic societies it is increasingly the case that no single 'national' culture is to be found. In other words, the argument has been that we cannot find it precisely because the myths are hegemonic, when the real answer should be that the search itself is rapidly becoming invalid.

A POLITICAL POSTSCRIPT

It is an irony that in spite of the supposed deformation of Scottish culture, Scottish political behaviour has never in post-war politics been so divergent from its southern counterpart, a situation seemingly achieved with little help from 'Scottish national culture'. Here, it seems, is a political manifestation which is not tied to a specific *cultural* divergence. It is a form of 'neo-nationalism' in which neither Scottish culture nor even the Scottish National Party plays the central part. Instead, it seems to be much more of a political manifestation, a concern with the practicalities of decision-making and control, although insofar as it celebrates and mobilises certain values (such as the Scottish myth), it is in that sense cultural.

Perhaps this expression of political difference – a nationalism if you want – has developed without the encumbrance of a heavy cultural baggage. It is as if, having looked to see what was on offer, the Scots have decided to travel light. No icons need to be genuflected at, no correct representation needs to be observed in this journey into the future. If what we have is so thoroughly tainted and deformed, then we will leave it behind. It is almost a cultureless, post-industrial journey into the unknown. In this respect, it seems to conform to a kind of 'post-materialist' politics (Inglehart 1977), not in the sense that it is unconcerned with economic issues, but that it seems to have left behind the kind of nationalist and culturalist agenda bequeathed from nineteenth and early twentieth century politics. Scotland, like other societies, may be entering a post-nationalist age. The vehicle on that journey, ironically, seems to be nationalism itself. That is the theme of the final chapter.

8

THE SOCIOLOGY OF A
STATELESS NATION

Scotland presents a puzzle for orthodox sociology. For nearly three
hundred years it has been part of the United Kingdom, one of
the most centralised and unitary states in post-1945 Europe, and
one dominated numerically and culturally by the English 'state-
people'. Scotland has less than one-tenth of the population of the
United Kingdom, and is largely bereft of that potent building
block of nationalism, a distinctive language, which has been eroded
since the unions of 1603 and 1707. It is true that it has inherited
what Nairn has called the old trinity of distinctive institutions –
law, education and religion – but their survival cannot explain the
assertion of Scottish identity in the second half of the twentieth
century, by which time the distinctiveness of these institutions has
been eroded. In crucial respects, then, Scottish political nationalism is a phenomenon of the late twentieth, not the nineteenth
century.

The theme of this book has been that what sociological research
there was on Scotland in the past three decades has been driven
by the need to explain the social, political and cultural divergence
of Scotland from England. Hence, theories of dependency and
developments were seized on in the 1970s and early 1980s as a
material means of explaining this divergence. If Scots were behav-
ing differently in their politics, if they were asserting distinctive
social values, then it seemed obvious to such theorists that these
superstructural expressions were resulting from more fundamental
material changes, specifically, in the colonial relationship between
Scotland and England. The thrust of Chapters 2, 3 and 4 in this
book, however, suggests that such a straightforward set of material
changes cannot be identified. Indeed, in its industrial and occupational structures, and its concomitant patterns of social mobility,

197

Scotland has far more similarities with than differences from its southern neighbour. Nevertheless, in its cultural expressions, and most obviously in its patterns of political behaviour, Scotland has become more not less distinctive in the late twentieth century. Indeed, it is possible to talk of Scotland's distinctive 'civil society' in which social and political values at virtually all levels of that society are different. The potency of the Scottish myth of egalitarianism described in Chapter 4, the assertion of a 'principled society' (Chapter 5), and most obviously the divergence of patterns of political behaviour (Chapter 6), all attest to the fact that Scotland is alive and well in sociological terms in the last decade of the twentieth century.

Is Scotland, then, a nation? This is a concept which sociologists have more trouble with. Even historians such as Hobsbawm find it slippery: 'Neither objective nor subjective definitions are ... satisfactory, and both are misleading' (1990: 8). There is good sense in his comment that 'nations do not make states and nationalisms, but the other way round' (1990: 10), hence there seems little value in pursuing an 'objective' set of criteria, and measuring Scotland against them. At the level of consciousness, however, the sense of Scotland is strong. Seven out of ten Scots give priority to being Scottish rather than British, and a further 19 per cent give equal weight to both identities, remarkable findings nearly three hundred years after Scotland lost its political identity (Moreno 1988: 171).

In many respects, the 'nation' is an aspiration rather than a historical fact. History is littered with examples of 'nations' which have died, and 'nations' which have been created, often out of very little. To borrow the perspective of the Welsh sociologists, Day and Suggett, a country (Wales or Scotland) should be seen as 'process' rather than 'place', that is, as an aspiration rather than a historical fact. Simply put, nations exist because nationalism says they exist. They are, in Benedict Anderson's phrase, creations of the imagination, imagined but certainly not imaginary. In this regard, nations can be conceived of as moving steadily up and down history (Anderson, B. 1983: 31). Events can be linked across centuries so that the 'Scottish people' can stretch across centuries. 'Remember Bannockburn' may seem a daft stricture in the late twentieth century when no one can imagine what it was like to be there. The Jacobite risings of the eighteenth century and the Highland Clearances of the nineteenth century are often employed to make sense of the present, not because the historical parallels are close (the divine right of kings, that most conservative of beliefs, has nothing to do with twentieth-century radicalism), but because the stress is on the continuity, the lineage, of events and processes. Social scientists and historians have little power to prevent this selective remembering, and confronting myths with 'facts' has little impact because myths survive almost in spite of facts rather than because of them. Rather, our task is to articulate and analyse different versions of 'Scotland', and to explain why different traditions survive in this way. It is, for example, noticeably difficult for historians to present the complexities of the Jacobite wars, or the Highland Clearances, particularly when playwrights such as John McGrath deliberately fuse together Bannockburn, 1707, the Clearances, industrialisation, emigration, the impact of North Sea oil, and de-industrialisation. In Renan's famous words, 'Getting its history wrong is part of being a nation'.

While it is important, for historians at least, to get the history right, national myths survive because they function to make sense of the present rather than the past. Scottish history has some splendid examples. Bruce and Yearley (1989) have argued that inventing ancient Scottish kings and queens had an important legitimating function for the Scottish monarchy faced with a predatory English state with designs on their allegiance. In particular, the DeWit portraits of the Scottish kings, real and imaginary, painted in 1684–6 and hanging in Holyrood House in Edinburgh, were commissioned by the Stewart monarchs to bolster their claim to the throne.

> The exact rules of succession . . . were subordinated to the sheer antiquity of the line . . . As it was elaborated and stories attached to names and dates, it became possible to use it for more elaborate ideological purposes.
>
> (1989: 185)

The Holyrood House portraits were designed to present an indubitably royalist legitimacy for the troubled Stewarts.

The late Marinell Ash argued that many of the symbols of Scottish history carried dubious factual accuracy. She argued, for example, that the St Andrew myth (there was very little to link him to Scotland) was largely invented to win papal approval for Scottish independence from England by claiming the intercession of St Peter's brother as the national patron, thereby upstaging the rather less than real St George. Even the so-called Declaration of Arbroath, she argued, should properly have been called the 'letter of Newbattle', for the decision was taken by king and nobles in 1320 at that place. The document disappeared for several centuries only to come into its own in the late seventeenth century, when a pamphlet war broke out over the proposed parliamentary union between Scotland and England. The 'Declaration' provided a godsend to anti-Union forces, 'not only because of what it had to say about freedom from English domination but also because of its statement that the crown was subject to the will of the people to be free of foreign subjection. Once again, modern concerns shaped views of the Scottish past'.

Truth to tell, all history can be subverted in the interests of the present, but Ash argues that Scottish history is especially prone to misconception. Her book, *The Strange Death of Scottish History*, argues that in the late nineteenth century, there occurred 'an historical failure of nerve' (1980: 10) causing Scottish history to become obsessed with the emotional trappings of the Scottish past. This occurred, she says, because in the late nineteenth century the Scottish middle classes were freeing themselves from 'history', for to be British was to be oriented to the future not the past. Nevertheless, if Scots were no longer prisoners of their past, neither were they free from it, for 'the past was inescapable' (1980: 11). As a result, Ash argues, Scottish history went underground and 'Instead, monuments were raised to meaningless or highly selective images of Scotland's past; images which did not endanger the newfound freedom from the past of which so many imperial Scots were proud' (ibid.).

Because there 'was no unified nation left to speak to'(1980: 124), a series of incomplete and competing histories emerged. Hence, Catholicism and Scottishness were judged by the nineteenth century to be incompatible, for, according to the myth, Catholics were the subverters of Scotland's ancient religious freedoms. Similarly, Scottishness and Unionism were not deemed in conflict, because the 1707 Union was seen by many bourgeois Scots as the culmination of Scottish history. Their aim was 'freedom'; in Ash's words, 'The Reformation was freedom, the Union was freedom, the Disruption was freedom, and the death of Scottish history was freedom' (1980: 150).

Whereas in the late nineteenth century, to be Scottish was to be oriented to the past, and therefore to be rejected by the progressive middle classes, a century later Scottishness has escaped from its historical prison, and reconnected with the present and the future. What we see are new versions of Scottishness emerging, with different political and cultural resonances. The notion that Unionism and Scottishness, for example, are compatible seems distinctly strange to late twentieth century eyes. Such are the shifting connotations of being Scottish, and why it is necessary to treat Scotland as changing 'process' rather than fixed 'place'. To make sense of these changes, it is necessary to set the debate within a discussion of nationalism, for the key lies there.

WHAT IS NATIONALISM?

What Ernest Gellner (1983) called the 'Dark Gods' theory of nationalism – that it derived from and mobilised atavistic, irrational instincts – has underpinned much intellectual analysis, both liberal, conservative and Marxist. Writing about nationalism in Spain, Pi-Sunyer pointed out, 'liberal scholarship has tended to look at nationalism, when it has done so at all, as an antique evil bound to give way to progress. Marxist theories generally treat nationalism as an ideological manifestation of some less-evident infrastructure' (1985: 254).

In his important book on nationalism, Benedict Anderson reinforced the point:

> In an age when it is so common for progressive, cosmopolitan intellectuals (particularly in Europe?) to insist on the near-pathological character of nationalism, its roots in fear and hatred of the Other, and its affinities with racism, it is useful to remind ourselves that nations inspire love, and profoundly self-sacrificing love.
>
> (1983: 129)

In large part, treating nationalism as tapping primordial sentiments in backward regions reflects the fact that nationalism (of the 'centre') is largely implicit in modern states, and that the explicit language of oppositional nationalism treats sovereignty as absolute and non-negotiable. In many respects, nationalists have been allowed to set the terms of the debate. Nationalism itself adopts a holistic, even ritualistic, understanding of the nation. It represents a doctrine that political and cultural boundaries should coincide, that every nation should have its state. This is a belief held by romantic nationalists and mystical unionists alike. Sovereignty in this regard is absolute and non-negotiable, a belief that brings nationalists into direct conflict with those of the centre who assert an alternative vision of what the nation is. The clash of competing, mutually exclusive interpretations allows little room for negotiation because the fundamentals are so starkly drawn. In this regard, the politics of nationalism can quickly degenerate into the politics of ritualism, which focus more on language and symbols than on pragmatic, negotiable politics. The riposte to the nationalist assertion of 'Independence, nothing less' is that it represents 'Independence, nothing else', because the goal of a separate, sovereign state takes precedence over everything else. Nationalism of this variety encourages a dichotomised view of the population: those who are not with us are against us. Those who would seek limited sovereignty or a slower pace of change are more dangerous than outright opponents who, at least, make their position plain and help to mobilise the people against it. Opponents need each other, and perhaps fear even more those who would redraw the rules of engagement.

The vocabulary of such nationalism includes concepts like 'betrayal' and 'sell-out' which are linked to the notion of the nation being the victim, the sacrificial lamb, whose fate is decided by others more powerful than itself. However, as one Lithuanian writer has pointed out, martyrs make poor politicians: 'the martyr complex is one of the elephants upon which the ritual politics of Sajudis [the Lithuanian nationalist movement] rides' (Sliogeris 1990). Both nationalists and counter-nationalists – those who would assert the sovereignty of the centre – are locked into a zero-sum game, which, this chapter argues, ignores fundamental changes in the nature of sovereignty in the late twentieth century.

IMAGINING THE NATION

Nationalism is *the* world historical force of the 20th century, however surprising that might be to the thinkers of the 18th century. Its only rival is socialism.

(Hall 1986: 217)

John Hall's statement catches the eye because it seems so much at odds with post-war experience and ideology, and since 1989, that rival has been gravely weakened. He argues that nationalism is neglected by academics, possibly because it is associated with many wars and much conflict in the twentieth century. His point of view is reinforced by Benedict Anderson who argues that 'nation-ness is the most universally legitimate value in the political life of our time' (1983: 12).

Anderson's fundamental point is that the nation is, above all, imagined, insofar as it has limited, political boundaries; it is a sovereign territory which the state claims legitimacy over; and it is a community, being conceived of as involving deep, horizontal comradeship with people one has never met. By defining the nation as imagined in this way, Anderson argues against two points of view. The first is the essentialist, nationalist one which treats the nation as a primordial, incontrovertible fact which has always existed. Patently, says Anderson, nations are created and imagined, through time and space. He also takes issue with the view expressed ('with a certain ferocity', 1983: 15) by Ernest Gellner that 'Nationalism is not the awakening of nations to self-consciousness: it invents nations where they do not exist' (Gellner 1983: 168). Anderson thinks that this formulation over-stresses nationalism as a masquerade, fabricated under false pretences. Invention here, says Anderson, should be interpreted as imagined or created rather than fabricated or false.

Whereas it is the nature of nationalism to claim that 'the nation' is a primordial, transcendental phenomenon which cannot be questioned, and 'which exists independently of the actual beliefs and actions of those supposed to be part of it' (Linz 1985: 249), an analytical interpretation has to demythologise nationalism. Hence, Giddens (who defines nationalism as, in Geertz's phrase, 'primordial sentiments' writ large) warns against confusing nationalism with the nation-state. Such a formulation arises from modernisation theory, which reduces it to the *realpolitik* of the interests of the state: 'to confuse it [nationalism] with the nation-state as such has just as disastrous consequences as regarding the nation-state as a mere epiphenomenon of capitalism' (Giddens 1981: 191).

Certainly, the nation-state as a 'conceptual community' is largely a modern concern, in which a shared common language and a common symbolic specificity are usual, if not vital. Nationalism has the important role of helping to 'naturalise the recency and the contingency of the nation-state through providing its myths of origin' (Giddens 1985: 221). Nevertheless, nationalism cannot simply be dismissed as a useful form of ruling class ideology.

The nation is primarily a psychological or symbolic concept, 'the affiliation of individuals to a set of symbols and beliefs emphasising communality among members of a political order' (1985: 116).

In Mackenzie's words, the nation 'is not merely a statement of fact; it is a state of feeling, a source of obligation. It demands loyalty within; externally it demands recognition by its peers, conferred through the juridical status of nation' (1973: 133). The successful nation demands exclusive jurisdiction internally, and independence externally, which together sum up the idea of sovereignty (Beetham 1984). Such a powerful fusion of nation with state is, of course, a modern phenomenon: the state is given exclusive jurisdiction over a territory, acting in the name of the nation which has the exclusive right of political allegiance. To nationalists, 'the nation' is the political expression of an eternal spirit – the *Geist* – of a people. Their national or cultural identity is a given. To Max Weber, a nation was 'a community of sentiment which would find its adequate expression only in a state of its own, and which thus normally strives to create one' (Beetham 1974: 122). This conception of nationalism which owed more to Weber's political beliefs than to his academic writing expresses the basic assumptions of committed nationalists. Both tend to assume the 'naturalness' of the nation, that it is an a priori given.

Patently, the attempts by nationalists to capture the 'inevitability' of the nation are not new. What is much more modern is the association of national sentiment with the state. Ernest Gellner has argued that mobilising this sentiment is a characteristic feature of modern societies. The size, scale and complexity of these societies require an explicit sense of loyalty and identification on the part of the population, and explicit binding of the state's citizens to it. Rapid rates of social change become a characteristic feature, and the state requires people to be sensitised to these rates. The agency of training for social change is the education system, which provides a shared, minimal culture. Education, then, becomes 'a universal condition of citizenship', and in modern society, 'every man is a clerc' (Gellner 1973: 10) who gains entrance to full social, economic and political citizenship on the basis of shared educational training.

There are echoes here of Michael Mann's notion of 'infrastructural power' in modern societies, in contradistinction to 'despotic power' in pre-modern or totalitarian societies. Mann contrasts these two types of power as follows: 'Great despotic power can be "measured" most vividly in the ability of all those Red Queens to shout "off with his head" and have their whim gratified without further ado – provided the person is at hand.' In the case of infrastructural power, on the other hand, the state can penetrate civil society: 'The state penetrates everyday life more than did any historical state. Its infrastructural power has increased enormously. If there were a Red Queen, we would all quail at her words – from Alaska to Florida, from the Shetlands to Cornwall there is no hiding place from the infrastructural reach of the modern state' (1984: 189).

Modern societies, then, are 'despotically weak, but infrastructurally strong' (1984: 190). In ideological terms, however, there is a price to pay. The system makes an assumption of social equality based on equality of citizenship. High rates of social change, and occupational mobility in particular, make permanent inferiority of social condition untenable in this context. Egalitarianism, says Gellner, becomes a 'kind of null hypothesis' an assumption made about the proper status of the citizen before the state. This is not to deny the extent or salience of economic inequality in capitalist societies, which does create problems of legitimacy, and tends to express itself in new ways:

> Inequality is moderated, camouflaged and tolerable unless visibly related to the kind of diacritical sign which deeds 'ethnic' conflict and generates self-conscious ethnicity. It then appears as 'nationalism'.
>
> (Gellner 1978: 108)

So, nationalism becomes more, not less, of a feature in modern societies because equality of status and a shared culture are preconditions for the functioning of complex advanced societies. These societies do not tolerate 'cultural fissures' within them which can become correlated with inequality and 'which thereby become frozen, aggravated, visible and offensive' (1978: 108).

Inequalities in pre-industrial societies, on the other hand, were more easily tolerated. They were endemic, and often created a cultural or ethnic division of labour. However, where social and cultural differences persist within modern societies, and where they correlate with inequality, they become markers for the alignment of conflict. The cultural and social markers of ethnicity become, in this context, crucial. They are the delimiters of social identity, the parameters around which social discontent forms. These delimiters, says Gellner – language, religion, culture – are not causes of nationalism or ethnicity in themselves; they are the raw materials which are used to shape social protest, and around which social movements can mobilise. Nationalism, therefore, is not simply the civic religion of the state (vital once the divinely ordained, dynastic realm had been destroyed). It also lends itself to alternative renditions based on other cultural criteria. As Giddens puts it, 'The advent of the nation-state stimulates divergent and oppositional nationalisms as much as it fosters the coincidence of nationalist sentiments and existing state boundaries' (1985: 220). The articulation of the struggle for statehood with the revival or rediscovery of an ethnic past – an 'ethnie' – has been perceptively analysed by Anthony Smith (1988).

Nationalism simply cannot be dismissed as reactionary or atavistic (Plamenatz 1973). As we pointed out in Chapter 6, citizens have to be bound legally and culturally in a way not required in pre-industrial states. Many states since 1945, particularly those which contained ethnic or national minorities with their own versions of social identity, sought to emphasise centralist nationalism. Pi-Sunyer called this the 'espanolista' position, a perspective which combines an emphasis on strong central control (in this instance, that of Castilian Spain) with a distrust of minority nationalisms on the periphery. A very similar position occurred in the United Kingdom, in the context of the relative failure of economic policies. Peripheral nationalisms flourished as the centre began to decay.

Nationalism provides a sense of historical continuity, in the words of Milan Kundera, a 'struggle of memory against forgetting'. It is a flexible ideology which is looking backwards as well as forwards to create the future. Alberto Melucci has argued that social movements, including nationalist ones, expose problems related to the structure of modern complex societies, while at the same time being rooted in history. Both dimensions are vital. If we treat movements as historical by-products (an obvious risk when dealing with nationalist movements), then we risk ignoring the issues of contemporary structural transformation which they reflect. And if we handle them simply as highlighting structural contradictions, we risk ignoring their origins in 'national questions'. Nationalist movements are especially complex in this regard. Melucci comments,

The etho-national question must be seen, therefore, as

206

containing a plurality of meanings that cannot be reduced to a single core. It contains ethnic identity, which is a weapon of revenge against centuries of discrimination and new forms of exploitation; it serves as an instrument for applying pressure in the political market; and it is a response to needs for personal and collective identity in highly complex societies.

(1989: 90)

Nationalist movements, therefore, can encapsulate cultural defence, the pursuit of political resources from the centre, as well as being vehicles for social identity in rapidly changing societies. Such movements will be multi-dimensional – political, economic, psychological and symbolic. Of particular importance, as Giddens points out, will be the search for areas of meaningful existence within the expansion of capitalism. Thus,

In conditions of day-to-day life in which routinisation has largely replaced tradition, and where 'meaning' has retreated to the margins of the private and the public, feelings of communality of language, 'belongingness' in a national community etc., tend to form one strand contributing to the maintenance of ontological security.

(1981: 194)

Manifestly, there is no 'single' explanation of nationalism, nor, indeed, one single type. Above all, however, it is important to remember that nationalism, or national identity, is not a characteristic, but imputes a relationship between different identities. To be Scottish, for example, is to be not English. In the next part of this chapter, the focus will be on nationalism of and in Britain. The purpose will be to show that only by understanding nationalism in a much broader way than hitherto, can we make sense of these phenomena.

NATIONALISM IN BRITAIN

At first glance, it may seem odd to focus a discussion of nationalism on Britain. After all, it is a centralised, unitary state with very little linguistic diversity. The conventional wisdom is that Britain and France are 'the two instances usually given of a smooth coincidence of "nation" and "state" ' (Giddens 1985: 270). Such wisdom does, however, read rather oddly in the late twentieth century when Scottish and Welsh nationalism, to say nothing of Irish, are potent forces in the British Isles, and when other senses of ethnicity are growing. It is not untypical to find such Anglocentric sentiments expressed in the literature (indeed, Giddens' account of nationalism in the British Isles is indexed under 'England/Britain').

Contrast this with these comments, made somewhat tongue in cheek, by W.J.M. Mackenzie, a Scottish political scientist:

> The French case might at first seem simpler. To the identity question, 'Who am I?', surely there is a confident answer, 'Je suis français'. (Whereas you are taught to be an American; and in the United Kingdom you are ridiculous if you say 'I am British', incomprehensible if you say 'I am English'.)
>
> (1978: 73)

What Mackenzie is getting at is that national identities in the United Kingdom are highly complex and ambiguous. Benedict Anderson (1983: 12) makes the point that 'United Kingdom', like 'Soviet Union' denies nationality in its naming, and is classically a non-national state. (The relationship of England to the UK is not unlike that of Russia to the Soviet Union.) Indeed, the ambiguity of the terms 'United Kingdom' and 'Britain', often interchangeable on the mainland, presents problems in Northern Ireland where the term 'British' is politically and ethnically loaded. There, the term has been captured by the Unionists (as in 'Ulster is British' – doubly incorrect because Northern Ireland is not Ulster, nor, geographically speaking, is it on the British mainland). 'British', in this context, is an aspiration, not a description of political geography.

The ambiguities of national identities in the United Kingdom ('British', 'Scottish', 'Welsh', 'Irish', and even 'English', the latter the most implicit and problematic of all) were highlighted in the late 1970s with the election of the Thatcher government. While for much of the post-war period nationalism, as in other western countries, had been largely implicit, the relative economic decline of the UK had made appeals to the national interest more urgent and explicit. Politics ceased to be a matter of electing the best team of economic managers, and became instead a struggle for the 'national soul'. The Thatcherite project set out to revolutionise British society and its economy by deliberately destabilising its institutional structures. Large sectors of the economy were opened up to international competition, state industries were privatised, trade unions deregulated, and considerable redistribution took place to the advantage of the better-off. Faced with this economic project, appeals to 'the national interest' became more urgent and explicit as an ideological means of enforcing social order. But which 'national interest'? Thatcherism has most usually been equated with extending market liberalism, but it contained within it a powerful strand of neo-Conservatism – whose motif is not 'freedom' but 'authority' (Elliott and McCrone 1987). Unlike economic liberals, Conservatives were not concerned with producing the minimal state, but re-establishing and extending the state's power over many aspects of social life – over matters of sex and morality, religion, the family, and race. The cultural counter-revolution of the 1980s drew upon neo-Conservatism not neo-liberalism. As Thatcherism developed, and particularly after the Falklands war of 1982, the neo-Conservative strand came to greater prominence.

Such nationalism, however, has depended upon a powerful enough sense of 'Britain' to encapsulate the minor national identities of these islands. It has, for example, depended historically upon the British Empire, the monarchy, and institutions such as the BBC. As Thatcher mobilised British nationalism, it became clear – at least to the 'periphery' – that it had become an empty shell, or at least was indistinguishable from English nationalism. As Conserative nationalism became more explicit, so competing nationalisms asserted themselves. Thatcher's success in England had its counterpart in electoral unpopularity in Scotland and Wales.

Much of the identity of 'Britain' depended upon its external reinforcement. In this context, the empire conferred an identity on the country which was, historically, divided. As Mackenzie has pointed out, 'One might add that commonwealth and colonies were symbols of "Britain", and that "Britain" is rather an empty word now that they have gone' (1978: 172). Such an imperial identity had helped to counter older, challenging national identities in Scotland and Wales, for example. In Scotland, a militaristic tradition had been developed after the Union in which 'Scottish' and 'British' were not incompatible (Kendrick and McCrone 1989). British national and imperial identity chimed quite nicely with a powerful strand of Scottish national identity, reinforced by Protestantism, Unionism and militarism.

Other symbols of 'Britain', like the monarchy, seem also to be losing their integrative force. As Tom Nairn points out in *The Enchanted Glass* (1988), the monarchy was 'invented' in the late seventeenth century to provide ideological cement in a fissile state (bringing Scotland into the Union in 1707, and Ireland, formally, in 1800), and frequent reinforcements were required thereafter. Associated with 'Britain' (Nairn calls it 'Ukania' to emphasise its artificiality, the non-correspondence of state and nation), the monarchy finds itself without a meaningful role as the sense of 'Britain' declines and counter-nationalisms grow. In this regard, 'Britishness' was almost wholly a political rather than a cultural phenomenon. It became a mobilising device, almost entirely defined by its external relations, without a substantive, cultural content. In the late twentieth century, its political carrier, the Conservative Party, has almost totally lost its Britishness, and its electoral strength is overwhelmingly concentrated in England, a feature not known since the late nineteenth century (Punnett 1985). Gamble concurs:

> What the Conservatives have learned ... and particularly during Thatcher's leadership, is that it is no longer necessary or possible to project themselves as the party of the Union in order to win elections. Unionism has declined with the Empire. Conservatism has had to find a new identity. The Conservative Nation now is no longer the nation of Empire and Union. The appeal is directed much more towards England, and towards certain regions of England, the old metropolitan heartland of the Empire.
>
> (1988: 214)

This Englishing of the Conservative Party is both the cause and the effect of the electoral success of Thatcherism in the 1980s, and helps to explain the disaffection of the electorate in the other countries of the UK. Bernard Crick has explained the lack of a specific English nationalism in the context of the British state in terms of its potential divisiveness. Englishness became submerged into a wider, and more artificial, sense of Britishness because, as the overwhelmingly dominant nationality within the state, its assertion, in the context of the Union, would have been divisive (Crick 1989). He argued that the cult of sovereignty and loyalty within English Toryism was directed towards the imperial identity, and in particular to the Crown – ambiguously referring to both the monarchy and the state. The demise of empire, the erosion of the monarchy, as well as the diminishing capacity of quintessential British institutions such as the BBC to reflect a unified and homogenised British culture have considerably weakened the sense of Britain. Indeed, the fortunes of the BBC and the monarchy have been closely intertwined since the 1920s (Cannadine 1984). In Ascherson's words, 'Britain is not so much a nation as a sort of authority, a manner of speaking rather than a matter of weeping' (1988a). Without the strong, centralised, unitary state, there is probably little that would remain of 'Britain'.

This section has argued that 'nationalism' in Britain is not simply the assertion of peripheral discontent. British nationalism is a highly problematic, even artificially constructed, concept of recent provenance. In many respects, the emergence of peripheral nationalism reflects the contradictions of the centre, and the lack of correspondence between the nation and a highly centralised state. The key to understanding political unrest in Britain lies as much at the centre as on the periphery. The British state highlights the growing contradictions confronting modern states in the late twentieth century.

NATIONALISM IN SCOTLAND

It is in this context, therefore, that we can begin to understand Scottish nationalism, not simply as the assertion of linguistic or cultural distinctiveness, but as a political challenge to the authority of the central British state. In many respects, Scottish nationalism should, according to conventional theories of nationalism, not have happened at all. In the first place, there is little to distinguish Scotland linguistically from England, since Gaelic is spoken by less than 2 per cent, and Scots struggles to remain a distinctive language (McClure 1988). Neither is Scotland differentiated by its religion, being Protestant although adopting the Presbyterian variant. Even if we were to make more than is possible of linguistic and religious differences, these cannot explain why nationalism has emerged in the late twentieth century rather than a century earlier when these differences were stronger. The old institutional trinity of law, education and religion which Scotland has retained in diluted form as part of its price for the Union of 1707 provide the basis for a civil society, but it is hard to claim that these are as powerful determinants of social life as they were even a century ago.

211

The last two decades have seen a burgeoning of Scottish culture – music, literature, theatre and the arts – but there is no direct connection between these and the waxing and waning of political nationalism. While Scotland has retained an embryonic civil society stubbornly resistant to incorporation into the wider British state, its new nationalism does not appear to stem directly from that. The relationship between cultural and political nationalism is complex. Since its formation in the 1930s the Scottish National Party has struggled to make political capital out of cultural concerns. The sense of being 'Scottish' (as has been pointed out, seven out of ten Scots give it priority over any sense of being 'British'; Moreno 1988) is not readily translatable into political nationalism, and the SNP's breakthrough in the late 1960s owed more to economic concerns over North Sea oil.

In Scotland, there is no significant cultural defence to be mounted against alien impositions of language, religion or, indeed, – with the exception of so-called white settlers in the north – people. Nevertheless, while complaints about the 'colonisation' of Scottish universities, cultural boards and public bodies by 'outsiders' have been long-standing in Scotland, the salience of the issue has grown in recent years (Nairn 1988b: 33). By and large, Scottish nationalism has eschewed a dependence on cultural issues (unlike the two other dominant nationalist formations in Ireland and Wales). As a result, cultural concerns provide some raw material for nationalism, but are rarely its *raison d'être*. As a consequence, the tariff for being a nationalist is much lower; one does not have to speak the language, nor to practise one religion, nor to undertake an examination in cultural capital.

The electoral fortunes of the SNP are, as a consequence, quite unpredictable. The 1970s was a much more profitable decade for the party than the 1980s, which were dominated at a British level by a thoroughly English Prime Minister. While the SNP took 30 per cent of the vote in October 1974, it could only muster 14 per cent in 1987. Certainly, this is not new, for, in the late 1940s when the Scottish Covenant seeking home rule was signed by two million people, the SNP was getting around 1 per cent of the vote (1.2 per cent in 1945, and 0.4 per cent in 1950). Neither does the SNP have a monopoly on those who want independence for Scotland. Opinion polls show a substantial minority of SNP voters claim not to want independence, while only a minority of those who want independence vote for the SNP (the Labour Party contains the largest number). Insofar as the SNP seeks to create an orthodox nation-state, its project fails to find favour with sufficient Scottish voters (McCrone 1991).

In many ways, the nationalist mantle has fallen on other parties in Scotland, notably Labour. Since Thatcher's election in 1979, and especially in 1987 when fifty Labour MPs were elected compared with ten Conservatives, it was an obvious political charge that the government had no mandate in Scotland. Labour's reliance on Scottish as well as Welsh MPs, set against the overwhelming strength of the Conservative Party in the south of England, reinforced the ethnic differences between the parties.

Since July 1988 Labour found itself playing the nationalist card in the Scottish Constitutional Convention, set up under the auspices of the Campaign for a Scottish Assembly. The convention was dominated by the Labour Party, with the support of the Liberal Democrats, the Green Party and the Communist Party, and included support from the churches and other bodies in Scottish civil society, while the Conservatives and the SNP declined to join. While the SNP argued that the convention's proposals did not go far enough, the Tories claimed that any change from the status quo was too much. The convention's testament, signed by all participants, has a nationalist thrust:

> We, gathered as the Scottish Constitutional Convention, do hereby acknowledge the sovereign right of the Scottish people to determine the form of government best suited to their needs, and do hereby declare and pledge that in all our actions and deliberations, their interests shall be paramount.
>
> (*A Claim of Right for Scotland* 1988)

The failure of the SNP to participate in this broader home rule movement has been signalled as a political failure by many nationalists. Tom Nairn has offered the following comment: 'All nationalisms have a purist wing: but I can think of no other where the wing has flown the bird so constantly, or with so little objective justification' (1990: 5). In many respects, the SNP has moved away from the gradualist position it held in the late 1970s when it argued for a step-wise progression to independence. By the 1980s the position of 'Independence, nothing less' had won the day, and the flirtation with devolutionists had ended, even though a significant number of the party's supporters (around one third) wanted an assembly within the UK rather than outright independence. In the words of one writer not unsympathetic to the party, 'The fundamentalism of Thatcher's unionism was the mirror image of the fundamentalism of the SNP's nationalism' (Mitchell 1990: 52). The marginalisation of the SNP – its standing in the polls was 17 per cent, one third of Labour's support in February 1990 – allowed the Labour Party to be much more enthusiastic about home rule within the convention than it would have been able to be if the Nationalists had been participants. The irony was that the SNP recognised the limited nature of sovereignty in its slogan – Independence in Europe – and argued for a 'Europe des patries' in which national sovereignty would inevitably be circumscribed. Nevertheless, the party, by its actions in standing outside the Scottish Constitutional Convention, refused to give up its claim to be the monopoly voice of the national movement. It seemed that, by default, it had been left to other parties, notably Labour and the smaller Liberal Democrats, to deliver home rule to Scotland, albeit in the first instance within the United Kingdom.

To sum up, nationalism in Scotland has unorthodox features. First, it draws very thinly on cultural traditions; there is virtually no linguistic or religious basis to nationalism. Second, there is no simple correspondence between desiring independence for Scotland and voting SNP; this was as true of the 1940s as it is of the 1990s. Third, the gathering desire for some measure of home rule, in large or small quantity, has been growing for twenty-five years. In that period Scotland has been governed by a 'semi-state' managed by the ruling Westminster party, often at odds with Scottish public opinion. Scottish electoral behaviour has diverged significantly from that of the English, and a distinct Scottish political agenda has emerged, distinctly at odds with the southern one. Finally, the rise of Thatcher, and her assault on the state came to be perceived in Scotland as an attack on the nation itself. Thatcherism shattered the harmony of the post-war years by politicising all aspects of state activity, and Labour has taken on the role of protector in this defensive battle, and with it the nationalist mantle. Insofar as Thatcherism became the political ideology of 'little England', it had few resonances north of 'the border. In crucial respects, then, Thatcher became, quite unwittingly, the midwife of Scottish Home Rule.

It would be easy to explain the relationship of different nationalisms within Britain purely in internal terms. This would be a mistake. The political, economic and social forces which are threatening to 'break up' Britain are not unique to it. Indeed, faced with strong centralised powers of the British state, it might seem fanciful to claim that Britain is the most susceptible to breakup. Nevertheless, we might argue that the reassertion of centralism in the Thatcher years marked the final desperate defence in a breached wall, rather than proof of the soundness of its fortifications. The strains and tensions in the fabric of the nation-state are, however, much broader than that. Fundamental changes are threatening to consign this political form to the dustbin of history, and usher in hitherto unthought-of new political formations.

NATIONALISM: THE GRAVEDIGGER OF THE NATION-STATE?

There was this Englishman who worked in the London office of a multinational corporation based in the United States. He drove home one evening in his Japanese car. His wife, who worked in a firm which imported German kitchen equipment, was already at home. Her small Italian car was often quicker through the traffic. After a meal which included New Zealand lamb, Californian carrots, Mexican honey, French cheese and Spanish wine, they settled down to watch a programme on their television set, which had been made in Finland. The programme was a retrospective celebration of the war to recapture the Falkland islands. As they watched it they felt warmly patriotic, and very proud to be British.

(Williams 1983: 177)

Raymond Williams is poking fun at the confused sentiments of nationalism which gather pace in the late twentieth century. However, Williams is careful to argue in his essay that nationalism is far from dead and provides the means for people to combat new, alienating and centralising powers in the modern world. In Benedict Anderson's words, 'the end of the era of nationalism, so long prophesied, is not remotely in sight' (1983: 12). We might, however, add a gloss to this comment – we seem to have entered a world of post-nationalism.

What is clear is that the historic creation of nationalism, the traditional nation-state, is losing its *raison d'être* (Marquand 1988). The nation-state, a historical product not a fact of nature, emerged as the dominant political formation between the mid-nineteenth

215

and the mid-twentieth centuries. The late nineteenth century in particular was a period of intense cultivation of national symbols – flags, anthems, ceremonies, holidays, and buildings (Hobsbawm 1984). The nation-state laid claim to territorial jurisdiction; its source of jurisdiction derived from the people or nation. As David Beetham has pointed out, the classical nation-state was a suitable adaptation to the economic, military and political circumstances of the nineteenth and early twentieth centuries. Those states were economically successful in that a free market was established based on a unified, national, system of law, taxation and administration. In military terms, nation-states succeeded if they asserted their autonomy, and mobilised its people in its defence. Politically, the population was incorporated into the citizenship of the nation-state by means of extending the franchise.

In many respects the nation-state has been undermined by precisely those forces which gave it strength. In the first place, the development of global, mobile capital, and a more complex international division of labour have reduced the capacity of the national state to determine its economic policy. Beetham has pointed out that multinational capital 'is able to optimise conditions for its operation without reference to the interests of particular national economies' (1984: 212). The introduction of the 1992 Single European Act will give further impetus to these developments. Further, transnational organisations such as the World Bank and the IMF have acquired substantial powers over national states.

The second factor which has helped to erode the nation-state derives from the *raison d'état* of the state itself, namely, its military strength. Beetham argues that while the modern state was largely the product of successfully waged warfare – 'control of the means of violence is par excellence the business of the state' (1984: 213) – in the late twentieth century the state has rapidly lost its power to protect its citizenry. Technological developments, and in particular the potential of nuclear weaponry, as well as the wider ramifications of localised conflicts have made limited warfare much more difficult to wage. The irony is that the more nation-states try to control their own means of destruction, the more they are vulnerable to others. Partly as a result, international law has developed to circumscribe the claims of the nation-states, thereby increasing the tension between national sovereignty and international law (Held 1988).

Finally, the relationship between national culture and the nation-state has been rendered virtually unworkable. Max Weber was a distinguished proponent of *kulturpolitisch* – whereby the state gave political expression to the individuality of the national community, its *Kultur*. It is difficult to find a simple correspondence between culture and the state anymore. Multi-culturalism is embedded in virtually all states, and claims that 'a people' have a single culture become harder to maintain. The globalisation of culture and media developments means that defending 'national culture' from alien influences becomes the labour of Canute. This does not, of course, prevent advocates of national cultures making their claims. The right-wing English Conservative politician, Norman Tebbit, drew scorn for his attempts in April 1990 to apply his 'cricket test' to measure national loyalty. Those of non-British ethnic origin were asked which team they would cheer if England were playing international cricket, the implication being that cheering the opposition was a sign of disloyalty and lack of social integration. What made the Tebbit test doubly ironic was that it did not seem to recognise the historically separate identities within the British Isles. 'Englishness' in this regard was not the name of the national-state identity, merely one of four possibilities. National identity has become much more complex. As Bernard Crick has pointed out, most people are required to live across cultures: 'Not only intellectuals can live in, or in and out of, two or more cultures. The migrant poor have done it for centuries' (1989: 34).

We have, however, to handle with care the argument that the nation-state is being eroded by economic, political-military and cultural changes in the late twentieth century. Externally, nation-states are still the key actors in modern geo-politics, and supra-national bodies (such as the European Community or the United Nations – witness the Gulf War of 1991) are still beholden to their military and economic power. Internally, too, the nation-state demands (and largely gets) the obeisance of its citizens. Nevertheless, the conditions which made the nation-state the creation of the nineteenth century have changed. David Held has argued that much has depended on the state's location in the international division of labour, and some international co-operation extends rather than diminishes the power of individual states (Germany being an obvious example, given its role in Europe). The implications, however, of these changes are clear. While the nation-state remains a key organising principle of modern politics, 'any conception of sovereignty which assumes that it is an indivisible, illimitable, exclusive, and perpetual form of public power – embodied within an individual state – is defunct' (Held 1988: 15).

The message is stark, not only for those in possession of nation-states. Thatcherism, as we have pointed out, was an uneasy mix of free market economics and Conservative nationalism. Britain, however, is by no means alone in facing these challenges. In the post-war years France, Belgium, Canada and even Germany (in an external form: the German state is not the German 'nation') have all been subject to these pressures. A long view of history would confirm the loose correspondence between nations and states. Many nations – like Scotland – did not survive as separate states. And many states were formed out of non-nations (the United States is an obvious example). The pressures on nation-states are likely to grow not diminish, and will come in two forms: centrifugal and centripetal. Supra-national government, such as that of the European Community, will erode the state's independence from above. At the same time, submerged nations or marginalised ethnic groups will become more vociferous in asserting their rights to self-determination, particularly if these can be shaped into territorial form. Juan Linz has argued that nationalism has shifted away from a simple emphasis on 'primordial ties' to a definition of the nation based on territoriality:

The definition would change from an emphasis on common descent, race, language, distinctive cultural tradition, in some cases religion, to one based on 'living and working' in an area, on a willingness to identify with that community, or on both.

(Linz 1985: 205)

This shift from 'ethnicity' to 'territoriality' (which manifestly lends itself to versions of ecological or 'green' politics) embodies the changes within nationalism itself. The implication of Linz's remarks is that simple – primordial – demands based on exclusivity are not suited to a multi-cultural, interdependent world. Nationalist movements which take that regressive, primordial route are doomed to fail. Those which mobilise new sentiments of resistance and cultural development based on new challenges are much more in line with Melucci's notion of social movements of the late twentieth century. It is a view echoed by Raymond Williams, himself a man of 'the border' fully equipped to live between cultures:

> It is clear that if people are to defend and promote their real interests on the basis of lived and worked and placeable social identities, a large part of the now alienated and centralised powers and resources must be actively regained, by new actual societies which in their own terms, and nobody else's, define themselves.

(1983: 197)

This is a plea for new forms of self-determination, of limited autonomy, and self-managing communities, based on the rights of people to govern themselves. Such plans are based on limited sovereignty in an interdependent world. The assault by nationalists on traditional nation-states is a symptom of the decay of these political formations, as well as the search for new forms as yet unimagined. Nevertheless, as the traditional nation-state decays, nationalism as a movement and ideology would seem to prosper. As Anthony Smith pointed out national identity is probably the most powerful force in the modern age 'to provide a strong "community of history and destiny" to save people from personal oblivion and restore collective faith' (Smith 1991: 161). The irony is that nationalism is probably the gravedigger of the conventional nation-state with its commitment to 'a world of sovereign, self-reliant nation-states claiming the right to assert themselves and pursue their essential national interests by taking recourse to force' (Mommsen 1990: 226). In its classical form, nationalism is pursuing precisely those political structures which are rapidly falling into disuse. As such, nationalism is probably destined to consume its own offspring. In this sense, these are post-nationalist times.

THE FUTURE OF SCOTLAND

Is, then Hobsbawm correct in dismissing nationalism as 'negative and divisive', as 'unstable and impermanent' (1990: 164, 179)? How accurate is his reading that Scottish nationalism is 'plainly a reaction to an all-British government supported by only a modest minority of Scots, and a politically impotent all-British opposition party' (1990: 179)? Such a reading addresses symptoms, not causes, for, as we have pointed out, the Nationalist party has not prospered under these conditions in the 1980s while the 'impotent' – Labour

– party has. But Hobsbawm's analysis is more deeply flawed than that. It is based on a centralised view of politics, which fails to see 'peripheral' nationalism as the mirror image of nationalism of the 'centre'. Ultimately, he falls back upon an Anglocentric centralist liberalism which, in Nairn's words, 'serves the big battalions' – the English, the French, the Russians (Nairn 1990: 30).

The key to understanding nationalism resides precisely in its unstable and impermanent features, the lack of correspondence between movement and party organisation, the failure of the political party to capture the idea of the nation. Both orthodox Nationalists and Unionists have a distorted view of what 'national sovereignty' is, a view that it is complete and absolute. However, as Lindsay Paterson has perceptively pointed out, sovereignty is a negotiated process, 'not a condition that is acquired or lost in one cataclysmic event' (1991: 104). Hence, one cannot say that before 1707 Scotland was in control of its own destiny, and that subsequent to the Union it was not. Instead, a series of complicated compromises were worked out to give Scotland (or more accurately, its elites) a high degree of social, economic and political autonomy. The debate about Scotland, as we have seen in this book, has largely been determined by the nationalist assumption that Scotland has been or is being 'lost' and has to be 'regained'. A more helpful argument would be that throughout its history Scotland's survival and identity have been the product of compromise and negotiation. In this respect, its 'identity' is not under threat of extinction.

In the last decade of the twentieth century, this process of negotiation has reached a new threshold. The almost inexorable move towards Home Rule, to a higher level of self-determination, has presented the British state with a crisis with regard to its own identity and governance. The irony – for it is not a coincidence – is that this 'internal' issue occurs just at the time when a strongly nationalist Conservative government is seeking to hold the line against further loss of British sovereignty to Europe. The British state is squeezed from above and below. What makes the Scottish case different and interesting is that it seems to involve what Tom Nairn has called a 'sideways and hesitant motion towards political nationalism', because the 'identity garments' of nationalism (language, religion, ethnic culture and so on) do not fit the Scots with any ease. And as we have pointed out in the previous chapter, the relationship between political nationalism and culture is unusually attentuated north of the border.

But the problem is not uniquely a British and a Scottish one. Those qualities of nationalism identified by Hobsbawm – instability and impermanence – point to the search for alternative principles of political restructuring in the twenty-first century. The rediscovery of 'popular sovereignty' and of democratic accountability, most noticeably in Eastern Europe, have a wider remit. If, instead of treating nationalism as a political party as Hobsbawm does, we view it as a social movement, as a fragile and heterogeneous construction, we might treat nationalist and autonomist movements as, in Melucci's words, 'nomads of the present', vehicles for collective action with an indeterminate end. The broad and diffuse, the 'non-political', appeal of nationalism seems to make it a movement of the twenty-first rather than the nineteenth century. Its commitment to the post-materialist values of autonomy, authenticity and acountability place 'post-nationalism' firmly in the future not the past.

And Scotland? Consider this comment made about the revolutions in Eastern Europe in the late 1980s:

Whenever the civil society becomes more confident, the state rapidly loses its grip; its structural weaknesss and powerlessness become evident. Civil society tends to swell rapidly from below. It feeds upon whatever gains it can wrench from the state, which normally lapses into confusion and paralysis.

(Keane 1988: 4–5)

Czechoslovakia in 1989; Scotland tomorrow?

BIBLIOGRAPHY

Adam, F. (1980) *The Scottish Clans and Their Tartans*, Edinburgh: W. & A. K. Johnston.

Anderson, B. (1983) *Imagined Communities: Reflections on the Origin and Spread of Nationalism*, London: Verso.

Anderson, E. (1979) 'The Kailyard revisited', in I. Campbell (ed.) *Nineteenth Century Scottish Fiction*, Manchester: Carcanet Press.

Anderson, M. and Morse, D. (1990) 'The people', in Fraser, W. H. and Morris, R. J. (eds) *People and Society in Scotland, volume 2, 1830–1914*, Edinburgh: John Donald.

Anderson, R. D. (1983) *Educational Opportunity in Victorian Scotland*, Oxford: Clarendon Press.

Anderson, R. D. (1985) 'In search of the "lad of parts": the mythical history of Scottish education', *History Today*, 19.

Anderson, R. D. (1991) 'Universities and elites in modern Britain', *The History of the Universities*, 10.

Arrighi, G., Hopkins, T. K. and Wallerstein, I. (1983) 'Rethinking the concepts of class and status group in a world-systems perspective', *Review*, 6(3).

Ascherson, N. (1985) 'Ancient Britons and the republican dream', John P. Mackintosh Memorial Lecture, reprinted in *Radical Scotland*, 18.

Ascherson, N. (1988a) 'The religion of nationalism', *The Observer*, 4 December.

Ascherson, N. (1988b) *Games with Shadows*, London: Hutchinson Radius.

Ash, M. (1980) *The Strange Death of Scottish History*, Edinburgh: Ramsay Head Press.

Ash, M. (1990) 'William Wallace and Robert the Bruce: the life and death of a national myth', in Samuel, R. and Thompson, P. (eds) *The Myths We Live By*, London: Routledge.

Ash, M. (n.d.) The St Andrews myth (mimeo).

Bain, R. (1968) *The Clans and Tartans of Scotland*, Glasgow: Collins.

Barth, F. (1969) *Ethnic Groups and Boundaries*, Bergen: Scandinavian University Books.

Bealey, F. and Sewel, J. (1981) *The Politics of Independence: A Study of a Scottish Town*, Aberdeen: Aberdeen University Press.

BIBLIOGRAPHY

Beetham, D. (1974) *Max Weber and the Theory of Modern Politics*, London: Allen & Unwin.

Beetham, D. (1984) 'The future of the nation state', in McLennan, G., Held, D. and Hall, S. (eds) *The Idea of the Modern State*, Milton Keynes: Open University Press.

Beveridge, C. and Turnbull, C. (1989) *The Eclipse of Scottish Culture: Inferiorism and the Intellectuals*, Edinburgh: Polygon.

Bochel, J. and Denver, D. (1970) 'Religion and voting: a critical review and a new analysis', *Political Studies*, 18.

Bold, A. (1990) *MacDiarmid*, London: Paladin.

Brand, J. (1978) *The National Movement in Scotland*, London: Routledge & Kegan Paul.

Brenner, R. (1977) 'The origins of capitalist development: a critique of neo-Smithian economics', *New Left Review*, 104.

Brewer, J. (1989) 'Conjectural history, sociology and social change in 18th century Scotland: Adam Ferguson and the division of labour', in McCrone, D., Kendrick, S. and Straw, S. (eds) *The Making of Scotland: Nation, Culture and Social Change*, Edinburgh: Edinburgh University Press.

Brown, C. (1987) *The Social History of Religion in Scotland since 1730*, London: Methuen.

Brown, C. (1988) 'Religion and social change', in Devine, T. and Mitchison, R. (eds) *People and Society in Scotland, volume 1, 1760–1830*, Edinburgh: John Donald.

Brown, C. (1990) 'Each take of their several way? The Protestant churches and the working classes in Scotland', in Walker, G. and Gallagher, T. (eds) *Sermons and Battle Hymns: Protestant Popular Culture in Modern Scotland*, Edinburgh: Edinburgh University Press.

Brown, G. D. [1901] *The House with the Green Shutters*, 1967 edn, London: Cassell.

Bruce, S. (1985) *No Pope of Rome: Militant Protestantism in Modern Scotland*, Edinburgh: Mainstream Press.

Bruce, S. and Yearley, S. (1989) 'The social construction of tradition: the restoration portraits of the kings of Scotland', in McCrone, D., Kendrick, S. and Straw, S. (eds) *The Making of Scotland: Nation, Culture and Social Change*, Edinburgh: Edinburgh University Press.

Bryden, J. (1979) 'Core-periphery problems: the Scottish case', in Seers, D., Schaffer, B. and Kiljunen, M-L. (eds) *Underdeveloped Europe: Studies in Core–periphery Relations*, Hassocks, Sussex: Harvester Press.

Buchanan, K. (1968) 'The revolt against satellisation in Scotland and Wales', *Monthly Review*, March.

Budge, I. and Urwin, D. (1966) *Scottish Political Behaviour*, London: Longman.

Bulletin of Scottish Politics, 2 (1981) 'The politics of tartanry'.

Burns, T. (1966) 'Sociological explanation', inaugural lecture, Edinburgh University, 8 February. Reprinted in Emmet, D. and MacIntyre, A. (eds) *Sociological Theory and Philosophical Analysis*, London: Macmillan, 1970.

Caird, J. B. and Moisley, H. A. (1961) 'Leadership and innovation in the crofting community of the Outer Hebrides', *Sociological Review*, 9.

Calder, J. (1988) 'Heroes and hero-makers: women in nineteenth century Scottish fiction', in Gifford,D. (ed.) *The History of Scottish Literature, volume 3, the Nineteenth Century*, Aberdeen: Aberdeen University Press.

Campbell, I. (1981) *Kailyard*, Edinburgh: Ramsay Head Press.

Campbell, R. H. [1980] *The Rise and Fall of Scottish Industry*, 2nd edn, 1988, Edinburgh: John Donald.

Cannadine, D. (1984) 'The context, performance and meaning of ritual', in Hobsbawm, E. and Ranger, T. (eds) *The Invention of Tradition*, Cambridge: Cambridge University Press.

Carroll, W. (1984) 'The individual, class and corporate power in Canada', *Canadian Journal of Sociology*, 9(3).

Carter, I. (1971) 'Economic models and the history of the Highlands', *Scottish Studies*, 15.

Carter, I. (1974) 'The Highlands of Scotland as an underdeveloped region', in DeKadt, E. and Williams, G. (eds) *Sociology and Underdevelopment*, London: Tavistock.

Carter, I. (1976) 'Kailyard: the literature of decline in 19th century Scotland', *Scottish Journal of Sociology*, 1(1).

Carter, I. (1979) *Farm Life in North-East Scotland, 1840–1914*, Edinburgh: John Donald.

Carter, I. (1981a) 'The Scottish peasantry', *Peasant Studies*, 10.

Carter, I. (1981b) 'The changing image of the Scottish peasantry, 1745–1980', in Samuel, R. (ed.) *People's History and Socialist Theory*, London: Routledge & Kegan Paul.

Caughie, J. (1982) 'Scottish television: what would it look like?', in McArthur, C. (ed.) *Scotch Reels: Scotland in Cinema and Television*, London: BFI Publishing.

Chapman, M. (1978) *The Gaelic Vision of Scottish Culture*, London: Croom Helm.

Checkland, S. and O. (1984) *Industry and Ethos: Scotland, 1832–1914*, London: Edward Arnold.

A Claim of Right for Scotland (1988) A Report of the Constitutional Steering Committee presented to the Campaign for a Scottish Assembly, Edinburgh.

Claval, P. (1980) 'Centre-periphery and space: models of political geography', in Gottman, W. (ed.) *Centre and Periphery: Spatial Variations in Politics*, London: Sage.

Clement, W. (1975) *The Canadian Corporate Elite*, Toronto: McClelland & Stewart.

Clement, W. (1983) *Class, Power and Property*, Agincourt, Ont.: Methuen.

Cohen, A. (ed.) (1982) *Belonging: Identity and Social Organisation in British Rural Cultures*, Manchester: Manchester University Press.

Cohen, A. (1985) *The Social Construction of Community*, London: Tavistock.

Coxon, A. P. M. (1982) *The User's Guide to Multi-Dimensional Scaling*, London: Heinemann.

Coxon, A. P. M. and Davies, P. M., with Jones, C. L. (1986) *Images of Stratification: Occupational Structures and Class*, London: Sage.

Craig, C. (1980) 'Fearful selves: character, community and the Scottish imagination', *Cencrastus*, 4.

Craig, C. (1983) 'Visitors from the stars: Scottish film culture', *Cencrastus*, 11.

Craig, C. (1990) 'Twentieth century Scottish literature: an introduction', in Craig, C. (ed.) *The History of Scottish Literature, volume 4, the Twentieth Century*, Aberdeen: Aberdeen University Press.

Craig, D. (1961) *Scottish Literature and the Scottish People, 1680–1830*, London: Chatto & Windus.

Craig, F. W. S. (1981) *British Electoral Facts, 1832–1980*, Chichester: Parliamentary Research Services.

Craig, F. W. S. (1984) *Britain Votes 3*, Chichester: Parliamentary Research Services.

Craig, F. W. S. (1989) *British Electoral Facts, 1983–1987*, Dartmouth: Parliamentary Research Services and Gower.

Crick, B. (1989) 'An Englishman considers his passport', in Evans, N. (ed.) *National Identity in the British Isles*, Occasional Papers in Welsh Studies no. 3, Harlech, Gwynedd: Coleg Harlech.

Crompton, R. and Mann, M. (eds) (1986) *Gender and Stratification*, Cambridge: Polity Press.

Davie, G. (1961) *The Democratic Intellect: Scotland and her Universities in the Nineteenth Century*, Edinburgh: Edinburgh University Press.

Davie, G. (1986) *The Crisis of the Democratic Intellect: The Problem of Generalisation and Specialisation in Twentieth Century Scotland*, Edinburgh: Polygon.

Davis, H. (1979) *Beyond Class Images: Explorations in the Structure of Social Consciousness*, London: Croom Helm.

Dickson, T. (ed.) (1980) *Scottish Capitalism: Class, State and Nation from before the Union to the Present*, London: Lawrence & Wishart.

Dickson, T. (1989) 'Scotland is different, OK?' in McCrone, D., Kendrick, S. and Straw, S. (eds) *The Making of Scotland: Nation, Culture and Social Change*, Edinburgh: Edinburgh University Press.

Donaldson, G. (1974) *Scotland: The Shaping of a Nation*, London: David & Charles.

Donaldson, W. (1986) *Popular Literature in Victorian Scotland: Language, Fiction and the Press*, Aberdeen: Aberdeen University Press.

Elias, N. (1978) *The Civilising Process*, Oxford: Basil Blackwell.

Elliott, B. and McCrone, D. (1987) 'Class, culture and morality: a sociological analysis of the new Conservatism', *Sociological Review*, 35.

Ellis, P. B. and Mac A'Ghobhain, S. (1970) *The Scottish Insurrection of 1820*, London: Gollancz.

Fewell, J. and Paterson, F. (eds) (1990) *Girls in their Prime: Scottish Education Revisited*, Edinburgh: Scottish Academic Press.

Firn, J. (1975) 'External control and regional policy', in Brown, G. (ed.) *The Red Paper on Scotland*, Edinburgh: Edinburgh University Students' Publications Board.

Fischoff, E. (1944) 'The Protestant ethic and the spirit of capitalism: the history of a controversy', *Social Research*, 11.

Flinn, M. (ed.) (1977) *Scottish Population History from the 17th Century to the 1930s*, Cambridge: Cambridge University Press.

Foster, J. (1989) 'Nationality, social change and class: transformations of national identity in Scotland', in McCrone, D., Kendrick, S. and Straw,

S. (eds) *The Making of Scotland: Nation, Culture and Social Change*, Edinburgh: Edinburgh University Press.

Foster, J. and Woolfson, C. (1986) *The Politics of the UCS Work-In: Class Alliances and the Right to Work*, London: Lawrence & Wishart.

Frank, A. G. (1969) *Capitalism and Underdevelopment in Latin America*, Harmondsworth: Penguin.

Fry, M. (1987) *Patronage and Principle: A Political History of Scotland, 1832–1924*, Aberdeen: Aberdeen University Press.

Gallagher, T. (1987a) *Edinburgh Divided: John Cormack and No Popery in the 1930s*, Edinburgh: Polygon.

Gallagher, T. (1987b) *Glasgow: The Uneasy Peace*, Manchester: Manchester University Press.

Gallie, D. and Vogler, C. (1990) 'Labour market deprivation, welfare and collectivism', in *Archives Européennes de Sociologie*, 21(1).

Gamble, A. (1974) *The Conservative Nation*, London: Routledge & Kegan Paul.

Gamble, A. (1988) *The Free Economy and the Strong State*, London: Macmillan.

Gellner, E. (1965) 'Nationalism', in Gellner, E. (ed.) *Thought and Change*, London: Weidenfeld & Nicolson.

Gellner, E. (1973) 'Scale and nation', *Philosophy of the Social Sciences*, 3.

Gellner, E. (1978) 'Nationalism, or the confessions of a justified Edinburgh sinner', *Political Quarterly*, 49(1).

Gellner, E. (1983) *Nations and Nationalism*, Oxford: Basil Blackwell.

Giddens, A. (1981) *A Contemporary Critique of Historical Materialism*, London: Macmillan.

Giddens, A. (1985) *The Nation-State and Violence*, London: Polity Press.

Gifford, D. (ed.) (1988) *The History of Scottish Literature, volume 3, the Nineteenth Century*, Aberdeen: Aberdeen University Press.

Goldthorpe, J. [1980] *Social Mobility and Class Structure in Modern Britain*, 2nd edn, 1987, Oxford: Oxford University Press.

Gordon, E. and Breitenbach, E. (eds) (1990) *The World is Ill-Divided: Women's Work in Scotland in the Nineteenth and Early Twentieth Centuries*, Edinburgh: Edinburgh University Press.

Gramsci, A. (1988) *A Gramsci Reader: Selected Writings, 1916–1935*, ed. D. Forgacs, London: Lawrence & Wishart.

Grant, W. and Murison, D. (1974) *Scottish National Dictionary*, Edinburgh: The Scottish National Dictionary Association Ltd.

Gray, J., McPherson, A. and Raffe, D. (1984) *Reconstructions of Secondary Education: Theory, Myth and Practice since the War*, London: Routledge & Kegan Paul.

Hall, J. (1986) *Powers and Liberties: The Causes and Consequences of the Rise of the West*, Harmondsworth: Penguin.

Hall, S. (1983) *The Politics of Thatcherism*, London: Lawrence and Wishart.

Harvie, C. (1975) 'The devolution of the intellectuals', *New Statesman*, 90.

Harvie, C. (1981) *No Gods and Precious Few Heroes*, London: Edward Arnold.

Harvie, C. (1988) 'Industry, religion and the state of Scotland', in Gifford,

D. (ed.) *The History of Scottish Literature, volume 3, the Nineteenth Century*, Aberdeen: Aberdeen University Press.

Harvie, C. (1990) 'The covenanting tradition', in Walker, G. and Gallagher, T. (eds) *Sermons and Battle Hymns: Protestant Popular Culture in Modern Scotland*, Edinburgh: Edinburgh University Press.

Hay, J. McDougall [1914] *Gillespie*, 1979 edn, Edinburgh: Canongate.

Heath, A. F., Jowell, R. M. and Curtice, J. K. (1985) *How Britain Votes*, Oxford: Pergamon Press.

Heath, A. F., Jowell, R. M. and Curtice, J. K. (eds) (1991) *Understanding Political Change: The British Voter, 1964–87*, Oxford: Pergamon Press.

Hechter, M. (1975) *Internal Colonialism: The Celtic Fringe in British National Development, 1536–1966*, London: Routledge & Kegan Paul.

Hechter, M. (1982) 'Internal colonialism revisited', *Cencrastus*, 10.

Held, D. (1988) 'Farewell to the nation-state', *Marxism Today*, Nov.–Dec.

Hesketh, C. (1972) *Tartans*, London: Octopus Books.

Hewison, R. (1987) *The Heritage Industry: Britain in a Climate of Decline*, London: Methuen.

Hobsbawm, E. (1969) *Industry and Empire*, Harmondsworth: Penguin.

Hobsbawm, E. (1972) 'Reflections on nationalism', in Nossiter, T., Hanson, A. and Rokkan, S. (eds) *Imagination and Precision in the Social Sciences*, London: Faber & Faber.

Hobsbawm, E. (1984) 'Mass-producing traditions: Europe, 1870–1914', in Hobsbawm, E. and Ranger, T. (eds) *The Invention of Tradition*, Cambridge: Cambridge University Press.

Hobsbawm, E. (1990) *Nations and Nationalism since 1780: Programme, Myth and Reality*, Cambridge: Cambridge University Press.

Hope, K. (1984) *As Others See Us: Schooling and Social Mobility in Scotland and the United States*, Cambridge: Cambridge University Press.

Houston, R. (1985) *Scottish Literacy and the Scottish Identity: Literacy and Society in Scotland and Northern Ireland, 1600–1800*, Cambridge: Cambridge University Press.

Hunter, J. (1976) *The Making of the Crofting Community*, Edinburgh: John Donald.

Hutchison, I. G. C. (1986) *A Political History of Scotland, 1832–1924*, Edinburgh: John Donald.

Hyma, A. (1937) *Christianity, Capitalism and Communism*, Ann Arbor, Mich.: G. Wahr – published by author.

Inglehart, R. (1977) *The Silent Revolution: Changing Values and Political Styles among Western Publics*, Princeton NJ: Princeton University Press.

Jamieson, L. (1990) 'We all left at 14: boys' and girls' schooling, 1900–30', in Fewell, J. and Paterson, F. (eds) *Girls in their Prime: Scottish Education Revisited*, Edinburgh: Scottish Academic Press.

Jones, T. (1977) 'Occupational transition in advanced industrial societies', *Sociological Review*, 25(2).

Keane, J. (1988) *Civil Society and the State*, London: Verso.

Keating, M. and Bleiman, D. (1979) *Labour and Scottish Nationalism*, London: Macmillan.

Kellas, J. [1973] *The Scottish Political System*, 1989 edn, Cambridge: Cambridge University Press.

Kellas, J. (1980) *Modern Scotland*, London: Allen & Unwin.

Kendrick, S. (1983) 'Social change and nationalism in modern Scotland', Ph.D. thesis, Edinburgh University, unpublished.

Kendrick, S. (1986) 'Occupational change in modern Scotland', in McCrone, D. (ed.) *Scottish Government Yearbook 1986*, Edinburgh: Unit for the Study of Government in Scotland.

Kendrick, S., Bechhofer, F. and McCrone, D. (1985) 'Is Scotland different: industrial and occupational change in Scotland and Britain', in Newby, H., Bujra, J., Littlewood, P., Rees, G. and Rees, T. (eds) *Restructuring Capital: Recession and Reorganisation in Industrial Society*, London: Macmillan.

Kendrick, S. and McCrone, D. (1989) 'Politics in a cold climate: the Conservative decline in Scotland', *Political Studies*, 37.

Kerevan, G. (1980) 'Whither Scotland?', *Bulletin of Scottish Politics*, 1.

King, A. (1976) 'The problem of overload', in *Why is Britain Becoming Harder to Govern?*, London: BBC Publications.

Kirby, M. W. (1981) *The Decline of British Economic Power since 1870*, London: Allen & Unwin.

Knowles, T. D. (1983) *Ideology, Art and Commerce: Aspects of Literary Sociology in the Late Victorian Scottish Kailyard*, Gothenborg: Acta Universitatis Gothoburgensis.

Kumar, K. (1978) *Prophecy and Progress*, Harmondsworth: Penguin.

Lash, S. (1990) *Sociology of Post-Modernism*, London: Routledge.

Lee, C. H. (1979) *British Regional Employment Statistics, 1841–1971*, Cambridge: Cambridge University Press.

Lenman, B. (1977) *An Economic History of Modern Scotland*, London: Batsford.

Levitt, I. (1989) 'Welfare, government and the working class: Scotland, 1845–1894', in McCrone, D., Kendrick, S. and Straw, S. (eds) *The Making of Scotland: Nation, Culture and Social Change*, Edinburgh: Edinburgh University Press.

Lindsay, I. (1991) 'Scottish migration: prospects for the nineties', in Brown, A. and McCrone, D. (eds) *Scottish Government Yearbook 1991*, Edinburgh: Unit for the Study of Government in Scotland.

Linz, J. (1985) 'From primordialism to nationalism', in Tiryakian, E. and Rogowski, R. (eds), *New Nationalisms of the Developed West*, London: Allen & Unwin.

Lythe, S. G. E. (1960) *The Economy of Scotland in its European Setting, 1550–1625*, Edinburgh: Oliver & Boyd.

McAllister, I. and Rose, R. (1984) *The Nationwide Competition for Votes*, London: Frances Pinter.

McArthur, C. (1981) 'Breaking the signs: 'Scotch myths as cultural struggle', *Cencrastus*, 7.

McArthur, C. (1982) *Scotch Reels: Scotland in Cinema and Television*, London: BFI Publishing.

McArthur, C. (1983) 'Scotch reels and after', *Cencrastus*, 11.

McClure, D. (1988) *Why Scots Matters*, Edinburgh: The Saltire Society.

McCrone, D. (1991) 'Politics and society in modern Scotland', in Day,

G. and Rees, G. (eds) *Regions, Nations and European Integration: Remaking the Celtic Periphery*, Cardiff: University of Wales Press.

McCrone, D. and Elliott, B. (1989) *Property and Power in a City: The Sociological Significance of Landlordism*, London: Macmillan.

McCrone, D. and Bechhofer, F. (1991) 'The Scotland–England divide: politics and locality in modern Britain' (mimeo).

McCrone, D., Kendrick, S. and Bechhofer, F. (1982) 'Egalitarianism and social inequality in Scotland', in Robbins, D. (ed.) *Rethinking Social Inequality*, Farnborough: Gower Publications.

McCrone, D., Kendrick, S. and Straw, S. (eds) (1989) *The Making of Scotland: Nation, Culture and Social Change*, Edinburgh: Edinburgh University Press.

McKenzie, N. (1977) 'Centre and periphery: the marriage of two minds', *Acta Sociologica*, 20.

Mackenzie, W. J. M. (1978) *Political Identity*, Harmondsworth: Penguin.

Mackie, J. D. (1978) *A History of Scotland*, Harmondsworth: Penguin.

Mackintosh, J. P. (1967) 'Scottish nationalism', *Political Quarterly*, 38(4).

Mackintosh, J. P. (1974) 'The new appeal of nationalism', *New Statesman*, 27 September.

Mackintosh, J. P. (1982) *John P. Mackintosh on Scotland*, ed. Drucker, H., Harlow: Longman.

MacLaren, A. A. (1974) *Religion and Social Class*, London: Routledge & Kegan Paul.

MacLaren, A. A. (ed.) (1976) *Social Class in Scotland*, Edinburgh: John Donald.

MacLaren, I. [1894] *Beside the Bonnie Briar Bush*, 1940 edn, New York: Dodd, Mead & Co.

McPherson, A. F. (1983) 'An angle on the Geist: persistence and change in Scottish educational tradition', in Humes, W. M. and Paterson, H. M. (eds) *Scottish Culture and Scottish Education, 1800–1980*, Edinburgh: John Donald.

McPherson, A. F. and Raab, C. (1988) *Governing Education: A sociology of Policy since 1945*, Edinburgh: Edinburgh University Press.

Mann, M. (1984) 'The autonomous power of the state', *Archives Européennes de Sociologie*, 25.

Mann, M. (1986) *The Sources of Social Power*, vol. 1, Cambridge: Cambridge University Press.

Marquand, D. (1988) *The Unprincipled Society: New Demands and Old Politics*, London: Fontana.

Marshall, G. (1980) *Presbyteries and Profits: Calvinism and the Development of Capitalism in Scotland, 1560–1707*, Oxford: Clarendon Press.

Marshall, G. (1982) *In Search of the Spirit of Capitalism*, London: Hutchinson.

Marshall, T. H. (1963) 'Citizenship and social class', in Marshall, T. H. (ed.) *Sociology at the Crossroads*, London: Heinemann.

Marwick, A. (1986) *British Society since 1945*, Harmondsworth: Penguin.

Marwick, W. H. (1931) 'Economics and the Reformation in Scotland', *The Scots Magazine*, 15.

Marx, K. (1959) *The Eighteenth Brumaire of Louis Bonaparte*, in Feuer, L.

(ed.) *Marx and Engels: Basic Writings in Politics and Philosophy*, New York: Doubleday.

Maxwell, S. (1976) 'Can Scotland's political myths be broken?', *Q*, 19 November.

Melling, J. (1983) *Rent Strikes: People's Struggle for Housing in the West of Scotland, 1890–1916*, Edinburgh: Polygon.

Melucci, A. (1989) *Nomads of the Present*, London: Hutchinson Radius.

Middlemas, K. (1979) *Politics in Industrial Society: The Experience of the British System*, London: André Deutsch.

Middlemas, K. (1986) *Power, Competition and the State*, vol. 1, London: Macmillan.

Midwinter, A., Keating, M. and Mitchell, J. (1991) *Politics and Public Policy in Scotland*, Edinburgh: Mainstream.

Miller, W. (1981) *The End of British Politics? Scots and English Political Behaviour in the Seventies*, Oxford: Clarendon Press.

Miller, W., Brand, J. and Jordan, G. (1981) 'Government without a mandate: the Conservative Party in Scotland', *Political Quarterly*, 52(2).

Mitchell, C. (1968) *A Dictionary of Sociology*, London: Routledge & Kegan Paul.

Mitchell, J. (1990) 'Factions, tendencies and consensus in the SNP in the 1980s', in Brown, A. and Parry, R. (eds) *Scottish Government Yearbook 1990*, Edinburgh: Unit for the Study of Government in Scotland.

Mommsen, W. (1990) 'The varieties of the nation-state in modern history', in Mann, M. (ed.) *The Rise and Decline of the Nation-State*, Oxford: Blackwell.

Moore, C. and Booth, S. (1989) *Managing Competition: Meso-corporatism, pluralism and the Negotiated Order in Scotland*, Oxford: Clarendon Press.

Moreno, L. (1988) 'Scotland and Catalonia: the path to home rule', in McCrone, D. (ed.) *Scottish Government Yearbook 1988*, Edinburgh: Unit for the Study of Government in Scotland.

Morris, A. (1989) 'Patrimony and power: a study of lairds and landownership in the Scottish Borders', Ph.D. thesis, Edinburgh University, unpublished.

Morris, R. J. (1990a) 'Scotland, 1830–1914: the making of a nation within a nation', in Fraser, W. H. and Morris, R. J. (eds) *People and Society in Scotland, volume II, 1830–1914*, Edinburgh: John Donald.

Morris, R. J. (1990b) 'Victorian values in Scotland and England', paper presented to a symposium, 'Victorian values', at the Royal Society of Edinburgh.

Mueller, W. and Karle, W. (1990) 'Social selection in educational systems in Europe', International Sociological Association, 12th World Congress of Sociology, Madrid, July.

Munro, A. (1984) *The Folk Music Revival in Scotland*, London: Kahn and Averill.

Murison, D. (1986) (ed.) *Scottish National Dictionary*, Aberdeen: Aberdeen University Press.

Nairn, T. (1977) *The Break-Up of Britain*, London: Verso.

Nairn, T. (1988a) *The Enchanted Glass*, London: Hutchinson Radius.

Nairn, T. (1988b) 'The tartan and the blue', *Marxism Today*, June.

Nairn, T. (1990) 'Identities', unpublished paper.

Newby, H. et al. (eds) (1985) *Restructuring Capital: Recession and Reorganisation in Industrial Society*, London: Macmillan.

Parry, R. (1981) 'Territory and public employment: a general model and British evidence', *Journal of Public Policy*, 1.

Parry, R. (1988) *Scottish Political Facts*, Edinburgh: T. & T. Clark.

Paterson, L. (1991) 'Ane end of Ane Auld Sang: sovereignty and the re-negotiation of the Union', in Brown, A. and McCrone, D. (eds) *Scottish Government Yearbook*, Edinburgh: Edinburgh University Press.

Payne, G. (1977) 'Occupational transition in advanced industrial societies', *Sociological Review*, 25.

Payne, G. (1987) *Employment and Opportunity*, London: Macmillan.

Pi-Sunyer, O. (1985) 'Catalan nationalism: some theoretical and historical considerations', in Tiryakian, E. and Rogowski, R. (eds) *New Nationalisms of the Developed West*, London: Allen & Unwin.

Plamenatz, J. (1973) 'Two types of nationalism', in Kamenka, E. (ed.) *Nationalism: The Nature and Evolution of an Idea*, London: Edward Arnold.

Poggi, G. (1978) *The Development of the Modern State*, London: Hutchinson.

Poggi, G. (1983) *Calvinism and the Capitalist Spirit*, London: Macmillan.

Poggi, G. (1990) *The State: Its Nature, Development and Prospects*, Oxford: Polity.

Punnett, M. (1985) 'Two nations? Regional partisanship, 1868–1983', in McCrone, D. (ed.) *Scottish Government Yearbook 1985*, Edinburgh: Unit for the Study of Government in Scotland.

Robbins, D. (ed.) (1982) *Rethinking Social Inequality*, Farnborough: Gower.

Roxborough, I. (1979) *Theories of Underdevelopment*, London: Macmillan.

Saunders, L. J. (1950) *Scottish Democracy, 1815–1840*, Edinburgh: Oliver & Boyd.

Scott, J. (1983) 'Declining autonomy: recent trends in the Scottish economy', in McCrone, D. (ed.) *Scottish Government Yearbook 1983*, Edinburgh: Unit for the Study of Government in Scotland.

Scott, J. and Hughes, M. (1976) 'The Scottish ruling class: problems of analysis and data', in MacLaren, A. A. (ed.) *Social Class in Scotland*, Edinburgh: John Donald.

Scott, J. and Hughes, M. (1980) *The Anatomy of Scottish Capital*, London: Croom Helm.

Scottish Trades Union Congress (STUC) (1989) *Claiming the Future: Scotland's Economy: Ownership, Control and Development*, London: Verso.

Shepherd, G. (1988) 'The Kailyard', in Gifford, D. (ed.) *The History of Scottish Literature, volume 3, the Nineteenth Century*, Aberdeen: Aberdeen University Press.

Skocpol, T. (1977) 'Wallerstein's world capitalist system: a theoretical and historical critique', *American Journal of Sociology*, 82(5).

Sliogeris, A. (1990) 'From ritual politics to pragmatism: a critique of Sajudis' politics of independence', *Radical Scotland*, 44, April–May.

Smith, A. (1986) *The Ethnic Origins of Nations*, Oxford: Basil Blackwell.

Smith, A. (1988) 'The myth of the "modern nation" and the myths of nations', *Ethnic and Racial Studies*, 11(1).

Smith, A. (1991) *National Identity*, Harmondsworth: Penguin.

Smout, T. C. (1970) *A History of the Scottish People, 1560–1830*, Glasgow: Collins.

Smout, T. C. (1980a) 'Scotland and England: is dependency a symptom or a cause of underdevelopment?', *Review*, 3(4).

Smout, T. C. (1980b) 'Centre and periphery in history', *Journal of Common Market Studies*, 18(3).

Smout, T. C. (1987) *A Century of the Scottish People, 1830–1950*, Glasgow: Collins.

Stewart, D. C. and Thompson, J. C. (1980) *Scotland's Forged Tartans: An Analytical Study of* Vestiarium Scoticum, Edinburgh: Paul Harris.

Taylor, A. (1986) 'Overseas ownership in Scottish manufacturing industry from 1950 to 1985', *Scottish Economic Bulletin*, 33, June.

Telfer-Dunbar, J. (1962) *History of Highland Dress*, London: Batsford.

Telfer-Dunbar, J. (1981) *Costume of Scotland*, London: Batsford.

Tilly, C. (1975) *The Formation of National States in Western Europe*, Princeton, NJ: Princeton University Press.

Tiryakian, E. and Rogowski, R. (1985) (eds) *New Nationalisms of the Developed West*, London: Allen & Unwin.

Touraine, A. (1981) 'Une sociologie sans société', *Revue Française de Sociologie*, 22(1).

Trevor-Roper, H. (1963) 'Religion, the Reformation and social change', *Historical Studies*, 4.

Trevor-Roper, H. (1984) 'Invention of tradition: the Highland tradition of Scotland', in Hobsbawm, E. and Ranger, T. (eds) *The Invention of Tradition*, Cambridge: Cambridge University Press.

Turner, R. (1960) 'Sponsored and contest mobility and the school system', *American Sociological Review*, 25(5).

Walker, G. and Gallagher, T. (eds) (1990) *Sermons and Battle Hymns: Protestant Popular Culture in Modern Scotland*, Edinburgh: Edinburgh University Press.

Wallerstein, I. (1974) *The Modern World System: Capitalist Agriculture and the Origins of the European World Economy in the 16th Century*, London: Academic Press.

Wallerstein, I. (1979) *The Capitalist World-Economy*, Cambridge: Cambridge University Press.

Wallerstein, I. (1980) 'One man's meat: the Scottish Great Leap Forward', *Review*, 3(4).

Watson, T. J. (1980) *Sociology, Work and Industry*, London: Routledge & Kegan Paul.

Watt, I. (1982) 'Occupational stratification and the sexual division of labour', in Dickson, T. (ed.) *Capital and Class in Scotland*, Edinburgh: John Donald.

Webb, K. (1978) *The Growth of Nationalism in Britain*, Harmondsworth: Penguin.

Wiener, M. (1981) *English Culture and the Decline of the Industrial Spirit, 1850–1980*, Harmondsworth: Penguin.

Williams, G. (1980) 'When was Wales?', BBC Radio Wales, annual lecture.

Williams, R. (1973) *The Country and the City*, London: Chatto & Windus.

BIBLIOGRAPHY

Williams, R. (1974) *Television: Technology and Cultural Form*, London: Fontana.

Williams, R. (1977) *Marxism and Literature*, Oxford: Oxford University Press.

Williams, R. (1983) *Towards 2000*, Harmondsworth: Penguin.

Winkler, J. (1976) 'Corporatism', *Archives Européennes de Sociologie*, 17(1).

Wittig, K. (1958) *Scottish Tradition in Literature*, Westport, Conn.: Greenwood Press.

Wood, S. (1987) *The Scottish Soldier*, London: Archive Publications.

Wright, P. (1985) *On Living in an Old Country: The National Past in Contemporary Britain*, London: Verso.

Young, J. D. (1979) *The Rousing of the Scottish Working Class*, London: Croom Helm.

Young, S. (1984) 'The foreign-owned manufacturing sector', in Hood, N. and Young, S. (eds) *Industry, Policy and the Scottish Economy*, Edinburgh: Edinburgh University Press.

Youngson, A. J. (1973) *After the Forty Five: The Economic Impact on the Scottish Highlands*, Edinburgh: Edinburgh University Press.

INDEX